지은이의 말

언어가 되면 새로운 세상을 경험할 수 있습니다. 중국, 한국, 일본, 베트남은 대표적인 한자 문화권 국가입니다. 각자의 토속어를 바탕으로 한자와 합쳐져서 각자의 언어로 발전해왔습니다. 그렇기 때문에 한가지 언어에 능통하면 다른 언어를 습득하는 시간도 짧아집니다. 개혁개방, 경제 발전, 관광 개발 등의 흐름에 따라 베트남어의 중요성도 많이 증가하였습니다. 따라서 자연스럽게 베트남을 방문하는 외국인들의 수도 증가하고 베트남어를 배우려는 학습자들도 늘고 있습니다.

많은 베트남어 학습자들이 첫 학습 단계부터 어려운 발음(6가지의 성조)과 어순 때문에 단어 습득에 어려움을 느껴 일찍이 포기하는 경우가 많습니다. 『베트남어 기본 단어(1043)』는 단어 습득을 효과적으로 할 수 있도록 6개의 성조별로 의미하는 뜻을 정리하여 흥미를 잃지 않고 단어를 습득할 수 있도록 도움을 줄 것입니다.

고등학교를 졸업하면 약 4만개의 단어를 습득한다고 합니다. 언어의 습득은 결국은 단어 싸움이며 무한 반복의 싸움입니다. 『베트남어 기본 단어(1043)』를 통해 단어를 습득하면 문법, 문장 등의 공부에 흥미를 잃지 않고 계속 정진할 수 있을 것으로 확신합니다.

끝으로 이 책의 출판에 도움을 주신 마음연결 출판사 김영근 대표님께 진심으로 감사의 말씀을 전합니다.

the author's words

    Languages open up new worlds. China, Korea, Japan, and Vietnam are all representative Chinese character cultures. Each of these countries has developed their own languages based on their indigenous languages, which have been influenced by Chinese characters. Therefore, being fluent in one language means that it takes less time to learn other languages. The importance of the Vietnamese language has increased with the trend of reformation, economic and tourism development. Therefore, the number of foreigners visiting Vietnam has increased, and the number of learners who want to learn Vietnamese has also increased.

    It is difficult to learn Vietnamese due to the diverse pronunciation (6 different tones) and word order from the first stage of learning. Students often give up early. "Vietnamese Basic Words (1043)" organizes the meaning of each of the six tones to help you acquire words effectively and without losing interest.

    It is said that by the time a person graduate from high school, he/she will have acquired about 40,000 words. Language learning is a battle of words, a battle of endless repetition. I am sure that if you acquire words through "Vietnamese Basic Words (1043)", you will be able to continue studying grammar, sentences, etc. without losing interest. Finally,

    I would like to express my sincere gratitude to Mr. Kim Young-geun, CEO of Nous and Mind Publishing House, for his help in publishing this book.

Tiếng Việt		中文		한국어	English
0001	a	a	1	낫. 작은 낫	sickle. small sickle
			2	모아서 쌓아놓다	collect and pile up
			3	베트남 알파벳의 첫번째 자	the first letter of the Vietnamese alphabet
		à	1	우르르 몰려오다	stampede come
			2	돌연히 무언가를 생각해 냈을 때 하는 말	Oh! I see
			3	문장뒤에 붙여 의문문을 만듦	question particle
		á	1	고통, 놀람 등을 나타내는 말	words that express pain, surprise, etc.
			2	아시아 (=Á châu)	Asia, Asian
		ả		낭자. 소녀	sister. she. her
		ạ		경의를 표하기 위해 문장뒤에 붙이는 말	a particle at the end of sentence to express formal politeness, especially to seiors
		â		베트남어 알파벳 중 3번째 자	the third letter of the Vietnamese alphabet, called "ớ" and written in the Latin script
		ă		베트남어 알파벳 중 2번째 자	the second letter of the Vietnamese alphabet
0002	ac	ác	惡(악)	1	잔인한. 가혹한. 흉포한	cruel. severe. fierce
				2	까마귀(烏)	crow
0003	ach	ách	脈(맥)	1	멍에	yoke
				2	과식하다	overeat
		ạch		1	털썩	thud
				2	땅에 넘어지거나 부딪칠때 나는 소리	the sound of being left on the ground or hit

0004	ai	ải	隘(애)	1	썩은	rotten
				2	좁고 거칠고 험한 장소 (길)	narrow, rough, and rough place (road)
		ai	哀(애)	1	누구. 누가	who. whoever. someone else
				2	불쌍한	poor
		ái	愛(애)	1	사랑하다	to love
				2	고통스런 소리를 나타내는 말	ow. ouch
0005	am	âm	音(음) 陰(음)	1	소리. 음향. 음성	sound
				2	부정의. 반대의. 소극적인	negative
		ấm	蔭(음) 附(부)	1	따뜻한. 미지근한	warm
				2	주전자	pot. kettle
		am	庵(암)		암자	small Buddhist temple
		ám	暗(암) 別(별)		(유령 등이) 출몰하다	to haunt
		ẩm	飲(음)		습기찬. 젖은. 축축한	humid. damp. moist
		ầm			시끄러운	loud
		ẵm			(아이를 품에) 안고 돌보다	to carry (a baby) in one's arms
		ằm			(아이를 품에) 안다	to hold (a baby) in one's arms
0006	an	an	安(안) 鞍(안)	1	편안한. 평화로운	relax
				2	말 안장	horse saddle
		án	按(안) 案(안)	1	형사상의 판결, 선고	sentence (judicial order for punishment)
				2	막다. 저지하다	keep out. block off
		ẩn	隱(은)	1	문을 밀어열다	push the door open

			2	숨겨진	hide out. latent. (computing) hidden
	ăn			먹다	to eat
	ân	恩(은)		은혜. 감사 (=ơn)	grace. thanks
	ấn	印(인)		누르다. 인쇄하다	to press. to print
	Ấn			인도(印度). Ấn Độ	India
0007	anh	ánh	映(영)	1	빛. 광선	light
				2	빛을 반사시키다	to reflect light
		anh	英(영) 瑛(영) 叛(반) 樱(영)	1	당신. 나	I, me, you (the same age as the speaker)
				2	형. 형님. 오빠	elder brother
				3	아내가 남편을 부르는 호칭	what wife calls her husband
				4	영국(Anh)	England. the United Kingdom
		ảnh	影(영)		(=hình). 사진	photo
0008	ang	áng		1	문학 혹은 문학적 의미를 가진 명사앞에 붙이는 말	a word that is put before a noun that has a literary meaning
				2	뛰어난 연구	outstanding research
				3	대략	approximately
		ǎng		1	가만히 있다	stay still
				2	말문을 닫고 있는	speechless
		ang			도자기	pottery
		ǎng			개의 울음소리	the cry of a dog when it's scared
		ảng			그릇. 도자기로 된 용기	ceramic container
0009	ao	ao		1	연못	pond
				2	가늠잡기 위해 재다	to measure approximately

		ào		1	(태풍, 홍수) 무섭게 몰려오다. 떼지어 몰려오다 (가다)	to rush
				2	맹렬한	impetuously
		áo			(상의)옷. 겉옷. 자켓	a top. an out fit
		Áo	奧(오) 襖(오)		오스트리아	Austria
		ảo			가상의	computing. virtual
0010	ap	áp	压(압)	1	억누르다. 압박하다	squeeze. to press against
				2	가까이 다가가다	to close in on
		ấp		1	작은 마을. 촌락. 부락	hamlet
				2	(새가) 알을 품다	to embrace. to hug
		ăp			가득하게. 찰랑찰랑하게. 넘칠 정도로	brimful
		ập			돌진해 들어오다	to rush in. to rush down
0011	at	át		1	(더 강한 것으로 인해) 약화되다. 제지하다. 억누르다	to overwhelm
				2	(카드게임의) 에이스	(card games) ace
		ất	乙(을)		십간의 을(乙)	the 2nd of Ten Heavenly Stem
		ăt			분명히. 확실히. 틀림없이. (=~là. ~hẳn)	clearly. surely. certainly
0012	au	âu	歐(구)	1	유럽	Europe
				2	아마	perhaps. just
		ấu		1	어린	young
				2	(식물) 마름의 일종	a plant
		ậu			문명사회와 격리되어 사는 부족	a trive that lives in isolation from civilized society
		ẩu	毆(구)		조심성 없는. 부주의한	careless
		au			đâu의 약어. 어디	where
		Âu			유럽	Europe. Euro-

0013	ay	áy		시든. 마른	withered. thin
		ấy		그분. 그것. 저것. 그. 저	that
0014	ba	ba	巴(파) 波(파)	삼(3)	three. 3
		bã		1 피곤해서 녹초가 된	tired out
				2 찌꺼기. 침전물	dregs. sedimentary matter
		bá	百(백) 伯(백)	1 아저씨. 백부	uncle
				2 아주머니. 백모	aunt
		bà	婆(파) 琶(파) 杷(파)	할머니	grandmother. she. woman. madam. Mrs. you (when addressing a woman significantly older then speaker)
		bạ	薄(박)	미장하다 (공사)	plastering work
		bả		작은 동물들을 죽이는데 쓰이는 독극물	a type of poison used to kill some kinds of small animal.
0015	bac	bác	博(박) 駁(박) 剝(박)	1 백부(伯父). 백모(佰母)	paternal uncle. father's elder brother. paternal aunt-in-law. father's elder brother's wife
				2 중년의 남자. 아저씨	a middle-aged man. uncle
		bắc	北(북)	1 북. 북부. 북쪽	northern. north
				2 (다리를) 놓다. 세우다	build (a bridge)
		bạc	泊(박) 薄(박) 箔(박) 爆(폭)	1 은	silver
				2 하얗다	white
		bậc		수준. 등급	level. rank
		bấc		코르크나무	cork
0016	bach	bách	百(백) 迫(박)	1 100	hundred
				2 억압하다(독자적으로 쓰이지 못함). 강요하다	to compel. to force. to constrain

		bạch	白(백) 袋(대)	1	부드럽고 무거운 물건이 떨어지는 소리	the sound of a soft heavy object falling
				2	흰. 하얀	white
0017	bai	bai		1	삽. 가래	spade
				2	늘어나다	stretch
		bài	排(배) 牌(패)	1	꼬리표. 판. 패. 카드놀이. 수업	tag. tablet. card. card game. lesson
				2	배제하다	to exclude
		bãi		1	바다와 강의 평탄한 둔덕. 더미	bank (of a river). shore. flat expanse. field. place
				2	그만두다	stop. cease. give up
		bái	拜(배)		절을 하다. (=lạy)	make a bow
		bại	敗(패)		마비되다. 저리다. 지다. 잃다	be paralyzed. to be defeated. to lose
0018	bam	bậm		1	나무의 일종	a kind of tree
				2	뚱뚱하고 어리석은. 견고한	fat and stupid. hard as nails
		băm		1	삼십(31에서 39사이의 숫자를 셀때 씀)	short for 30 ("thirty...")
				2	잘게 자르다	cut into small pieces
		bẩm	稟(품)	1	윗사람에게 아뢰다	tell one's superiors
				2	천부의. 타고난	natural. inborn
		bầm		1	상처의	scarred
				2	상처	wound. scar. hurt
		bám			꽉잡다	to cling to
		bâm			비웃다	laugh at
		bẳm			(작은 조각으로) 쪼개다	split up
		bấm			누르다	to press. to push (a button, a key, etc.)

		bặm		물다	bite (with one's mouth)
0019	ban	bận	1	바쁜	busy, occupied
			2	입다 (남부 방언)	(Southern Vietnam) to wear (clothes)
		ban	班(반) 般(반) 頒(반)	1	시간의 한 부분을 가리키는 말	a word that refers to a part of time
				2	(같은 일을 하는 사람들의) 그룹	group (of people doing the same work), band, board, squad, committee
				3	(황제가) 하사하다, 부여하다, 주다	be granted (an imperial favor)
		bàn	盤(반) 槃(반)	1	탁자, 책상	table, desk, board
				2	토의하다, 의견을 교환하다	to discuss, to talk over
		bần	貧(빈)	1	가난한, 빈궁한	poor, poor as a poor
				2	코르크나무	cork
		bẳn		1	까다로운	tricky
				2	화를 내다	lose one's temper, get angry
		bán	半(반)		팔다	to sell
		bẩn			더러운	dirty, unclean, filthy
		bấn			곤궁한, 힘든	in need, needy
		bạn	伴(반) 絆(반) 叛(반)		친구, 동료	friend, companion, comrade
		bản	本(본) 板(판) 版(판)	1	원고	manuscript
				2	판 (版)	edition
		bắn			사격하다	to fire, to shoot
0020	bang	băng	氷(빙) 崩(붕)	1	얼음	ice
				2	밴드, 테이프	band, tape

			3	임금이 붕어(崩御)하다. (=băng hà)	the death of a king
		bằng	朋(붕) 棚(붕)	1	큰 새	a big bird
				2	증명하다	prove
				3	동등비교 (A는 B만큼 ~하다. ~ 서로 같다. ~만 하다)	equal to. equals
		báng	謗(방)	1	머리를 때리다	to hit the head
				2	(의학)복수 (腹水)	(medicine) aseites
		bẵng		1	잊어버리다	to forget
				2	소식이 없는	unannounced
		bang	邦(방) 搗(도)		연방내의 주	a state (a state within a federation)
		bằng			~를 이용하여. ~로	by way of. with~
		bàng	旁(방) 謗(방) 飯(반) 龐(방) 傍(방)		나무이름	tree name
		bẵng			날려보내다. 나무를 옮겨심다. (=bứng)	blow away. transplant a tree
		bảng	榜(방) 板(판)		판	board (for writing, listing)
0021	banh	banh		1	(남부 방언) 공	(Southern Vietnam) ball
				2	넓게 열다	to open
		bành		1	열어젖히다	fling (a door) open
				2	코끼리 등에 얹는 안장	a saddle on the back of an elephant
		bánh			빵. 케이크. 떡	bread. cake. rice cake
		bạnh			열다. 벌리다	to open
		bảnh			멋부리다. 몸치장 하다	put on airs. dress oneself up

0022	bao	bao	包(포) 褒(포)	1	천으로 만든 가방. 자루	bag. sack
				2	(~을) 싸다	wrap (up). pack (up)
				3	얼마나	how. how much. how many
		báo	報(보)	1	신문	newspaper
				2	보고하다. 공표하다. 알리다	to report. to tell
		bão	抱(포) 飽(포)	1	태풍	(weather) storm
				2	배부른. 꽉찬	be full. be stuffed
		bào	鮑(포) 泡(포) 袍(포) 咆(포)	1	대패	plane
				2	대패질하다	to plane (wood)
		bạo	暴(폭)		과감한	bold. daring
		bảo	保(보) 堡(보) 寶(보) 抱(포)		명령하다. 말하다 시키다 (bảo+사람+동사 : 사람에게 동사하라고 시키다)	to tell. to say to make someone do something
0023	bap	bắp			옥수수 (인디언 옥수수)	corn. popcorn
		bập			빠르게 베다. 자르다	cut quickly
0024	bat	bát	八(팔) 撥(발) 迫(박)	1	여덟	eight
				2	오른쪽으로 노를 젓다	row to the right
		bất	不(불)	1	~이 아닌	not ~
				2	부러뜨리다	to break
		bạt	拔(발) 跋(발)	1	발 (햇빛 가리개)	sun shade
				2	땅을 고르다	level the ground
		bật	弼(필)		(반동에 의해) 뻗다. 튕겨나가다. 뻗어나가다. 틀다. 켜다	be carried out by reaction. bounce out to switch on (lights)
		bặt			정적이 흐르는	still. silence
		bắt			잡다. 체포하다	to seize. to catch
0025	bau	bầu			조롱박	gourd

		bàu	1	연못	pond
			2	선출하다	to elect
		bâu	1	밀집하다. 떼를 짓다. 착 달라붙다	to assemble. to gather into one place
			2	옷의 목 칼러. 옷의 호주머니	collar of dress
		báu	1	소중한	precious
			2	소중히 여기다	to cherish
		bấu		할퀴다	to scratch
0026	bay	bay	1	흙손. 미장삽	a trowel
			2	날다	to fly
		bây	1	너 (예의바르지 않은 표현). 네놈들	you
			2	지저분하게 하다	make a mess
		bẫy	1	올가미. 덫	trap. snare. pitfall
			2	들어올리다	lift
		bấy	1	어린	young
			2	그때. 그정도	then. that much
		bày		배치하다. 배열하다. 진열하다	to arrange. to dispose. to display
		bầy		무리. 떼	flock. herd
		bậy		틀린. 부적당한	morally wrong. false
		bảy		일곱. 7	seven
		bẩy	1	지레로 올리다	to raise with a lever
			2	덫을 놓다. 덫에 걸리게 하다	set a trap. set in a trap
			3	지렛대 (=đòn bẩy)	leverage

0027	be	be	1	논두렁을 쌓다. 보수하다	to build a mud embankment with one's hands
			2	병 (위스키 등의 납작한 휴대용)	wine flask
		bệ	1	(학교)교단. 단	(teacher's) platform
			2	옮기다. 들어 옮기다	move. shift. take. lift and transfer
		bể	1	바다	sea, ocean
			2	깨지다. 파멸하다	to break. to be broken
		bé		작다. 작은	small. little. tiny
		bè		뗏목 서로 연결된 사람들 집단, 그룹	raft (floating structure) group
		bế	閉(폐)	안아주다	to hug
		bề		크기. 가장자리	side. surface
		bẻ		부러뜨리다	to break into two
		bẽ		부끄러운	shameful
		bẹ		코코넛, 바나나, 옥수수 등의 잎 줄기	leaf stem of coconuts, bananas, etc.
		bễ		송풍기. 풀무기	fan
		bê	1	송아지	calf (baby bull/cow)
			2	(무거운 물건을) 가져 가다	take a heavy object
0028	bech	bệch		창백한	sickly white
0029	bem	bẻm		수다스러운	talkative
0030	ben	bén	1	날카로운. 예리한	sharp
			2	닿다. 바짝 붙이다	reach. stick fast
		bèn		즉시	right off
		bển		그곳	that side
		bẹn		사타구니	groin

		bện			(머리를) 땋다	braid up
		bền			지속적인. 질긴. 견고한. 내구력있는	durable. strong. solid. firm
		bến			정거장. 부두	a station. a port
		bên		1	편. 면. 옆. 이웃한	side. edge. face
				2	가까이에. 곁에	at hand. by one's side
0031	benh	bềnh			들어올리다	lift
		bệnh	病(병)		병. (=bịnh(病))	disease. illness. sickness. defect. bad habit
		bênh			편들다	to take sides with
0032	bep	bẹp			찌그러진	be crushed. be flattened
		bếp			부엌	stove. cooker. kitchen
0033	bet	bét		1	얼굴을 서로 피하다	avoid each other's faces
				2	최하의	be the last, or the worst (at something)
		bẹt		1	열어젖히다	fling (a door) open
				2	평평한	flat
		bết		1	지친	tired
				2	(옷이) 달라붙다	one's clothes stick together
		bệt		1	땅에 눕다. 땅에 앉다. 달라붙다	lie on the ground. sit on the ground. stick together
				2	피곤한. 지친. 어리석은	tired. foolish
0034	beu	bệu			근육이 약한. 연약한	weak-muscled. weak and fragile
		bêu			부끄러운. 수치스러운	shameful. disgraceful
0035	bi	bi	悲(비) 卑(비)	1	(장난감) 구슬. 당구공	a marble (spherical ball). (billiards, snooker) a ball
				2	슬픈. 불쌍한	sad. poor

		bí	秘(비) 悶(비)	1	신비한. 비밀스러운. 알 수 없는	mysterious. secret. unknown
				2	호박	pumpkin
		bì	皮(피) 疲(피)	1	봉투. 자루	bag. sack. envelope
				2	(돼지, 소 등의) 껍데기 (음식)	(of pig, cow, etc) skin (as food)
		bỉ	披(피) 秕(비)	1	경멸하다.	to disdain. to despise
		Bỉ			벨기에	Belgium. Belgian
		bĩ			나쁜	bad. (only in compounds) unlucky. unfortunate
		bị	備(비) 裨(비) 被(피)	1	바구니	basket
				2	불쾌하거나 재난의 일을 겪다. 당하다 (수동태 문장을 만들 때 사용함)	to suffer an unpleasant or disastrous event. (used to create passive sentences)
00 36	bia	bia		1	묘비. 비석	tombstone. gravestone. stele. monument
				2	맥주	beer
		bi-a			당구	billiards
		bìa			껍질. 껍데기. 커버	book cover. cardboard. frame
		bịa			(이야기, 주장 등을) 지어내다	to make up (a story, claim, etc.)
00 37	bich	bịch		1	세게 치다	to hit hard
				2	대나무로 만든 기둥모양의 바구니	a pillar-shaped basket made of bamboo
		bích	壁(벽) 璧(벽)		벽	wall
00 38	biec	biếc			하늘색의. 푸른	sky-blue
00 39	biem	biếm			비난하다. 풍자하다. 강등되다	to denounce. make a satire. be demoted

0040	bien	**biến**	變(변) 遍(편) 編(편)	1	사라지다. 증발하다	disappear
				2	변하다	to turn into. to change into
		biện	辯(변) 辨(변) 卞(변)		준비하다	to prepare
		biển	扁(편)		바다. 해양	sea
		biền	弁(변) 便(편)		바다 가운데 섬. 강가의 오지	an island in the middle of the sea
		biên			쓰다	to write
0041	bieng	**biếng**		1	흥미를 잃다	to lose interest in
				2	태만한. 게으른	negligent. lazy
0042	biet	**biệt**	別(별)	1	떠나다	to leave
				2	흔적없이 사라진. 별도의	gone without trace. separate
		biết			알다	to know. to realize. to understand
0043	bieu	**biểu**	表(표) 襄(양)	1	~표. 색인	table. index
				2	말하다. 일러두다	to tell. to say
		biếu			진심으로 선물하다	to cordially give (a present, usually to someone of higher status)
0044	bim	**bím**		1	변발. 길게 땋은 머리	pigtail. plait of hair. long braided hair
				2	달라붙다. 잡고 늘어지다	stick together. hang on one's heels
0045	bin	**bin**			곤로를 임시로 받쳐주는 것	temporary support of a cooking stove
0046	binh	**bịnh**	病(병)		병. (=bệnh)	disease. illness. sickness. defect. bad habit
		bình	平(평) 評(평) 瓶(병) 屏(병)	1	꽃병	vase
				2	비평하다. 평가하다	make a remark. evaluate

		binh	兵(병)	1	사병	soldier. army
				2	지키다. 지지하다. 편들다	to keep. support. side with
		bính	丙(병) 炳(병) 柄(병) 餅(병)	1	10간중의 하나인 "병"(갑, 을, 병)	the third of Ten Heavenly Stem
				2	(옷, 신발 등을) 빌려온	lending (clothes, shoes, etc.)
		bình	秉(병)		쥐다. 잡다	take hold of
0047	bo	bo			팁 (고맙다는 뜻으로 주는 돈)	money tip, extra money given in appreciation for a rendered service
		bố	布(포) 佈(포) 怖(포)	1	아버지. 아빠	father. dad
				2	쓸어내다. 쓸어내어 깨끗이 하다	sweep off. sweep clean
		bộ	步(보) 部(부) 薄(박)	1	한벌. 세트	set (of something)
				2	걷다	to walk
		bổ	補(보) 浦(포) 圃(포)	1	보약	supplementary medicine
				2	보충하다	to supplement
		bõ		1	늙은 (남자) 하인. (=bõ già)	old manservant
				2	(~할만한) 가치가 있다	to be worthwhile, to be worth (the trouble)
		bơ		1	버터	butter
				2	도움을 빌리다	ask for help
		bò		1	(사람이나 동물이) 기다, 기어다니다	to crawl
				2	소	ox. cow
		bó		1	다발. 묶음. 꾸러미	pack. bundle
				2	다발짓다. 묶다	to pack. press (fruit)
		bở		1	부서지기 쉬운. 무른	friable
				2	썪다	decay

		bợ		1	들어올리다	to lift
				2	작은 바구니	a small basket
		bỏ			버리다. 내놓다	to put. to place. to leave. to abandon. to quit
		bồ	葡(포) 匍(포)		동료. 친구	mate. pal. buddy
		bọ			벌레. 곤충. (=sâu bọ)	insect. bug
		bờ			둑. 제방. 논두렁길. (=bờ ruộng)	a bank. embankment. a rice paddy road
		bớ			아우성치다	crowd
		bô			(어린아이용) 변기	a potty (children's chamberpot)
0048	boc	bộc	爆(폭)	1	계단	stairs
				2	폭파하다. 폭로하다	blow up. to expose
		bốc	卜(복)	1	복싱. 권투	boxing
				2	손에 쥐고 골라내다	to pick something up with hand
		bọc		1	자루. 가방. 손가방. 꾸러미	sack. bundle
				2	덮다. 싸다. 감싸다. (~으로) 두르다. 싸넣다	to cover
		bóc	剝(박)		껍질을 벗기다. 벗겨지다	to peel (fruits)
0049	boi	bói		1	점(占)	divination. fortune-telling
				2	점치다	to tell fortunes. to divine. to take an augury
		bội	倍(배) 焙(배) 背(배)	1	닭장	chicken cage
				2	배반하다	to betray
				3	(수학) 배수	(mathematics) multiple
		bối	貝(패) 輩(배) 背(배)	1	(배위에서 치기전문의) 도둑	thief
				2	둥글게 하다	to round

		bồi	1	웨이터	waiter
			2	합지하다(合紙)	to stick more than two sheets of paper together to make it thicker
		bơi		헤엄치다. 수영하다	to swim (move through water)
		bòi		농촌의 젊은이	a young peasant
		bởi		~에 의해	by. because of. because
		bới		(삽이나 손가락으로) 땅을 파다. 헤치다	to dig to search for something
		bôi	1	지우다	to clean (board, etc.)
			2	바르다. (=thoa. xức)	to apply. to coat
0050	bom	bom		폭탄	bomb. (dated) apple
0051	bon	bón	1	인분. 비료	human excrement. fertilizer
			2	비료를 주다	fertilize
		bon		빙글빙글 돌다	turn round and round
		bơn		(강) 작은 모래섬	a small sand island (by the river)
		bòn		조금씩 모으다	to save (every bit of). to glean. to collect (bit by bit) to lay up
		bọn		무리. 한 무리의 사람들. 일파 (특히 범죄를 목적으로 하는) 일당. 갱단	group. gang. cohorts. associates
		bỡn		조롱하다. 비웃다. 농담하다. (=giỡn, bỡn cợt)	make a mockery of
		bốn		넷. 4	four. 4
		bồn		주발. 그릇. 용기	bowl
		bộn		바쁜	busy
		bợn		더러움. 오물. 불순물. (=bợn dơ)	dirty. filth. impurities

0052	bong	bỗng	1	돌연	all of a sudden
			2	갑자기. 우연히. (=tình lình)	suddenly. by accident
		bóng	1	공. 축구공	ball. soccer ball
			2	(대리석, 금속 등이) 빛나는. 번쩍이는. 광이 나는	flashing (marble, metal, etc.). bright. polishing
		bộng	1	구덩이	pit
			2	손이 빈. 공동(空洞)의	empty-handed
		bỏng	1	화상	burn
			2	화상입다. (=phỏng)	get burned
		bổng 俸(봉)	1	녹봉. 봉급	a stipend. salary
			2	(목소리) 맑고 높은. 드높은	clear and high-pitched. high as a church mouse
		bồng 蓬(봉)	1	바닥이 낮고 가는 화분	a low-bottom, thin flowerpot
			2	비등하다. 부풀리다	blow up
		bong		떨어지다. 분리되다	fall. drop. drip. come apart
		bòng		자몽. (=bưởi)	grapefruit
		bõng		물같은	watery
		bọng		자루. 아랫배	sack. the lower abdomen
		bông	1	꽃	(Southern Vietnam) bloom. flower
			2	목화꽃	cotton flowers
			3	면	cotton
0053	bop	bốp	1	돈지갑	wallet
			2	화려한	(colloquial, rare, of clothes) foppish. dandified. swell
		bóp	1	지갑. 손가방 (남부 방언)	(southern Vietnam) wallet (containing money, documents, etc.)

		bọp	2	(누구의) 손으로 누르다	to press (with hands)
		bọp		(물건이 높은 곳에서 떨어져) 부서지는 소리	the sound of an object falling from a high place and breaking up
		bộp		환한 모습으로	with a bright face
		bớp		손바닥으로 때리다	to slap lightly. to box lightly. to slap. to smack
0054	bot	bọt	1	색이 바래다	fade in color
			2	(옷이 오래되어서) 너덜너덜 해지기 쉬운	old and ragged
		bớt	1	(태어날때 몸에 있는) 점. 반점	birthmark
			2	줄이다. 감소시키다	to diminish. to cut down. to decrease. to reduce
		bột	1	가루. 빻은 가루 (밀가루. 녹말 등)	powder. flour. starch
			2	돌연히	suddenly
		bót	1	경찰서	police station
			2	(청소용) 브러쉬. 솔	(dated) brush (used for clean up)
		bọt		거품. (맥주. 바다의) 거품. (비누의) 거품	foam. froth
		bốt		패션 부츠. 병영	(fashion) boot. (military, obsolete) post. troop station
0055	bu	bù	1	보상하다. 갚다	to compensate
			2	(머리) 얽히고 설킨	(hair) tangled up
		bu	1	모친 (북부 방언)	(nothern Vietnam) mother
			2	조립하다. 한 곳에 모이다	to assemble. to gather into one place
		bú	1	새의 보금자리	a nest of birds
			2	우유를 먹으려고 (젖을) 빨다	to suck (at a breast) to consume milk

		bự	1	권력이 있다. 영향력을 지니다	have power. have influence
			2	큰. 굵은	big. thick
		bư		멍청이. 바보 같은	silly. stupid
		bụ	1	포동포동한 아이	a plump child
			2	토실토실한. 살찐	plump. chubby
		bủ		(남.녀) 늙은이. 노인. (=lão, cụ)	the aged
0056	bua	bừa	1	써레	rake. harrow
			2	끌다. 써레질하다	to rake. to harrow
		búa	1	망치	a hammer
			2	거짓말하다	tell a lie
		bùa		부적. (=bùa chú)	charm. amulet
		bữa		밥. 식사	meal
		bưa		적당한. 알맞은. (=vừa)	proper. appropriate
		bủa		(주위를) 싸다. 펼치다	nest of forked-twigs
		bựa		치석(齒石). 이똥. 찌꺼기	floss. tartar. scale. plaque
		bửa		쪼개다	to split. to cleave
		bứa		야생 망고스틴 나무	wild mangosentin tree
		bũa		낮. 주간	daytime. day
0057	buc	bực	1	계급	class
			2	성가신. 화가 난	vexious. angry
		bục	1	(홀, 식당의) 단. 연단. 교단	(hall, dining) platform. podium
			2	무너지다	collapse
		bức	1	뜨거운	hot
			2	빛	light
		bực		화가나다	get angry

0058	bum	bủm	1	방귀를 뀌다	to fart
			2	방귀	fart
		bụm	1	손으로 움켜쥐다	grasp by hand
			2	한 줌의	a handful of
0059	bun	bùn		진흙	mud
		bún		쌀국수	rice vermicelli. rice noodle
		bủn		부패하다. 쇠퇴하다	become corrupt. decline. dacay
0060	bung	bưng	1	양손을 이용하여 들다. 손으로 막다. 가리우다	hold with both hands. block with one's hand
			2	매우 어두운. 캄캄한	as dark as night. dark as night
		bung	1	안에서 밖으로 부풀어 오르다	to swell from inside out
			2	터지다. 찢어지다	to burst
		búng	1	(가볍게) 치다. 찰싹 때리다	strike lightly. give a person on the face
			2	민물조개	fleshwater clam
		bùng		폭발하다. 타오르다	explode. blow up
		bụng		(신체) 배. 위	belly
		bứng		완전히 쓰러뜨리다	knock down completely
		bựng		더미	a heap. a pile. a stack. a rick. an accumulation
		bủng		축 늘어진. 연약한	limp as a ramrod. tender
		bừng		갑자기 열리다. 갑자기 분출하다. 갑자기 번지다	to suddenly flare up. to wake up suddenly
0061	buoc	buộc	1	작은 묶음	a small bundle
			2	묶다. 매다	to bind. to tie
		bước	1	한 걸음	step. pace
			2	걷다	to step

ID					Korean	English
0062	buoi	buổi			하루의 반	half a day
		bươi			긁다. (땅을) 파다	scrape. dig (the ground)
		buòi			남자의 생식기	male genitalia
		bưởi			자몽	grapefruit
0063	buom	buồm	1		돛	a sail
			2		달아나다. 도망가다	to run away
		bươm			너덜너덜 헤진	ragged-out
		bướm			나비	butterfly
0064	buon	buồn	1		바라다. 내키다. 원하다	hope. be tempted to do. to want
			2		슬픈. 우울한	sad
		bươn			급히가다. 빨리가다	hurry along. go fast
		buôn			구입하다. 거래하다. 처리하다	to buy in. to deal in. to trade in
0065	buong	bương	1		큰 대나무	large bamboo
			2		완전히 잃다. 다 날려보내다	lose completely
		buồng			송이. 다발	(of bananas or areca nuts) bunch. bundle
		bướng			완고한. 고집이 센	stubborn. headstrong
		buông			풀어놓다. 놓다	to release from one's hand
0066	buou	bướu			혹	bump. lump. (anatomy) gizzard. (pathology) goiter. (of a camel) hump
		bươu			부풀어 올라 혹이 되다	to swell into a bump
0067	but	bút			펜. 붓 등 (분필 제외)	a pen, writing brush, etc. (any piece of equipment used for writing with one's hand, except chalks.)
		bứt			잡아뽑다. 찢다. 자르다	to take off. to pluck
		bụt			부처	(religion) the Buddha

0068	buu	bửu			명령하다	give orders
		bưu			우편	post (service or system that parcels or letters)
0069	buyt	buýt			버스	bus
0070	ca	cà	袈(가)	1	문지르다. 비비다	to rub
				2	가짓과의 각종 식물	nightshade
		cá	個(개)	1	물고기	fish
				2	내기하다	to bet
		ca	歌(가)		노래하다	to sing
		cạ			문지르다. 마찰시키다	rub up
		cả			모든	all
0071	cac	các		1	(접두어로 복수를 나타냄) 모든. 전부의	(a prefix of the plural) all
				2	신분증. 증명서	an ID card. identification card
		cặc			남자의 성기. 음경(陰莖)	dick
		cắc			다임(dime). 10센트 (美 화폐단위). (=hào)	10 cents. dime
		cạc			카드	card
0072	cach	cách	革(혁) 格(격) 隔(격)	1	격식. 양식. 방법. 길. 수단	way. manner. fashion
				2	먼. 떨어진	to be distant from. to be seperated from
		cạch			포기하다	to give up
0073	cai	cái		1	(종별사) 스스로 움직일 수 없는 물체의 종류와 성질을 나타내는 종별사	(classifier) indicates inanimate noun
				2	(종결사) 조각. 부분	piece (of). partial

		cai	該(해) 營(영) 垓(해)	1	직장(職長). 십장. (군대의) 상병(上兵)	overseer. foreman. supervisor
				2	포기하다	to give up
		cài			묶다. 매다. 달다	to pin. to fasten
		cải	改(개)		수정하다. 바꾸다	to change. to alter
		cãi			논쟁하다. 반항하다	to answer back. to argue
0074	cam	câm		1	바퀴의 살	a spoke of a wheel
				2	침묵하는. (=câm mồm)	silent
		căm		1	원한을 품다	hold a grudge
				2	(차바퀴의) 살	a spoke of a wheel
		cầm	禽(금) 琴(금)	1	새 (날짐승)	bird (a flying animal)
				2	손에 들다. 손으로 집다	to hold. to keep. to capture. to arrest
		cam			오렌지	orange
		cảm	感(감)		느끼다	to feel
		cấm	禁(금)		금지하다	to prohibit. to forbid. to ban
		cằm			턱 (=càm)	a chin (bottom of a face)
		cắm			꽂다. 찔러넣다. (=giắt)	to stick an object onto a surface
		cẩm	錦(금)		경찰청(長) (프랑스 식민지 하에서)	police officer
		cạm			덫(올가미). (=cạm bẫy)	trap. snare. pitfall
		cám			(쌀, 보리 등의) 겨	bran (of rice, barley, etc.)
		càm			턱. (=cằm)	a chin (bottom of a face)
0075	can	cân	筋(근) 斤(근)	1	저울	scale
				2	(무게를) 달다	weigh
				3	킬로그램	kilogram

	cần	芹(근) 勤(근)	1	미나리	water parsley. water celery. water dropwort
			2	근면한	industrious
			3	필요하다	to need
	can	干(간)	1	캔	a can
			2	지팡이	walking stick. cane
	cán		1	(햄머 등의) 손잡이	handle
			2	치이다	to be crushed (by a vehicle, etc.)
	càn		1	엉터리의. 경솔한	illogical. imprudent
			2	무섭게 돌진하다	rush furiously
	cạn		1	얕은	shallow
			2	육지에(서)	on land
	cản		1	제어하다. 방해하다	to prevent. to bar. to hinder
			2	완충판. 덮개	buffer plate. a cover
	cấn	艮(간)	1	팔괘의 간(艮)	of the Eight Trigrams for divination
			2	빚을 탕감하다. 공제하다	forgive the debt. make a deduction
	căn	根(근) 間(간)	1	사이	gap (between). space (between)
			2	채 (집 단위)	a unit of counting houses, building, etc.
	cẩn	謹(근) 僅(근) 槿(근)		상감세공을 박아넣다. 새기다	carve
	cẳn			크지 않은	not much
	cặn			앙금. 침전물	dregs. lees. sediment
	cắn			물다. 깨물다	to bite
	cận	近(근)		이웃의. 부근의. 인접하는	neighboring. contiguous

0076	cang	căng		1	잡아당기다. 팽팽하게 하다	pull. tighten
				2	캠프	camp
		cáng		1	가마(輿(여), 駕(가)). 들것	palanquin. sedan chair. stretcher
				2	들것으로 운반하다	carry by stretcher
		càng		1	더욱더	all the more
				2	(게의) 집게발. 집게	nipper. pincer
		cảng	港(항)	1	항구	port. harbor
				2	정박하다	to anchor
		câng			무례한	impudent
		cẳng			사지(四肢)	the (four) limbs
		cǎng			잡아당기다	pull
0077	canh	canh	庚(경) 更(경) 警(경)	1	국	broth
				2	지키다. 지켜보다	to watch. to guard
		cành			(나뭇)가지	tree branch
		cánh			날개	wing
		cảnh	景(경)		장면. 풍경	scenery. view. landscape. state. situation plight
		cạnh			모퉁이. 가장자리. 면(面)	corner. edge. face. side
0078	cao	cao	高(고)	1	높은. 큰	high. tall
				2	존엄한	dignified
				3	고약. 연고	(medicine) ointment. salve
		cào		1	갈퀴	rake
				2	(갈퀴로) 긁어 모으다	to rake. to scratch
		cáo		1	여우	a fox

			2	구실을 대다	give an excuse
		cảo	縞(호)		사본. 손으로 쓴 것	a duplicated form. a copy. handwritten matter
		cạo			깎다 (머리, 수염 등)	shave off
0079	cap	cấp	給(급) 級(급) 急(급)	1	급수	rank. level. class
				2	허가하다. 발행하다.	to grant. to issue
		cặp		1	한쌍 (짝이 갖추어진 것을 나타내는 말)	pair. duo. couple
				2	다가오다	approach
		cáp			철사. 전선	cable
		cập	及(급)		미치다(이르다)	reach
		cạp			씹다	to chew
		cặp			팔에 껴안다	hug one's arms
0080	cat	cật		1	허리. 등	waist. back
				2	대나무의 결층. 나무껍질	outer layer of bamboo bark
		cát	割(할) 吉(길) 佶(길)		모래	sand
		cất			세우다. 짓다. 건축하다. 집을 짓다	build
		cắt			자르다	to cut
0081	cau	cẩu	狗(구) 苟(구) 垢(구)	1	기계로 무거운 물건을 올리거나 내리거나 혹은 옮기다	to lift with a crane
				2	(동물) 개	a dog (animal)
		câu	鉤(구) 驅(구) 溝(구) 俱(구)	1	구(句). 문장	sentence
				2	낚시질하다	to hook. to fish
		cáu		1	화난. 성난	to be upset. to be angry
				2	오물. 쓰레기	dirt. filth

		cầu	求(구) 球(구)	1	다리. 교각(橋)	pier
				2	원하다. 바라다. 기원하다	to want. make one's wish
		cau			빈랑나무	areca
		cậu			숙부. 외삼촌(어머니의 남동생)	a maternal uncle (mother's brother)
		cấu	構(구) 購(구) 詁(고) 返(후) 觀(관)		비틀다. 꼬집다	to craw. to pinch
0082	cay	cày		1	쟁기	plow
				2	쟁기질하다	to plough
		cầy		1	(식용의) 개	dog. chow (as food)
				2	경작하다	farm. plow
		cay			매운	spicy. peppery. hot
		cáy			게의 종류	small crabs in Searmidae family
		cây			나무. 수목	tree. plant
		cấy			이식하다. 옮겨심다	to transplant
		cậy			의지하다. 의존하다	rely on. depend on
		cạy			비집다	squeeze in
0083	cha	chà		1	마찰하다	to rub. to cleanse
				2	와! 야!	wa! yah!
		chạ			뒤섞인. 혼재된	mixed up. mixed
		cha			아버지	father. dad
		chả			짜 (고기, 생선, 새우 등을 다져서 조미료를 넣고 굽거나 튀긴 음식)	a dish made of meat, fish or shrimp that is sliced, chopped or ground, seasoned, then fried or grilled
0084	chac	chạc		1	나무에서 가지가 갈라져 나간 부분	tree fork

			2	남의 호주머니 돈으로 얻어먹다	to beg
		chắc		확실한. 확신한	sure. certain
		chậc		~한 일에 마지못해 동의할 때 내는 의성어	(onomatopoeia) tsk. tut
0085	chach	chạch		작은 민물 뱀장어	small freshwater eel
0086	chai	chai	1	병. (손.발의) 못. 굳은살	bottle. callus
			2	(흙) 매우 단단한. 잘 갈라지지 않는	very hard (soil). hard to crack
		chài	1	투망	a kind of fishing net
			2	마법에 홀리다. 마술로 홀리다	be enchanted by magic
		chái		벽에 붙인 곁방. 곁채	an adjoining room
		chải		솔로 닦다. 빗질하다	brush with a brush. to comb
0087	cham	chăm	1	부지런한	diligent
			2	벼의 일종	a kind of rice
		chăm	1	점	put a punctuation mark on
			2	구둣점을 찍다	to put a punctuation mark on
		chằm	1	늪지	swampy land
			2	여러겹으로 꿰매다	sew in layers
		chẩm	枕(침) 葉(엽)	1	베개	pillow
				2	후두의. 목부분의	neck-shaped
		châm	針(침) 鍼(침)		불을 붙이다	light a fire
		chàm			인디고. 남색	indigo (color)
		chẩm			독침을 가진 새의 일종	a kind of poisonous bird
		chạm		1	새기다. 조각하다	carve. inscribe
				2	터치하다. 누르다 (스마트폰 등의 아이콘 이나 숫자 등)	to touch. to make physical contact

		chặm			물 독	water poison
		chậm			느린. 천천히	slow
0088	chan	chân	眞(진)	1	발	foot. leg
				2	진실한	true to nature
		chăn		1	담요	a blanket or a duvet
				2	가축을 몰고 나가다. 가축을 기르다	to lead and guard a free-range livestock animal(s)
		chằn		1	여자 도깨비	a woman goblin
				2	펼치다. 잡아당기다. 잡아당겨 넓히다	spread out. pull open
		chắn		1	방해하다. 막다. 차단하다	to shield. usually of a road to block
				2	도박의 일종	a kind of gambling
		chẩn	賑(진) 診(진) 疹(진)	1	돕다. 고통을 덜어주다	to help. ease the pain
				2	반점. 얼굴의 점	a dot. a mole on one's face
		chẵn		1	정확하게	with accuracy
				2	짝수	an even number
		chán			지루한. 지친. 귀찮은	dull. boring. bored. tired. to be tired of
		chấn	震(진) 振(진)	1	깎다. 삭감하다	cut back
				2	흔들다	to shake. to vibrate
		chận			막다. 멈추게하다	keep out. block (up). stop (up). bring to a halt
		chạn			(부엌) 찬장. (닭장) 홰	cupboard. perch
		chần			반숙하다. 끓는 물에 살짝 데쳐내다	be half-boiled. blanch sth lightly in water
		chan			담그다. 쳐넣다	dip
		chặn			차단하다. 막다	to block. to stop. to intercept

0089	chang	chang		햇빛이 쫙 내리쬐는. 쨍쨍한	bright and sunny
		chăng	1	의문사 (예 혹은 아니오)	(interrogative) yes or no
			2	의심을 나타내는 의문사	a questionable matter that expresses doubt
		chẳng	1	쭉 벌리다. 짝 벌어지다	spread out. spread wide
			2	아주 뜨거운. 아주 더운	hot as a hot. very hot
		chàng		그. 3인칭 남자, 젊은 신사, 자기	he. young gentleman. you (used by woman to call her husband or young lover)
		chạng		다리를 벌리다	spread one's legs apart
		chằng		묶다. 매다	to tie
		chặng		항정(航程)	section (of road). stage
		chẳng		강한 부정. 결코 ~아니다	not at all. even if not. if not
0090	chanh	chanh		레몬	lemon
		chạnh	1	감정을 불러 일으키다. 측은한 생각이 발동되다	arouse feelings. feel pity for
			2	놓치다. 빗나가다	to miss
		chánh	1	正(정) 政(정) 정식의. 우두머리의. 중요한. (=chính)	head. chief
			2	작은가지	small branch
0091	chao	chao	1	흔들어 헹구다	shake and rinse
			2	절인 두부	pickeld tofu
		cháo		쌀로 만든 죽. 해장국	rice porridge. hangover soup. rice congee
		chào	1	인사하다	to bow. to greet. to salute
			2	인사말	greeting (good morning, good afternoon. good evening. hello. Hi)
		chạo		호박, 생선, 새우를 다져 만든 음식의 한종류	a kind of food made by mincing pumpkins, fish and shrimp

		chảo			후라이팬	a pan-like item of cookware, a pan, a wok
		chão			밧줄, 케이블	rope, cable
0092	chap	chặp		1	순간, 찰나	moment, in a moment
				2	하나로 묶어 제본하다	bind and bind together
		chắp		1	연결하여 덧붙이다	to join two things together
				2	눈다래끼	sty
		chấp			무조건으로 대결하다	to confront unconditionally
		chập		1	끼우다, 서로 묶다	to join two things together
				2	잠시, 순간	for a moment, moment
		chạp			음력 12월	the 12th month of the lunar year
0093	chat	chất	質(질)	1	본질, 특질	substance
				2	쌓다, 축적하다	gain, accumulate, amass, build (up)
		chặt		1	자르다	to cut, to fell, to chop
				2	탄탄한, 빈틈없는	on the ball
		chắt		1	증손	great-grandchild
				2	물을 빼내다, 물을 붓다	to drain water off a water container
		chát			(냄새나 맛) 독한	acrid
		chạt			소금을 채취하기 위해 여과된 바닷물	seawater filtered to collect salt
		chật			좁은, 작은	tight, tightly
0094	chau	châu	洲(주) 州(주) 走(주) 珠(주) 舟(주) 周(주)	1	대륙	continent
				2	귀한 돌, 보석, 진주	precious stone, gem, jewel, pearl
		chầu		1	임금을 보좌하다	assist the king

				2	기간. 시기. 기회	round. bout. session. period. season
		cháu			손자	a nephew. a niece or a grandchild
		chầu			입을 삐죽 내밀다. 뽀루퉁하다	get sulky
		chậu			세면기. 목욕통. 나무분재용 큰 화분	basin (for water). pot. vessel
0095	chay	chầy		1	늦은	late
				2	절구공이. 방앗공이	a pestle
		chấy		1	머리의 이	head louse
				2	(버릇) 계속 쌓이다. 주어모으다	(habit) pile up
		chạy		1	달리다	to run (to move quickly on two feet. also said of a machine)
				2	잘 나가는. 순조로운	smooth
		cháy			불이나다. 태우다	to burn. to become burnt. to burn out
		chây			일을 안하려고하다. 남의 말을 안듣는다	try not to work. shut one's ears to a person
		chày			절구공이. 방앗공이. 종치는 곤봉	a pestle. a bat
		chảy			흐르다	to flow. to run (liquid). to melt. to leak
		chay			채식주의의	vegen
0096	che	chẽ		1	잔가지. 작은 송이	twigs. small brunches
				2	이익과 운수가 따르는	accompanied by profit and luck
		che			덮어서 안보이게 하다	to cover. to hide
		chè			푸른 땅콩과 설탕으로 만든 후식용 음식	a thick. sweet dessert soup or pudding. often made with glutinous rice and/or beans

		ché			술통	a wine bottle
		chế	制(제) 製(제)	1	조롱하다. 비난하다	make a mock of. to criticize
				2	만들다	to manufacture. to parody. to ivent (a new thing)
		chẻ			베다. 자르다	to slit. to cleave
		chê			험담하다. 비난하다	speak ill of. to criticize. belittle
0097	chech	chếch			비스듬한. 기울은	oblique. askew
		chệch			비스듬한. 경사진. 원래위치에서 벗어난	oblique. slope. out of place
0098	chem	chém			자르다	to cut. to slash. to chop. to behead
		chêm		1	쐐기를 박아 고정시키다	drive a wedge
				2	끼워넣다. 첨가하다	put in. add
0099	chen	chén			떼밀다. 밀어부치다	to get into a crowd. to elbow into. to jostle
0100	chenh	chênh			같지않은. 격이 다른	unequal. of different levels
0101	cheo	chèo		1	노	oar. paddle
				2	노를 젓다	to row (a boat)
		cheo			결혼식 때 여자쪽에서 신랑의 마을에 증표로 내는 기부금	a donation from the women as a token to the groom's village at the wedding
		chéo			대각선의	diagonal
0102	chep	chép			베끼다. 복사하다	copy
0103	chet	chết		1	죽다	to die
				2	죽은	dead
		chẹt		1	질식시키다. 목을 조르다	to choke. to strangle
				2	(사람을) 덮치다	to run over (a person)
				3	몸에 꼭 맞는	close-fitting

01 04	chi	chi	支(지) 肢(지) 之(지) 芝(지)	1	무엇. 어떤 것	what
				2	사지. 수족	limb. legs and arms
		chí	志(지) 至(지) 誌(지)	1	의지	will. spirit
				2	매우. 꽤	quite. pretty
		chỉ	只(지) 枳(지) 止(지) 指(지) 趾(지) 紙(지) 沚(지) 脂(지)	1	바느질실	sewing thread
				2	가리키다	to point
				3	단지	only
		chì			납	lead (chemical element)
		chị			언니. 누님	elder sister
01 05	chia	chĩa		1	포크	pitchfork
				2	겨냥하다	to point (a weapon at). to aim (at)
		chìa		1	쭉 뻗다. 내밀다	stretch forth (one's hand). hold out
				2	열쇠	key
		chia			나누다. 분배하다	to divide
		chia			작살	harpooning
01 06	chich	chích			(바늘 따위로) 따끔하게 찌르다	to prick
01 07	chiec	chiếc		1	하나. 한쌍	one. a pair
				2	외로운. 고독한	lonely
				3	(종별사) 주로 차량, 선박, 비행기, 교량, 옷가지 등의 명사 앞에 쓴다	category word use before nouns nuch as vehicles, ships, airplanes, bridges, and articles of clothing
01 08	chiem	chiếm	占(점) 償(상)		장악하다. 차지하다	to occupy

01 09	chien	chiến	戰(전)	1	싸우다	go to war. war
				2	훌륭한. 멋들어진	excellent
		chiên			튀기다. 볶다	to fry
110	chieu	chiếu	照(조) 詔(조)	1	깔개. 깔판. 요	straw mat for sleeping. seat. rank
				2	빛나다. 비추다	to shine. to light up. to illuminate. to project (images)
		chiều		1	오후	afternoon
				2	공손히 하다. 다른 사람의 의견에 따르다	be respectful of
				3	방향. 코스	direction. course
		chiểu			~에 따라. ~에 의거하여	according to
		chiêu		1	속임수	trick
				2	씻다	to wash down (with)
01 11	chim	chim			새	(zoology) bird
		chím			가라앉다	to sink
01 12	chin	chỉn		1	실. 실밥	thread. threadbare
				2	다만 ~을 우려하다	be concerned only that
		chín		1	아홉. 9	nine
				2	요리된. (과일, 작물 등이) 익은	(of food) well done. (of fruit or crops) ripe
		chin			다리. (=chân)	leg
01 13	chinh	chính	正(정) 政(정)	1	본질적인. 주요한	main. major. chief
				2	바로. 금방	right away. soon
		chỉnh	整(정)	1	정리하다	clean up
				2	옳은. 맞는. 정연한	be correct

		chinh	征(정) 鉦(정)	전쟁(혼자 쓰이지 않는 단어)	war(a word not used alone)
		chĩnh		항아리	jar
01 14	chip	chíp		짹짹 울다. 찍 하는 소리	chirp. peep
01 15	chiu	chịu	1	참다. 이겨내다. 맡다	to endure. to put up with. to make do with
			2	신용으로. 믿음으로	on trust. by faith
			3	동의하다	to agree (to). to consent (to)
01 16	cho	cho	1	주다	to give
			2	~에게. ~을 위하여	dear. for the sake of
		chó		개	dog
		chò		고무나무 비슷한 나무. 집을 만들거나 배를 만드는데 사용	rubber tree-like tree. used to make a house or a ship
		chõ		찜통	steamer
		chộ		보다. 인지하다. (=thấy, trộ)	see. perceive
		chờ		기다리다. (=đợi chờ, chờ đợi)	to wait
		chợ		시장	market
		chớ		하지 마라	don't do that
		chở		수송하다. 운반하다. (차에) 태우다, 태워주다	transport. carry away. take. a ride. pick up
		chỏ		팔꿈치	elbow
		chỗ		장소. 곳. 자리. 좌석	place. seat
01 17	choac	choạc		크게 열리다. 크게 벌리다.	open wide
01 18	choan	choán		장소를 차지하다	occupy a place
01 19	choang	choang		눈부신. 매우 밝은	dazzling. glaring. blinding. bright as a beetle
		choàng	1	두르다. 걸치다	wear sth (about/ around)
			2	갑자기	all of a sudden

		choáng	1	어질어질하다	(medicine) shock. dazzled. overwhelmed. stunned. shocked
			2	반짝반짝 빛나는. (광택) 반질반질한	twinkle. smooth and smooth
		choạng		벌리다. 펼치다	open up. spread out
		choàng		두들겨패다	beat up
0120	choat	choắt		왜소해지다	become dwarfed. stunted. shriveled
0121	choc	chóc	1	말라서 단단해지다	dry up and harden
			2	(한약재) 나무이름	(medicinal herbs) tree name
		chốc		순간	moment. short while
		chọc		찌르다. (과일) 찔러서 구멍을 내다. 누군가를 화나게 하다.	to prick. to puncture. to make someone angry
0122	choi	chói	1	귀가 아플 정도로 높은 소리	an ear-sickening sound
			2	눈부시다. 빛나다	be dazzling
		chõi	1	받쳐주다. 버팀목이 되다	support
			2	철봉	an iron bar
		chơi		놀다	to play
		chòi		오두막	hut
		chổi		빗자루	broom
		chỗi		일으키다. 봉기하다	cause. rise in revolt
		chói		쓰러지거나 붕괴하지 않도록 받쳐주다. 지지해주다	support
		chồi		새싹. 씨앗	sprout. seed
		chọi		부딪치다. 던지다. 싸우다. 되어가다	blow up. to throw. (of animals) to fight. come along
		chối		부인하다. 부정하다	to deny

01 23	chom	**chõm**	1	가늘고 길다	be thin and long
			2	탈취하다	take away
		chòm		(과실. 꽃 따위의) 송이. 다발	bunch (of). cluster (of)
		chờm		뒷다리로 서다. 한계를 벗어나다	go out of bounds
		chồm		뒷발로 서다	to spring up. to prance
		chớm		시작하다. 출발하다	to start to. to begin to
		chỏm		꼭대기. 상투머리	top (of something). peak. summit
		chôm		훔치다. 도둑질하다. (=chôm chỉa. ăn cắp)	to steal
01 24	chon	**chồn**	1	족제비	(zoology) weasel
			2	지치다	to get tired
		chờn	1	마모가 되어 기계의 톱니가 잘 안맞는	the teeth of the machine are worn out and don't fit well
			2	감히 엄두를 내지 못하다	dare not even think about it
		chợn		떨다. 두려워하다	tremble. be afraid of
		chốn		장소 (=chỗ, nơi)	place. spot. destination
		chọn		고르다. 선택하다	to choose. to select
		chôn		(시신을) 묻다. (누구를) 여의다. (땅 속에) 숨기다	to bury
01 25	chong	**chổng**	1	거꾸로 올리다	raise upside down
			2	강물위에 떠 있는 송장	a (dead) body floating on the river
		chống	1	반대하다. 저항하다	to against something
			2	적대적인	anti-
		chồng	1	남편	husband
			2	여러겹으로 쌓다. 중복되어 겹치다	to stack up

		chổng	1	거꾸로 올리다. (=chỗng)	raise upside down
			2	강물에 띄운 송장	a (dead) body floating on the river
		chong		불을 켠채로 두다	leave the light on
		chóng		빠른 (=nhanh chóng, mau chóng)	quick. fast. rapid
		chõng		긴의자. 대나무의자 또는 침대	a long chair. bamboo chair or bed
		chòng		조롱하다. 희롱하다	make a mock of. taunt. ridicule. jeer (at)
		chông		창. 작살	spike. spear. lance. harpoon
0126	chop	chớp	1	곧 ~할 지경이다	be on the verge of doing
			2	섬광. 번개	lightning
		chóp		맨앞. 정상	the very front. top. summit
		chôp		빼앗다. 훔치다	take away. steal
		chợp		선잠을 자다. 잠깐 눈을 붙이다. (=chợp mắt)	have a light sleep. take a nap
		chộp		(붙)잡다	to catch. to seize. to snatch. to grab. to nap
0127	chot	chót	1	정상. 선단. 끝부분	top. end
			2	마지막. 최후의	the last
		chốt	1	나무못. 걸쇠. 빗장	bolt. fastening pin
			2	빗장을 걸다. 닫다	to bolt
		chột		한쪽 눈이 먼	blind in one eye
		chợt		갑자기	suddenly
0128	chu	chu	周(주) 週(주) 朱(주)	1	반복. 주기	repetition
				2	공급하다	supply
		chủ	主(주)	1	주인	owner. proprietor. master. employer. boss

				2	가장 중요한. 핵심의	of prime importance. core
		chứ		1	문장 끝에 붙여서 의문을 나타내는 말. (=phải không) ~하죠?, ~하겠죠?	used at the end of a sentence to create an interrogative sentence (you do, right?. You'll do it, right?)
				2	(확인의 의미로 쓸 때) 확실하다. 물론이다	(the meaning of confirmation) I'm sure. of course
		chú	註(주) 鑄(주) 注(주) 炷(주)		숙부. 삼촌. 외삼촌	paternal uncle (father's younger brother). maternal uncle-in-law (mother's sister's husband). used to address an older man
		chư			모든. 온갖	all. every
		chữ			글자. 말. 문자	alphabet. writing system. script
		chừ			지금. 현재	now. the present
0129	chua	chua		1	시큼한. 신맛나는. 신랄한	sour. acid. vinegary
				2	주석을 달다	to annotate
		chúa		1	주인. 영주. 신	god. lord. Christ
				2	(혼자서는 사용되지 않음) 매우. 극단적으로	excessive. too much
		chửa		1	임신하다. 새끼를 배다	to be pregnant
				2	아직. (=chưa)	yet. alternative form of chưa
		chùa			불교사원	temple
		chưa			~했습니까? (평서문의 문장끝에 위치하여 시간적 개념을 가진 의문문을 만든다)	yet. not yet Did you do? (Located at the end of a plain sentence, it creates a question with a temporal concept)
		chứa			담고있다. 저장하다	save
		chữa			수리하다. (=chữa bài)	to repair. to mend. to treat. to cure

		chừa			버리다. 그만두다	to give up (a bad habit). to abstain from. to quit
01 30	chuan	chuẩn		1	표준. 기준	standard. criterion
				2	인가하다	permission. approval. licence. permit
01 31	chuc	chúc	祝(축)	1	축하하다	to wish
				2	햇불	torchlight
		chức	職(직) 織(직)	1	직무	office (position). rank
				2	짜다. 뜨다. 엮다	weave. knit
		chực			기다리다. 항상 대기하다. 항상 ~할 태세에 있다	to wait. stand by at all the time
		chục			10단위	ten units
01 32	chui	chui			살살 기어들어가다. 기어나오다	to creep (in or out)
		chúi			몸을 앞으로 내밀다	to lean forward
		chùi			닦다	to wipe. to scour. to cleanse
		chửi			모욕하다. 욕하다	to insult. to abuse. to curse. to scold
01 33	chum	chum			병. 항아리	a kind of vase used to contain water
01 34	chun	chun		1	(고무줄처럼) 늘이다	stretch (like a rubber band)
				2	고무줄	rubber band
		chủn		1	기준. 표준	criteria. standard
				2	매우 짧은. 키가 매우 작은	very short
		chùn			움츠리다. 천천히 걷다. (=~bước)	shrink back. to walk slowly
01 35	chung	chung	終(종) 鐘(종)	1	술잔	a drinking glass
				2	모으다	gather
				3	일반적인. 대중적인	general. common. public
		chùng		1	느슨한	loose

			2	몰래. 살짝		on the quiet. secretly. furtively
		chưng	1	끓이다. 삶다		boil
			2	뽐내다. 증류시키다		to show off. to sport. to distill
		chừng	1	한도. 절도. 계량		limit. metering
			2	대략. 거의		about. approximately
		chủng	1	인종. 종족		race. ethnicity. species
			2	종두(우두)를 하다. (=chủng đậu)		to vaccinate
		chững	1	어린아이가 서서 걷기 시작하다		a child begins to walk on his feet
			2	우아한. 안정된		elegant. graceful. stable
		chúng	衆(중)		사람들. 그들. (=chúng nó)	they. them
		chừng			그만큼. 그정도	that much
		chứng	證(증) 症(증)		증명. 증언	proof. verbal evidence
		chựng			어린아이가 서서 걷기 시작하다. (=chững)	a child begins to walk on his feet
01 36	chuoc	chước	着(착)	1	모략. 계략	a plot. a stratagem. a trick. a scheme
				2	참작하다. 면제해주다	take into account. exempt from
		chuộc			대속하다. 몸값을 치루다	to redeem (by payment). to ransom. to atone
		chuốc			술을 따르다	to pour out (wine) for guests
01 37	chuoi	chuỗi			일련. 사슬	chain. string. series
		chuối			바나나	banana
		chuồi			미끄러지다	to slip
		chuội			찌다	steam

		chuôi			(칼의) 손잡이. (=cán)	the handle of a knife
01 38	chuong	chướng	障(장) 腸(장) 誦(송)	1	불쾌한. 꼴불견인	unpalatable. unseemly
				2	장애가 되다. 막다	be an obstacle. hurdle
		chương	章(장) 璋(장)	1	책의 목록을 나누어 놓은 각 장	chapter (of a book)
				2	빛나는. 밝은	shining. bright
		chưởng	掌(장)	1	장악하다	take hold of
				2	손바닥	palm
		chuộng			좋아하다. 애호하다	to prefer. to like
		chuồng			가축우리	a domesticated cage
		chường			드러내 보이다. 쑥 내밀다	appear. show up. stick out
		chuông			종	musical instrument bell
01 39	chup	chụp		1	잡다	to seize. to catch
				2	(사진, X레이를) 찍다	to photograph
01 40	chut	chút			소량. 조금	very small. tiny
		chụt			입맞춤할 때 나는 소리	the sound of a kiss
01 41	chuy	chùy			곤봉	mallet. hammer. blow. thrashing
		chủy	匕(비)		비수	dagger
01 42	chuyen	chuyện		1	일. 사건	story. talk. matter. affair. thing
				2	이야기하다	to talk to
		chuyến			한차례의 이동. 이동편	trip (to the mountains, abroad, etc.)
		chuyền			건네주다. 건너가다	to pass on (to)
		chuyển			건네주다. 옮기다. 보내다	to move. to transfer. to shift. to switch over. to change
		chuyên			전공의. 전문의	to specialise in. to be expert in

0143	co	có		1	가지다. 있다. 존재하다	to have
				2	긍정의 대답을 할때 사용하는 말	do
		cố		1	할아버지. 할머니	a great-grandparent
				2	저당잡히다. 세를 얻다. 소작하다	put up a mortgage on. rent. raise crops
				3	필사적으로 노력하다	to try
		cò		1	우표	a postage stamp
				2	어린	young
		cổ	古(고) 鼓(고)	1	(사람, 동물, 병 등의) 목	neck
				2	옛날의. 오래된	old
		cồ		1	뚫고 나오다	break through
				2	잘먹인. 잘기른	well-fed. fine-grained
		cọ		1	비비다. 마찰하다. (=cạ)	to rub. to scrub. to scour
				2	야자수과의 식물로 잎으로 지붕을 하거나 모자를 만듦	palm tree
		cỏ		1	잔디. 풀. 초목	grass
				2	야생의	negligible
		co			줄어들다. 수축하다	to shrink (to become smaller)
		cơ	基(기) 機(기) 飢(기)	1	하트형(카드)	heart type (card)
				2	근육	a muscle
		cỡ			(총, 총알 등의) 구경 (口徑)	(a gun, bullet, etc.) caliber
		cờ			장기	a board game in which there are pieces, such as chess, go, shogi, xiangqi, etc.
		cộ			차. (=xe)	car
		cớ			이유. 원인. 동기	reason, excuse, pretext
		cỗ			짝. 벌	pair, set

		cô	1	고모	paternal aunt. father's sister
			2	젊은 여성. 아가씨. 여교사	Miss. madam. female teacher(formal, to a woman)
0144	coc	cóc	1	두꺼비	a toad
			2	~아니다. ~않다. 아니다	not. no
		cọc	1	말뚝. 막대기	stake. post
			2	계약금. (=tiền cọc)	down payment. deposit
			3	자라지 않는	ungrown
		cốc	谷(곡) 穀(곡) 梏(곡)	1	손가락 관절로 어떤 사람의 머리를 때리다	hit a person on the head with the knuckles
				2	컵	class. tumbler
		cọc		간단한. 짧은	simple. short
0145	coi	coi		보다	to look. watch (over)
		cơi	1	쟁반	tray
			2	쌓아올리다. 들어올리다. 높게 하다	pile up. lift. make high
		còi	1	발육이 그친. 왜소한	underdeveloped. dwarfed. small. undersized
			2	기적. 경적. 싸이렌	a whistle (device used to make a whistling sound). a horn (loud alarm, especially on a motor vehicle)
		cời	1	(장대나 막대기로) 떨어뜨리다	drop (with a pole or stick)
			2	찢어진	torn
		cỗi	1	뿌리. 근원. (=cội)	root. source of origin
			2	늙어서 발육이 그친	out of development with age
		cõi		지방. 영역. 분야	large region. country. large area or space. world. depth (of the heart)

		cói			등심초. 골풀	a rush
		còi			돌기	bump. swelling
		cối	會(회)		절구	a mortar
		cội			뿌리. 기원	root. source of origin
		cởi			벗다. (=cối)	to disengage. to untie. to unfasten. to take off. to set off
		cối			벗다. (=cởi)	to disengage. to untie. to unfasten. to take off. to set off
		cỡi			타다. (=cưỡi)	ride
01 46	con	con		1	아이. 자식	child (daughter or son)
				2	(경멸의 의미로) 여성에 붙이는 단어	words attached to a woman as a sign of contempt
				3	작은	small
				4	(생물체의) 단위 명사	unit noun of living things
		còn		1	남다. 유지하다	to remain. to be left. to still have or exist
				2	여전히. 아직	yet. still
		cốn		1	벌채하다	cut down
				2	사다리 난간	a ladder rail
		cớn		1	무디어지다	be worn out
				2	설익은	underdone
		cỡn			(동물) 암내를 내는. 발작적으로 암내를 내는. (=động cỡn)	make the odor of a female animal in heat
		cồn			알코올	alcohol
		cộn			겹치다. 겹쳐입다	dress in layers
		cọn			수차(水車)	waterwheel

		cơn		(상태, 심리, 자연현상 앞에 붙이는 명사로 단독으로는 쓰이지 않는다)	a noun that preceds a state. psychological. or natural penomenon and is not used alone
		côn		곤봉	club (weapon). stick. cudgel. fighting stick
01 47	cong	cong	1	굽은. 구부러진	curved. be bent
			2	구부러지다	bend over
		còng	1	족쇄	a foot shackle
			2	허리가 굽은	bent at the waist
		cóng	1	(손이) 곱은	(of a body) frosty. be frozen
			2	작은 유리병. 도자기로 만든 용기	a small glass bottle. ceramic containers
		cọng	1	줄기	stem
			2	보태다. (=cộng)	add up
		cộng	共(공) 1	잎꼭지. 대	the leaf of a plant
			2	가산하다. 합계하다	to add. plus
		cống	貢(공) 1	용수로(用水路). 하수로	sewer. drain
			2	조공을 바치다	to pay tribute
		cõng		등으로 나르다. 허리에 싣고 나르다	to give someone a piggyback
		cổng		문. 입구	entrance. gate
		cồng	鉦(정)	징(鉦). (=chiêng nhỏ)	gong
		công	1	공공의	public
			2	공평한. (=công bằng)	just. fair. impartial
			3	보수. 대가	pay. cost. price
01 48	com	còm	1	굽히다	bend over
			2	야윈	thin

		cộm		1	부푼. 튀어나온	bulging
				2	부풀다. 부풀게하다	swell up. inflate
		cớm		1	햇볕이 들지 않는. 발육불량의.	sunless. undeveloped
				2	경찰을 부르는 은어	(law) enforcement. (slang) a cop
		cơm			밥	meal. cooked non-glutinous rice
		cốm			찐 쌀. 햅쌀로 만든 떡	steamed rice. rice cake made from newly-cooked rice
		cưm			부은	swollen
		cọm			허리가 굽은. (=khọm)	bent at the waist
0149	cop	cóp			복사하다. 표절하다. 도용하다	make a copy. plagiarize. steal away
		cợp			털이 무성한. 머리칼이 귀까지 덮힌	hairy. hair covered to ears
		cọp			호랑이	tiger
		cốp			(자동차의) 트렁크	trunk. boot (of a car, motorbike, etc.)
0150	cot	cột		1	기둥	pillar. column. pole
				2	매다. 묶다	to fasten. to strap in. to bind. to tie
		cót			대나무 매트	bamboo mat
		cợt			놀리다. (=trêu ghẹo)	make fun of. kid. tease. provoke
		cốt	骨(골)		뼈	bone. skeleton
0151	cu	cú	句(구)	1	올빼미	owl
				2	머리를 때리다	to knuckle one's head
		cự	拒(거) 巨(거) 距(거)	1	욕설을 퍼붓다	scold, oppose, resist
				2	거리. 간격	distance. interval

		cù	苦(고) 苟(구) 瞿(구)	1	팽이. 회전기	humming top. spinning top
				2	흥을 돋구다. 간지럽히다	to tickle
		cừ	渠(거)	1	운하	canal
				2	능숙한. 뛰어난. 말쑥한	skillful. excellent. neatly
		cữ		1	주기. 기간	period, cycle
				2	삼가하다. (음식을) 가려먹다	refrain from. pick one's food
		cu			음경 (수컷의 생식기관)	penis
		cư	居(거)		거주하다	to live. to dwell
		cũ			고대의. 낡은. 오래된. (=cũ càng)	old
		củ	矩(구)		구근 (球根)	root. bulb
		cứ		1	계속하다	to continue to do something
				2	그냥	just
		cử	擧(거)		지명하다	to appoint. delegate
		cụ	具(구) 懼(구)		나이 많은 노인에게 붙이는 용어	Sir, madam, Mr, Mrs (when addressing a very old person)
01 52	cua	cua		1	게	crab
				2	모퉁이. 곡선. 굴곡. (경로가 급격하게 변하는 지점)	corner. curve. bend (point where a route changes sharply)
		cưa		1	톱	saw
				2	자르다	to saw
		của		1	재산. (=của cải)	property. belongings
				2	(소유격) ~의. ~에 속하는	of (belonging to or associated with)
		cựa		1	움직이다. 탈출구를 찾다	move. find a way out
				2	(싸움닭) 싸울때 사용하는 곁발가락	spur (of roosters)

		cứa		무딘 칼로 자르다	to cut little by little. to saw off
		cửa		문	door. any entrance into a building or room
0153	cuc	cúc	菊(국) 鞠(국)	1	국화	chrysanthemum
				2	단추	button
		cực	極(극)		극	pole
		cục	局(국)	1	사무실. 부처. 부서	office. ministry. department
				2	조각. 덩어리	indicates feces balls. small stones. erasers. flour balls
0154	cui	cúi		1	구부리다. 숙이다	to bend (one's body)
				2	불쏘시개	a firecracker
				3	돼지	(zoology) pig
		cùi		1	과일의 일부. 과심. 과육 포함	part of the fruit, include the core and/or the flesh
				2	나병의	leprosyous. leprosy
		cũi		1	굴. 우리	cage (specifically for a quadruped)
				2	(우리에) 집어넣다	put in (a cage)
		cửi		1	베짜는 기계	weaving machine
				2	소공예식으로 비단을 짜다	weave silk in a small-scale fashion
		củi			장작. 땔나무	firewood
0155	cum	cùm		1	족쇄. 속박	fetters
				2	족쇄를 채우다	fetter
		cum			볏단	a sheaf of rice
		cúm			유행성 감기. 인플루엔자	(medicine) influenza. flu
		cụm			수풀. 덤불	cluster. bunch

0156	cun	**cun**		므엉족의 추장. 옛날 므엉(Mường)족의 관리 계급 이름	a chief of the Mường tribe
		cùn		둔한. 무딘	(of a knife) be blunt
		cún		강아지. (=chó con)	puppy
0157	cung	**cung**	宮(궁) 供(공) 弓(궁) 恭(공)	1 궁전	palace
				2 공급하다	supply
		cùng	窮(궁)	함께	with
		cưng		하고싶은대로 하게 하다. 비위를 맞추다	curry favor to with
		cũng		역시	also. too
		cúng	供(공)	공급하다	supply
		củng	鞏(공) 拱(공)	손가락 마디로 이마나 머리를 때리다	hit sb on the forehead or head with a knuckle
		cứng		단단한. 딱딱한	hard. tough. rigid
		cụng		치다. 때리다	to hit
0158	cuoc	**cuốc**		1 괭이	hoe
				2 괭이로 밭을 일구다	to hoe
		cuộc		1 모임 등에 쓰이는 말 (대규모, 다인 행사)	a large-scale or multi-person event
				2 내기걸다	make a bet
		cước	脚(각)	다리	leg
		cược		(돈을) 걸다	bet money on. put money on
0159	cuoi	**cuội**		1 조약돌	pebble
				2 교묘하게 거짓말을 하는	deftly lying
		cười		1 웃음	a smile
				2 웃다. 미소짓다	to smile

		cuối			끝	end. terminal part. bottom. lowest part
		cưỡi			(말, 자전거 등) 타다	to ride (an animal)
		cưới			결혼하다	to marry. to wed
0160	cuong	cương		1	말굴레. 고삐	a bridle. a halter. a reins
				2	부풀은	(of a penis) erect
		cuống	桂(계) 戒(계)	1	잎꼭지	petiole. leafstalk
				2	당황하다. 안달복달하다	be in need of doing something that one start to do it quickly.
		cuồng	狂(광)		미친. 이성을 잃은. 무모한	crazy. mad. bonkers
		cường	强(강)		강한	strong. vigorous
		cưỡng	强(강)		강요하다. 강제하다	to coercion. to pressure. to force (sb to do)
0161	cuop	cướp		1	강도	robber. mugger
				2	빼앗다	to rob
0162	cup	cúp		1	컵(운동경기에서 우승의)	cup (competition reward). trophy
				2	자르다. 베다. 끊다	cut (down/off/out/away)
		cụp		1	(잎) 오므리다. (꼬리) 내리다	fold up (the leaves). lower (one's tail)
				2	즐거운. 상쾌한	joyful. fresh
0163	cut	cút		1	작은 굴뚝새	small chimney bird
				2	갑자기 떠나다	make a sudden departure
		cụt			단절되어 짧아진. 꽉막힌	shortened
		cứt			(사람, 동물의) 대변. 똥	feces. shit
0164	cuu	cưu	鳩(구)		(마음) 지니다	have a mind
		cửu	九(구) 玖(구) 久(구)		아홉. 9	nine. 9

		cửu	柩(구) 臼(구)		관. 관가(棺架). 영구차	coffin. casket. hearse. funeral coach
		cứu	救(구)		구하다. 구제하다	to save. to rescue. to relieve
		cừu			(동물) 양	sheep
		cựu	舊(구)	1	오래된. 낡은	old
				2	(접두사) 전	(prefix) ex-
01 65	da đa	đá		1	돌	rock. stone
				2	단단한	hard
				3	얼음	ice
				4	(발로) 차다	to kick without using the sole
		dà		1	뱃밥을 채우거나 천, 실을 물들이는데 쓰이는 나무	a tree used to fill oakum or to dye cloth or thread
				2	친근한 의미로 부정을 나타내는 말. "안 그런데요"의 뜻	a word that expresses negative meaning of "I don't think so." in friendly sense
		đa	多(다)	1	많이	much
				2	용수(열대아시아에 분포하는 뽕나무과의 교목). (=da)	the mulberry tree of tropical Asia.
		dã	野(야)	1	야만의. 미개의	wild. savage. rustic
				2	(알코올, 독약 등을) 중화하다	to neutralize the effect of (alcohol)
		đà		1	뜀박질	run. dash
				2	잡아당기다. (칼싸움) 속임수를 잘 쓰다	pull at. be clever at deception
		đã		1	이미 ~을 했다 (문장의 과거형을 만든다)	a past tense marker. already. done
				2	우선	first
		da			피부	skin (outer covering of the body)
		dạ	夜(야)		예. 네. (정중한 대답)	an initial particle to express politeness and respect.

		đả	打(타)		때리다. 치다. (=đánh)	to hit. to strike
01 66	dac đac	đặc	特(특)	1	고체의. 고형의	solid
				2	응축하다	condensed
		đạc	度(도) 鐸(탁)	1	(경지면적을) 측량하다	measure (land area)
				2	목탁	wooden percussion instrument used for chanting by Buddhist clergy
		dác			나무의 껍질 다음에 형성된 나무살	a tree trunk formed after the bark of a tree
		dặc			잡고 팽개치다	throw away at
		đắc	得(득)		획득하다. 얻다	to acquire. to obtain. gain
01 67	dai đai	dãi		1	침, 타액	saliva. especially sticky or slimy saliva
				2	햇볕에 쬐다	be bathed in the sun
		đai	帶(대)	1	업다	to carry something on one's back
				2	띠	belt
		đái	帶(대) 戴(대)	1	소변을 보다. (=đi đái)	to pee. to urinate
				2	끈	string
		dại		1	햇볕에 쬐다	be bathed in the sun
				2	광견병의	having rabies
		đại	大(대) 代(대) 袋(대)	1	큰	big. great
				2	무작위로. 무책임하게	randomly, or in a irresponsible way
		dai			강한. 질긴	persistent. (of dood) tough
		dài			긴	long
		đài	台(태) 鮟(안)		태	calyx. flower cup. tower. monument
		dải			띠. 끈. 리본	ribbon. band. belt

		đãi	待(대) 怠(태) 殆(태)		헹구다. 씻다	to rinse off (unwanted parts in water). to wash out. to pan off. to flay (soybean)
01 68	dam đam	dầm		1	(비에) 젖다	be wet (with rain)
				2	(건축) 동륜(銅輪)	a copper wheel
		dăm		1	대패밥	shavings
				2	다소의	a few. some
		dặm		1	거리의 단위	mile (measure of length). league (distance)
				2	청혼하다	propose
		dằm		1	쪼개진 조각	fragment
				2	날카로운 꽃챙이로 헤치다	plow through with a sharp stick
		đảm	擔(담)	1	부담하다. 담당하다	be in charge of
				2	~할 능력있는	capable. resourceful
		đầm		1	늪. 못. 습지	swamp
				2	흠뻑 젖다	to be soaking. to be sopping wet
		đậm		1	진한(색)	(of colors) deep
				2	심하게. 격차가 크게	badly. a wide gap
		dam			논에 사는 게	a crab (living in a rice paddy)
		dàm			(동물) 입마개. 고삐	muzzle. bridle
		dám			감히 ~하다. 대담하게 ~하다	(somewhat informal) to dare to do something
		dâm	淫(음)		음란한. 음탕한	lustful. lecherous. voluptuous
		đam			빠지다. 열중하다	be absorbed in. be intent on
		đăm			우측	(of a direction) right
		dẫm			짓밟다	trample (on/over)
		đâm			찌르다. (=trở nên)	to stab. to crash into

		đàm	痰(담) 談(담) 譚(담) 潭(담)	1	말하다. 이야기하다	to talk. to discuss. to negotiate
				2	담. 가래. 점액. (=đờm)	phlegm. mucus
		dấm			식초	vinegar
		đám			떼. 무리	cluster. heap
		đắm			(배가) 가라앉다. (=say đắm)	(of ship, boat) to sink (completely)
		đấm			주먹으로 때리다	to punch. to beat
		đậm			진한. 짙은	deep. dark
		đạm	淡(담) 澹(담)	1	질소	nitrogen
				2	단백질	protein
		đẫm			흠뻑 젖다	be soaked
		đằm			(수렁, 모래, 물속에서) 뒹굴다	to roll (about in a mire, sand or water)
		đầm			조용한. 평정한. (=ướt đầm)	quiet
		dạm			미리 예측하다. 측정하다	predict beforehand
		dậm			(발을) 구르다 (giậm)	to stamp
01 69	dan đan	dãn		1	길이나 양은 증가하나 부피는 불변인 상태	a state in which the length or quantity increases but the volume remains unchanged.
				2	늘어난	stretched
		dần	寅(인)	1	호랑이	tiger
				2	두드리다	to beat (repeatedly). to thrash
		đan	丹(단) 單(단) 握(악)	1	짜다. 뜨다. 엮다. 뜨개질하다	to weave
				2	신청서. (=đơn)	application form
		đàn	彈(탄) 檀(단) 壇(단)	1	무리. 떼	flock. herd
				2	연주하다	to play (a string instrument)

	dạn		1	익숙해지다	get used to
			2	대담한. 철면피의	bold. brazen. not shy
	đản	誕(탄) 亶(단)	1	생일	birthday
			2	황당무계한	absurd
	đần		1	멍청한. 어리석은	dull-minded. very stupid
			2	꾸짖다	give a person a scolding
	đẵn		1	자르다	to cut
			2	마디	joint. knuckle
	đẫn		1	살이 너무 쪄서 둥글다	be fat and round
			2	어느 한토막	one piece
	dan			(팔, 날개) 뻗다. 늘이다. 펴다	(arm, wing) extend. stretch. spread
	dán			풀로 붙이다. 붙이다	to paste. to glue
	dân	民(민)		민족. 국민. 시민	people. citizen
	dàn			배열하다. 정돈하다	to display. to put in order. to arrange
	dăn			주름진. (=nhăn)	wrinkled
	đán	旦(단) 港(권)		여명. 아침	dawn. morning
	dặn			충고하다	to recommend. to advise
	dẫn	引(인)		이끌다. 안내하다	to lead. to guide
	dằn			억제하다	to restrain
	dấn			~에 (몸을) 두다. (=nhấn)	rest oneself in
	dận			발로 밟아 누르다	stamp on
	đận			한때. 한참. 한시기	once
	đặn			어르다. 어르고 뺨치다	to humor. to coax
	đẳn			누르다	to press
	đạn	彈(탄)		구슬(볼베어링)	bullet

		dãn	1	원래의 피부를 유지하면서 길이나 양이 늘어난	(physics) expanding. stretched
			2	팽창하다. 늘어나다	increase. rise
01 70	dang đang	dáng	1	외형. 모습	an outward form. figure
			2	흡사 ~같다. (=dáng như)	look like a
		đăng	登(등) 燈(등)	1	기대하다	to anticipate
				2	어랑 (물고기 잡는 장치)	fishing basket. creel
		đặng		1	~할 수 있다. (=được)	can
				2	~하기 위해서. (=đặng cho)	in order to. so that
		đẳng		1	방면. 측	direction. side
				2	팽팽하게 잡아당기다	pull tight
		dang			(손. 발을) 펴다. 뻗다	(of limbs) to stretch out
		dâng			(수면이) 오르다	usually of water level to rise
		dăng			길게 펴다	stretch out
		đang	當(당) 倦(권)		~하는 중이다	be doing
		dạng	樣(양)		외견. 형상	form. shape
		đáng			~할 가치가 있다. ~해야 마땅하다	worthy. worth. to deserve. to merit
		dặng			헛기침을 하다	clear their throat
		dẳng			끌어당기다	draw in
		đàng			~쪽. ~편. 길. 도로. (=đường)	road
		đãng	蕩(안)		잊기 쉬운. 통제하지 못하는	easy to forget. out of control
		đảng	黨(당)		정당 (=chính đảng). 政黨	political party
		đẳng			재능이 있고 큰 일을 하는 인물에 붙는 말	used for gods, heros, talented people, etc.
		đẳng			(맛) 쓰다	bitter
		đẳng	等(등)		등	rank. grade. class

0171	danh đanh	đành		1	순순히 동의하다. 묵인하다	acquiesce in
				2	마음에 드는. 흡족한	satisfied. pleased. content
		danh	名(명)		이름. 명성. (=tăm tiếng)	name. fame. reputation
		đanh			단단한. 견고한	hard. hard and dry. sharp (of sounds)
		dành			대비하다. 저축하다	to save up. to reserve
		dảnh			벼의 모	transplant rice seedlings
		đánh			때리다. 치다. 두드리다	to beat. to strike
		đảnh			꼭대기. (=đỉnh)	top
0172	dao đao	đảo	島(도) 倒(도) 禱(도)	1	섬	island
				2	모순된. 정반대되는	contradictory. conflicting. diametrically opposed
		đào	桃(도) 逃(도) 淘(도) 陶(도) 萄(도)	1	복숭아	peach
				2	파다. 발굴하다	to dig up. to unearth
		dạo		1	시기. 기간	time period. times
				2	(총을) 시험삼아 쏴보다	try (a gun)
		đáo	到(도)		도달하다	come to. to reach. arrive (at/in)
		đạo	導(도) 道(도) 盜(도) 稻(도)	1	길	street. way. road
				2	빼앗다. 훔치다	to take. to steal
		dao	刀(도)		칼. (=con dao)	knife
0173	dap đap	đập		1	댐. 둑	dam
				2	깨부수다. 때리다	to beat. to strike
		đáp	答(답) 塔(탑)		대답하다	to answer
		dập			묻다. 덮다	to bury. to cover (with soil or sand)

		dấp			(물에) 적시다	to soak (in the water)
		đạp			(발로) 밟다	to kick, trample or push using the sole
		đắp			덮다	to cover something with a layer
0174	dat đat	dật	逸(일) 溢(일) 佚(일)	1	주색에 빠진, 음탕한	indulge in boozing and womanizing, lewd
				2	도주하다	make one's getaway
		dát			얇게 만들다	make thin
		dắt			(손을 잡고) 데리고 가다	to lead
		dặt			채워넣다	fill up
		dạt			오래되어 찢어지기 쉬운	old and fragile
		đặt		1	두다, 놓다	to place, to put, to lay
				2	예약하다, 예매하다, 주문하다	make a reservation, to command, to order
		đất			토지, 땅	earth, soil, land
		đắt			(값이) 비싼	expensive, dear, costly
		đạt	達(달)	1	보내다, 전달하다	to send, deliver
				2	도달하다	reach, attain
0175	dau đau	đau		1	아프다	to be hurt, to be wounded
				2	고통, 아픈	hurt, wounded, sore, aching
		dầu		1	기름	oil
				2	~이긴 하지만, 비록 ~ 일지라도, ~에도 불구하고	even if
		đậu	豆(두) 逗(두) 痘(두)	1	주차하다. (=đỗ)	to park
				2	두부. (=đậu phụ)	tofu
				3	콩, 견과	bean, nut

		đấu	斗(두) 鬪(투)	1	(곡물, 액체를 재는) 되. 말	(measuring grain, liquid) ladle. scoop. dipper
				2	혼합하다	mix up
				3	싸우다	to battle. fight
		dàu			시들다	wither (away)
		dâu			며느리. 새색시. 뽕나무. 딸기	bride. mulberry. strawberry
		dậu	酉(유)		닭 (十二支의 하나)	chicken
		dẫu			비록 ~이지만	although~
		dâu			(의문) 어디	where
		dấu			성조	mark. sign. diacritic. tone
		đầu	頭(두)		머리	head
01 76	day đay	đây		1	여기에	here
				2	이번. 금번	this
		đầy		1	가득찬. 충분한. (=đầy đủ)	full. filled
				2	~이내에. ~의 범위안에	within the confines of
		đay		1	(식물) 황마(黃麻)	jute
				2	중얼중얼 말하다. 같은 말을 자꾸 지껄이다	to mutter. murmur
		dây		1	줄. 선. 끈. 밧줄	rope. cord. wire. string
				2	때가 묻다	be stained with dirt
		dẫy			밀물이 되다	be in high tide
		day			돌리다. 돌다	to turn. to spin
		dày			두꺼운. 짙은	thick. deep. dense
		dãy			열. 행렬	a set. a chain. a series
		dấy			일어나다. 일으키다	to raise. to rise up
		dậy			일어나다. (=thức dậy)	to wake up. to rise
		dạy			가르치다. (=dạy học)	to teach. to train

		dày		두꺼운. (=dầy)	thick
		đáy		바닥. 밑바닥	bottom
		dảy		(갑자기) 밀다	to push (suddenly)
		đày		귀양가다	to be exiled
		đãy		자루. 가방	bag. sack
		đẩy		밀다	to push. to shove. to thrust
		đấy	1	저기. 그쪽	there. that place. that
			2	문장끝에 붙여 의문문을 만들때 쓰임	used at the end of sentence to create an interrogative sentence
		đậy	1	빚을 갚다. (=trả nợ đậy)	pay the debt
			2	대신하다	to substitute. to replace
		đẫy		뚱뚱한	fat. full
01 77	de đe	dẽ	1	단단히 조이다	tighten up
			2	딱딱하게 굳은	harden
		đệ	弟(제) 第(제) 1	남동생	a younger brother
			2	제출하다. 품신하다	to submit
		để	1	두다. 남기다. 위치하다. 놓다	to place. to set. to let. to leave (alone)
			2	~하기 위해서 (목적, 방법)	in order to. so that
		đẻ	1	태어나다	to birth
			2	출산의	to give birth to
		đe	1	(대장간의) 모루	anvil
			2	으르다	to warn. to threaten
		dễ	1	말귀를 빨리 알아듣다	quickly catch a person's drift
			2	용이한. 쉬운	easy. simple

		đế	帝(제)	1	황제. (=hoàng đế)	emperor of an empire
				2	첨가해 쓰다 (연극 공연 중) 대사와 대사사이에 끼어드는 말을 하다	add to one's (ad-lib) interject between a line and line
		đề	題(제) 提(제)	1	표제. 주제	subject
				2	기입하다. 쓰다	to write
		de			육계피 (보통 침대 또는 상자용으로 사용)	usually used as a bed or box
		dè			경제적으로 쓰다	use something economically
		dế			귀뚜라미	cricket
		dễ			경시하고 깔보다. (=coi thường)	look down on
		đè			강요하다. 강제하다	to press
		dẻ			개암나무. (과일) 밤의 일종	chestnut
		dệ			~가. 가장자리	edge
		đễ	悌(제)		(윗 사람에게) 순종하는. 잘 따르는. (=hiếu đễ)	obedient. be a good follower
		dê			염소	goat
		đê			제방. 제방 길	embankment. embankment path
01 78	dem đem	đệm		1	깔다. 동행하다	to place (under). to accompany
				2	완충지. 매트리스. 요	mattress. cushion
		đem			들고 가다. 가지고 오다(가다)	to bring. to carry
		dém			(커튼) 양쪽 폭을 당겨 꼭 조이다	tighten the curtains by pulling both widths
		đếm			(숫자를) 세다	to count (one by one). to number. to enumerate
		đêm			밤. 야간	night

0179	den đen	dền		1	시들지 않는 꽃. 아마란	amaranth
				2	(빵, 떡) 부드러운	(bread, rice cake) soft
		đến		1	도착하다. 오다	to arrive. to come
				2	~까지. ~할 정도로. 심지어 ~까지도	to
		đền		1	궁전. (=đền rồng)	palace
				2	보상하다. 갚다	compensate. pay back
		đen			검은	(of the color) black
		đèn			램프. 등불	lamp
		dện			거미. (=nhện)	spider
		đẹn			(의학) 아구창	thrush. oral candidiasis
		đẻn			뱀의 한 종류 (독이 많은 작은 뱀으로 물속에서 서식한다)	a species of snake
0180	dep đep	dép			샌들. 신발	sandal
		dẹp		1	정리하다	to clean up
				2	평평한	be flattened. flat
		đẹp			아름답다	beautiful (possessing charm and attractive)
		đệp			(대나무로 만든) 작은 바구니	a small basket (made of bamboo)
0181	det đet	đét		1	말려서 시든	dried and withered
				2	채찍으로 치다	to whip
		dệt		1	방직	weaving
				2	짜다. 뜨다	to weave
		dẹt		1	평평해지다. 움푹꺼지다. (=bẹt)	flatten out. a dip in the ground
				2	납작한	flat bottom
		đẹt		1	곱사병의. 구루병의	rachitic
				2	살짝살짝 때리다	give a slight slap

0182	deu deu	đều		1	규칙적인. 고른	equal. even
				2	둘 다. 모두	both. all
		đểu			교양이 없는. 천박한. 사기성의	uncultivated. shallow. fraudulent
0183	di đi	di	移(이) 遺(유) 夷(이) 怡(이)	1	옮기다	to move. shift
				2	오랑캐	barbarian
		đi		1	가다. 걷다	to go
				2	동사뒤에 붙여 명령, 권유를 나타냄 (~해라. ~하자)	posted on the back of a verb, indicating command, exhortation.
		đì		1	꾸짖다. 비난하다	to scold. criticise
				2	음낭. 고환	a scrotum
		đĩ		1	음탕한	lewd. lascivious
				2	매춘부. 창녀	(vulgar) a whore
		dì			이모	maternal aunt. mather's sister
		dĩ	以(이) 已(이)		사용하다. 취하다	to take. to employ
		dỉ			속삭이다. 작은 소리로 말하다 (소근거리다)	to whisper
		dị	異(이) 易(이)		기이한. 이상한	eccentric. strange
0184	dia đia	đìa		1	많은	numerous. over head and ears (in debt)
				2	연못	pond (in the field)
		dĩa		1	접시. 받침접시	a plate. a dish. a saucer. etc.
				2	둥글납작한 판. 원반	a disc. a disk. etc.
				3	포크	a fork
		đĩa			접시. (=dĩa)	a plate. a dish. a saucer. a disc. a disk. etc.

		địa	地(지)		지리. Địa lý의 약(略)	geography
		đỉa			거머리. (=con đỉa)	(zoology) leech
0185	dich đich	dịch	譯(역) 役(역) 易(역) 疫(역) 液(액)	1	번역하다. 통역하다	to translate
				2	전염병. 유행병	infectious diseases
				3	액체	fluid. liquid
		địch	笛(적) 敵(적)	1	피리. 플루트	pipe. flute
				2	적	enemy. adversary. foe
		đích	的(적) 嫡(적)		과녁. 표적	(sports, of a race) a goal
0186	diec	diếc			험담하다. 나무라다. (=nhiếc)	speak ill of. to scold
		diệc			백로. 해오라기. (=con diệc)	egret. white heron
		điếc			귀머거리의. 청각 장애가 있는	deaf
0187	diem điem	điểm	点(점)	1	견해. 의견. ~점	point. dot. (academic) mark
				2	불을 붙이다. 점화하다	light a fire
		điềm		1	징후	signs
				2	조용한	quiet
		điếm		1	(창녀차림으로) 유혹하려고 차려입다	dress up as a prostitute
				2	매춘부. 창녀. (=gái điếm)	prostitute
		diễm			(단독으로 쓰이지 않음) 예쁜. 아름다운	pretty. beautiful
		diềm			가장자리 장식	edge decoration
		diêm			성냥	match. matches (device to make fire)
0188	dien đien	diện	面(면)	1	관점. 면. 부분	aspect. area
				2	멋을 부리다	to dress up (in). to be well-dressed (in)

		điển	典(전)	1	경전	classical book
				2	전형적인. 표준적인	typical
		điền	田(전)	1	밭. 논	land. field
				2	기입하다. 써넣다	fill out
		diễn	演(연)		(무대에서) 연기하다. 역을 맡다. 공연하다	to act. to perform
		điện	電(전) 殿(전)	1	궁전. 어전	palace
				2	전기	electricity
		điên			미친. 실성한	rabid. insane. mad
01 89	dieng đieng	diềng			정월. (=tháng Giêng)	the first month of the year
		điếng			기절할 만큼의. 격심한. (=điếng người)	intense
01 90	dieu đieu	điệu	調(조) 悼(도)	1	태도	attitude
				2	강제로 데리고 나가다. 잡다	force out. take by force
				3	멜로디. 곡조. 공기	melody. tune. air
		diệu	妙(묘)	1	익숙한. 교묘한	effective. marvellous. wonderful
				2	과시하다	show off. parade
		điếu	弔(조) 釣(조)	1	문상하다. 애도하다	to condole on someone's death
				2	담뱃대	hookah. pipe (for smoking)
		diều		1	솔개	(zoology) kite
				2	연	kite (flying toy on string)
		điều	條(조) 調(조)	1	말	word. sentence
				2	(무형적, 추상적) 것 (=cái). 일. 사건. 문제. 점	pretext
		điểu			새의 이름	a bird's name
		điêu			정직하지 않은. 거짓의	prone to lying. untruthful
		diễu			지나가다	to parade

0191	dinh đinh	đinh	丁(정) 釘(정)		못	a nail
		dính		1	밀착하다. 달라붙다	to stick. to glue
				2	끈적끈적한. 접착성의. 이어진	sticky. gluey
		đính	訂(정) 頂(정) 錠(정)	1	정정하다	to correct
				2	부착된. 동봉한	enclosed
		đình	廷(정) 停(정) 庭(정)	1	정자	village shrine
				2	정지하다	to stop. to postpone
		định	定(정)	1	결정하다. 정하다	to fix. to appoint. to set. to assign
				2	지정된. 정해진	designated. setted
				3	~하려고 한다. ~할 작정이다 (가까운 미래의 계획, 예정)	to intend (to). to plan (to). to be about (to)
		dinh	營(영)		(군대) 진영. 캠프	(military) camp
		dĩnh	穎(영)		영리하다. 영 (穎). 영포 (穎苞)	clever. eleutherosteglum
		đỉnh	頂(정)		정상. 꼭대기. 정점	a top (uppermost part). a summit (peak, top of the mountain). (geometry) a vertex
0192	do đo	đó		1	통발 (물고기잡는 도구)	a weir made of willow or bamboo. a fish trap
				2	그. 저	there. they. those
		đỗ	杜(두) 汲(급)	1	주차하다	to park
				2	임시로	temporarily
		đố		1	천의 가로줄 무늬	horizontal line pattern of cloth
				2	결코 ~않다 (강한 부정)	by no way (a strong denial)

	dò		1	새잡는 덫	a bird trap
			2	꼼꼼히 확인해보다	to check carefully
	dơ		1	더러운. 불결한. (=nhơ)	dirty. filthy
			2	(손을) 들다	to raise (one's hand)
	dở		1	(책을) 열다	open (a book)
			2	시시한. 나쁜. 좋지 않은	bad. uninteresting
	độ	度(도) 渡(도)	1	도 (열, 기온 등)	unit degree. degree Celsius
			2	대략. 약	approximately. about
	đồ	徒(도) 塗(도) 屠(도) 圖(도)	1	물건	thing
			2	징역에 처하다	sentence sb to prison
	đỏ		1	붉은. 빨갛다	red
			2	붉게 타오르다	burn red
	do			~에 의해. ~으로써. 왜냐하면 ~ 때문에	(neutral passive voice marker) by. because of. due to
	dó			나무껍질을 종이만드는데 사용하는 식물	a plant that uses bark to make paper
	đo			측정하다. 재다	to measure
	đò			나룻배. 거룻배	a kind of small boat
	dỗ			감언으로 설득하다. 어르다	to coax. to entice. to allue
	dọ			의뢰하다. 조사하다	make a request. investigate
	dỡ			(집의) 지붕을 허물다	to dismentle. to demolish
	đơ			경직된. 마비된. (=đờ)	sttifen
	đõ			벌집	honeycomb
	đổ			앞으로 돌진하다	rush forward
	đờ			경직된. 무표정한. 말문이 막힌	expressionless
	đớ			말문이 막히다. 바짝 얼어붙다	be speechless. be frozen

		đỡ		(대답, 재난 따위를) 피하다	to prop. to help. to reduce
		đợ		저당 잡히다	be mortgaged
		đọ		경쟁하다. 비교하다	to compete. to compare
		đô	1	도시	(capital) city
			2	달러	dollar
		đổ		붓다. 쏟다. (기름을) 넣다	to pour. fill up
0193	doa	doa		드릴로 구멍을 넓히다	widen a hole with a drill
		dọa		위협하다. 협박하다	make a threat. to threaten (with). to intimidate
		đóa		떨기. 송이. 다발	a bunch. a indicates cluster (of flowers)
		đọa		(지옥으로) 떨어뜨리다	drop (to hell)
0194	doan đoan	đoan	端(단)	1	관세 부문(프랑스 식민시대)	the customs sector of the french colonial government
				2	곧바른. 단정한	neat and tidy
		đoạn	斷(단) 段(단) 緞(단)	1	부분조각	section. portion
				2	끝나다	to end. to finish
		doãn	允(윤) 尹(윤)	1	순응하다. 따르다	adapt oneself to
				2	(봉건시대) 일정한 지역의 통치관리	the governance of a certain area in feudal times
		đoàn	團(단) 段(단) 鍛(단)	1	단체. 무리	group. party. corps
				2	단련하다	train oneself
		doan			우아한. (=duyên)	elegant. graceful
		đoán	斷(단)		예상하다. 추측하다	to guess. to predict
		đoản	短(단)		짧다	short
0195	doanh đoanh	doanh	營(영)		군주둔지. (=dinh)	a military compound
		doành			물의 흐름. (=duềnh)	the flow of water
		đoành			꽝(폭죽과 소총의 작은 소리)	bang. thump (the sound of fireworks)

0196	doc đoc	dốc		1	경사진	slope
				2	비우다. 비다. 털어놓다	to pour out. to empty. to exhaust
		độc	獨(독) 讀(독) 毒(독)	1	고독한. (=cô độc. đơn độc. cô đơn)	lonely
				2	독악(毒惡)한. 잔인한. (=độc ác)	cruel. brutal. cold-blooded
				3	읽다	to read. to pronounce
		dọc		1	길이	length
				2	~와 나란히. ~의 옆에. 곁에. ~을 따라	alongside. side by side
		đốc	督(독) 篤(독)	1	독촉하다. 재촉하다	to urge
				2	뾰족한 부분	a sharp point
		dóc			(재미있게) 떠벌리다. 허풍치다	to lie
		đọc			읽다	to read
0197	doi đoi	đòi		1	요구하다. 청구하다. 조르다	to claim back. to demand. to ask. to require
				2	많은	many. all
		đối	對(대)	1	반대의. 역의	to be contrary to. to be against. to oppose
				2	~에 대해서. (=đối với)	about
		đời		1	일생. 삶. 세대	life. generation
				2	속세(俗世)의	worldly
		doi		1	갑(岬). 강가에 토사가 쌓인 긴층	a level of soil by the river
				2	(체구) 아담한. 작은	small-bodied
		dõi		1	혈통. 대(를 잇다)	succeed to one's family
				2	(단독으로 쓰이지 않음) 뒤쫓다. 추적하다. (=dõi bước)	to follow closely. to pursue

	dội		1	붓다. 쏟다	pour out
			2	시간. 때	time
	dối		1	거짓말하다	to lie. deceive
			2	거짓의	false
	dồi		1	순대	(colloquial) intestines (as (food)). korean sausage (Sun-dae)
			2	(공) 계속 쳐올리다	keep hitting (the ball)
	dọi		1	(수직을 측정하기 위해) 끈의 끝에 붙인 연옥	a thing at the end of a string to measure the perpendicularity
			2	부딪히다. 치다	be crushed
	đội	隊(대)	1	(모자를) 쓰다	to wear. to put on (only used with pieces of headwear)
			2	들어올리다	to carry on one's head
			3	팀	team
	dòi			파리의 유충	the larva of fly
	dơi			박쥐	(zoology) bat
	đói			(배) 고프다. (=đói bụng. đói lòng)	hungry (desirous food)
	dời			이사하다. 이전하다	to move (to a different place) . to transfer. to shift
	dỗi			토라지다. 삐치다	to be sulky. to be in a sulk
	đổi			바꾸다. 교환하다	to change. to exchange
	đợi			기다리다. (=chờ đợi. đợi chờ)	to wait for. to await
	đỗi			끝까지	until the end
	đồi			언덕	a hill (elevated location)
	đôi			쌍. 커플. 켤레	double. pair. two

01 98	dom đom	dom			[해부] 직장(直腸)	(rare) anus. prolapse of the rectum
		đơm		1	대로 엮은 고기잡는 도구	a bamboo-woven fishing tool
				2	고기잡이 도구로 물고기를 잡다	to fish with a fishing tool
		dợm		1	무슨 일을 하기 위해 준비자세를 취하다	stand ready to do something
				2	곧 ~할 태세인	on the verge of~
		đốm		1	반점. 자욱	spot
				2	반점이 있는	spotted
		đởm		1	유능한. (=đảm)	competent. able. capable. talented
				2	쓸개	gall bladder
		dóm			불을 일으키다. (운동. 캠페인) 불같이 일어나다. (=nhóm)	create a boom. rise like a fire
		dòm			(틈사이로) 들여다보다	to see. to peek
		đóm			불쏘시개. 담뱃불 붙이개	a firecracker
		đòm			소총소리	the sound made by a gun
		đờm			가래. 담	sputum
		đỏm			멋을 내는. 잘빗고 차려입은	neatly dressed
01 99	don đon	don		1	시든. (=héo don, héo)	withered
				2	조개류	shellfish
		đơn	單(단)	1	신청. 청원. 요청	application. petition. request
				2	단독의	single
		độn	鈍(둔) 遁(둔)	1	채워 넣다. 채우다	fill (in/up)
				2	우둔한	stupid. foolish

		đớn	1	아픈	painful
			2	비열한. 천한	despicable. vulgarity
		đốn	1	벌채하다	to fell (a tree)
			2	가엾은	poor fellow
		đờn		기타를 치다	play the guitar
		dòn		부서지기 쉬운. 깨지기 쉬운	fragile
		dơn		(식물) 글라디올러스꽃	gladiolus flower
		đon		(벼의) 작은 다발	a small bundle
		dồn		쌓다. 저축하다. 모으다.	to gather (together). save up
		đòn		지레. 운반용 장대	lever. carrying pole
		dợn		(머리카락의) 물결같은 결. (나무) 엽맥. 결	grain
		dọn		정돈하다. 깨끗이 하다. 청소하다	to clear (a table, etc.)
		đón	1	맞이하다	to welcome. to greet
			2	마중하러 가다	to pick up (to collect a passenger)
		đồn	屯(둔)	1	초소	(military) post. (police, frontier) station
				2	소문을 퍼뜨리다	to spread a rumour
		đọn		작은	small
		đôn		화분 받침	a pot stand
02 00	dong đong	đong	1	(체력, 물량을) 재다. 측정하다	take. measure. gauge
			2	(양을 재는) 되	a gauge for measuring volume
		dõng	1	용감한. (=dũng)	brave
			2	곧장	straight

	động	洞(동) 動(동)	1	동굴	a cavern
			2	만지다	to touch
			3	움직이다	to move
	dong		1	호송하다. 동행하다	drive, escort
			2	(잠자는) 나무평상	(sleeping) a wooden bench, a wooden tablet
	dòng		1	물결, 전류	current, stream, line, strain, descent
			2	(로프 등을) 내리다	(a rope) lower
	dọng		1	칼등	the back of a knife
			2	용기속의 물을 심하게 흔들어 밖으로 튀도록하다	shake the water out of a container
	dộng		1	물건을 뒤집어 엎다. 쾅 하고 울리다. 부딪히다	turn a thing upside down, to bang, to bump
			2	누에 번데기. (=nhộng)	silkworm pupae
	đồng	銅(동) 同(동)	1	동, 구리	copper
			2	똑같게 만들다	make the same
			3	베트남 화폐 단위	the unit of currency in Vietnam, Vietnamese dollar
	dóng			대나무가지	bamboo branch
	đóng			닫다, 폐쇄하다	to close, to shut, to be closed (a door, lid, border)
	dỏng			(귀를) 쫑긋 세우다. (꼬리를) 들다	pick up one's ears, raise one's tail
	đồng			논. (=đồng lúa)	a rice paddy
	đọng		1	(물, 공기가) 고여 있는	stagnant
			2	(물, 공기가) 고이다	to stagnate
	đống			(돌, 흙, 나무 등의) 더미	heap, pile

		đông	東(동) 冬(동) 凍(동)	1	동	east. orient
				2	겨울. 동	winter
				3	동결하다. 응고(응결)하다. 얼다	freeze up
				4	붐비다	crowded
		dông			심한 뇌우	a thunderstorm
02 01	dot đot	đót		1	응고된. 굳어진	coagulated
				2	응고되다	become coagulated
		đốt		1	멍청한	ignorant. slow-witted. stupid
				2	머리가 둔하다	be slow-witted
		đốt		1	태우다	to burn
				2	마디와 마디 사이의	(of fingers, trees) a joint. a internode
		đột	突(돌)	1	돌출하다	stick out
				2	갑자기	suddenly
		dột			비가 새다	(of a holed roop) drippy. leaky
		dợt			(색이) 바래는. 연해지는. 창백해지는	fading. lose color
		đợt		1	새싹. 새눈	sprout
				2	바느질하다. 꿰메다	to sew. to stitch
		đớt			불완전한	incomplete
		đợt			단계	wave. stage. step. round
02 02	du đu	du	遊(유) 兪(유) 攸(유) 悠(유) 諛(유) 猶(유) 油(유) 楡(유)	1	느릅나무	elm
				2	갑자기 밀다	push suddenly

	đu		1	그네	swing
			2	앞 뒤로 흔들리다	to swing. to seesaw. to teeter
	dù		1	우산	umbrella
			2	어쨌든. 어떻든	althouth. in spite of
	dự	與(여) 予(여) 預(예) 譽(예)	1	참가하다	participate (in). join (in)
			2	작은 쌀	small rice
	dữ		1	사나운	fierce. ferocious
			2	매우	really. so. very
	dừ			(음식) 푹 익은. (=nhừ)	well-done
	dụ	諭(유) 誘(유) 喩(유) 裕(유)	1	(임금의) 칙령	an edict of wages
			2	유혹하다	to entice. to lure
	đủ		1	충분한	to be sufficient. to be enough
			2	모두. 전부	all
	dư	餘(여) 予(여) 與(여) 余(여)		남아있는. 여분의	residual. left over
	dử			미끼. (=nhử)	bait. lure
	đú			짖궂다. 장난치다. (=đua nghich)	be obstinate. fool around
	dứ			(미끼) 내보이다	give a bait
	đừ			녹초가 된. 기운이 빠진	out of shape. out of spirits
	đứ			즉시	right off. immediately
	đụ			결합하다. 성교하다 (상대를 심하게 욕할 때, cha 또는 mẹ와 함께 사용한다)	to fuck

02 03	dua đua	đứa		1	나이어린 사람 또는 손아랫사람에게 붙이는 말	indicates young person. child. an inferior person
				2	놈. 녀석	guy. fellow
		dua			아첨하다. (=dua nịnh)	to flatter. butter up
		đua		1	경쟁하다. 겨루다	to compete. to vie
				2	진열하다. 뽐내다	to display. to show off
		dùa			모으다. 모이다	gather up
		dưa			메론. (=dưa chua)	melon
		dũa			갈아 다듬다	grind up
		đưa		1	건네주다	to bring. to take. to give. to hand
				2	이끌다. 안내하다. 운전하다	to lead. to guide. to drive
				3	손을 뻗다	to reach out (to extend one's hand, foot, etc.)
		đũa			젓가락	chopstick
		đùa			농담하다	to joke. to play
		dừa			야자	coconut
		dứa			파인애플. (=thơm)	pineapple
		dựa			기대다	to lean on. to base on
02 04	duc đuc	dức		1	조롱하다. 학대하다. 모욕하다. 비난하다.	to deride. to abuse. to insult. to reprove
				2	몹시 쑤시는	aching
		đực		1	수컷	male
				2	멍청한	foolish
		đục		1	끌. 정	chisel
				2	끌로 깎다	to carve. to chisel
		đúc			주조하다	to cast. to mold (metal)

		dục	欲(욕) 育(육) 浴(욕) 煜(욱) 昱(욱)	1	원하다. 바라다	to want. to wish
				2	열망. 성욕. 탐욕	desire. lust. greed
		dực	翼(익) 翊(익)		(단독으로 쓰이지 않음) 날개	wings
		đức	德(덕)		덕	virtue. righteousness
02 05	dum đum	dúm		1	한줌. 한움큼	a handful
				2	한데 모아 묶다. (=nhóm)	to team up. to form a group
		đùm		1	포장. 싸개	packet
				2	싸다. 포장하다	to wrap around
		đúm		1	안에 솜을 넣고 꿰멘 인형	a stuffed doll with cotton inside
				2	(놀이) 모여들다	(play) flock together
		dụm			쪼그리다	give a crouch. squat (down)
02 06	dun đun	dun		1	밀다	to push
				2	약봉지용으로 쓰기 위한 종이	paper for medicinal purposes
		dùn		1	느슨한	loose
				2	(일을) ~에게 돌리다. (=đùn)	leave (one's work) to another
		dún		1	구부리다	to bend
				2	배꼽. (=rốn)	navel. belly button
		đun			가열하다	to heat
		đùn			밀다. 밀어 올리다	to push. push up
		đụn			(물건) 쌓아 놓은 더미	a pile of (things)
02 07	dưng đung	dưng			바쁘지 않다. 한가하다	be not busy. free
		dung	容(용) 蓉(용) 庸(용) 融(융)	1	허용하다	to permit. to allow
				2	관용을 베푸는	tolerant

	dũng	勇(용) 湧(용) 俑(용)	1	용기. (=dũng khí)	courage
			2	용감한	brave
	dùng		1	사용하다. 이용하다	to use. to employ. to take (medicine). to apply
			2	드시다 (먹다. 마시다)	to eat or drink. to consume (meal)
			3	느슨한	loose
	dứng		1	(초벽의) 대나무 틀	bamboo frame
			2	칸막이를 하다	partition off
	dừng		1	멈추다. 서다	to stop. to halt
			2	대나무가리개. (=dứng)	a bamboo screen
	dúng			담그다	to dip. to soak. immerse
	dựng		1	세우다. 짓다	to build
			2	똑바로 세우다	set upright
	đưng			(식물) 풀의 일종. 집을 짓거나 돗자리를 만들때 씀	a kind of grass. used to build a house or make a mat
	đúng			올바른, 정확한	correct. to be right
	dửng			(깃털을) 세우다	set up a feather
	dụng	用(용)		이용하다. 고용하다	to use. to employ. to hire. take on
	đứng			일어서다	to stand
	đừng			(동사앞에 사용) ~하지 말라. ~해서는 안된다	do not. don't
	đựng			넣다. 포용하다. ~을 함유하다	to contain. to hold
	đũng			(바지의) 궁둥이 부분	to hip area (of trousers)
	đụng			부딪히다. 충돌하다	to bump against. to collide (with)

02 08	duoc đuoc	duốc		1	유독성 물질로 물고기를 잡는 것	catching fish with toxic substances
				2	독성물질로 물고기를 잡다	to fish with a toxic substances
		duộc			액체를 푸는 큰 주걱	ladle
		dược	藥(약)		약	medicine
		đuốc			횃불	torch
		đước			맹그로부나무(mangrove)	mangrove tree
		được			(문장어순이 주어+được+명사+동사의 형식으로 주어측에 유리한 내용을 담고 있는 경우. 유리한 피동태) ~할 수 있다 (동사+được=có thể+동사=có thể+동사+được)	to obtain. to get. to gain. to be. to be all right. be able to -
02 09	duoi đuoi	duỗi			늘이다. 뻗다. (=ruỗi)	to stretch
		dưới		1	하급의	low-class. lower. junior
				2	~의 아래에	under. below
		duối			뽕나무과의 일종	a kind of mulberry family
		đuối			뒤떨어지다	much weakened. doing very badly
		đuổi			쫓다. 쫓아가다	to chase. to pursue. to kick out. to chivy. to expel
		đuôi			꼬리. 끝부분. 결말. 종결	tail. (of a ship, boat, etc.) stern
		dưới			이하	less than
02 10	duong đuong	dương	陽(양) 羊(양) 洋(양) 楊(양) 揚(양)		양(陽)	yang (of yin and yang)
		dường			~처럼 보이다 (hình như)	to seem (like). to appear (to)
		dướng			껍질로 종이를 만드는 나무	a tree that makes paper out of its bark

		dưỡng	養(양)		기르다. 키우다. (=nuôi)	to raise. rear. bring up. keep. grow
		dượng			계부. (=bố ghẻ)	stepfather. stepdad
		đương			~하는 중이다. (=đang)	be doing
		đường	糖(당)	1	길. 도로	road. path
				2	설탕	sugar
02 11	dut đut	đứt		1	(실, 로프 따위가) 끊어지다	to be break off. to be cut off
				2	완전히. 확실히	completely. certainly
		đút			집어넣다. 끼워 넣다.	to plug into. to put into something
		dứt			끝내다. 끝나다. 끊다	to cease. to end. to come to an end
		đụt			몸을 피하다	to dodge
02 12	duy	duy	唯(유) 維(유) 惟(유)	1	유일하게. 단지. ~만	the only. only
				2	사유하는. 사고하는	think. thought. thinking
02 13	duyen	duyên		1	매력. 우아함	charm. grace
				2	운명의. 인연의	predestined affinity
02 14	duyet	duyệt	閱(열) 悅(열)		검사하다. 검열하다	to examine. inspect. review. to censor
02 15	e	è		1	목이 막힌듯이 숨쉬기 어려운	choked with breathless
				2	아주 힘겹게 견디다	to bear with great difficulty
		é			겁을 먹다	be frightened
		ế		1	잘 팔리지 않는	(of goods) unmarketable. unsalable. unable to find customers. sluggish
				2	혼령기를 지난 미혼자	a single person who has passed the age of marrriage
		e		1	걱정하다	to be afraid
				2	em (아우, 연하의 사람)의 줄임말	an abbreviation for one's "em" (a young man)

		ẻ		협박이나 독촉해서 부르는 소리	threatening or forcing words
		ẻ		설사하다	have diarrhea
		ẹ		더러운 (어린애들의 말)	dirty (chidren's words)
		ê	1	어이 야	hey
			2	부끄러운. 수줍어 하는	shameful. shy
02 16	ec	éc		돼지 울음소리	(of a pig) squeal
02 17	ech	ếch		개구리	(zoology) frog
02 18	em	em	1	아우. (=em gái, em trai)	younger sibling
			2	(애칭) 연하의 사람	(a familiar younger person) I. me. you
		ém		(사건 따위) 입막음을 하다	shut one's mouth
		ếm		효력을 마비시키다	paralyze the effect
		êm	1	부드러운	soft
			2	고요한. 차분한. 침착한	calm
02 19	enh	ènh		몸을 펴다	to stick out. to swell
		ễnh		부풀다. 크게 부풀리다	to swell
02 20	ep	ép		강제로 ~시키다	to force someone. to press something
		ệp		쇠약하다	fall into decline. weak. feeble. infirm
		ẹp		쇠퇴하다. 시들다	go to seed. decline. decay. wither. wilt
02 21	eo	eo	1	허리	waist
			2	(한가운데가) 꽉 조여들다	be tight in the middle
		ẹo		몸을 구부리다	bend over

02 22	ga	ga		역. 정거장	train station. station
		gá		공작물을 선반에 고정시키다	fix a work piece to a lathe
		gã		(경멸적 의미) 녀석. 놈	lad. bloke
		gà		닭	chicken
		gả		시집보내다	to give (one's daughter) in marriage
		gạ		교언영색하다	to entice. to trick with words
02 23	gac	gác	1	계단	stairs
			2	~에 놓다	to put something on something
			3	지키다	to guard. to watch
		gạc	1	사슴뿔	antler
			2	거즈	gauze (medicine)
02 24	gach	gạch	1	선을 긋다	to rule (a line)
			2	~을 지우다	to strike off
			3	괘선(가로, 세로의 선)이 있는	rule lined
			4	벽돌	brick (hardened block used for building)
02 25	gai	gai		가시	thorn. prickle
		gãi		긁다. (=cào)	to scratch
		gài		잠그다. (문을) 걸다	to pin. to fasten. to set (trap)
		gái		여성의 총칭	an unspecified female. females, girls, etc.
		gại		예리하게 하다	sharpen
02 26	gam	gam		그램 (무게의 단위)	gram (unit of mass)
		găm	1	끝이 뾰족한 물건	a pointed object
			2	숨기다	to hide

		gầm		1	(맹수가) 포효하다	to roar
				2	아래에	the place under beds or cabinets
		gấm			무늬를 두드러지게 짠 비단. 능라	brocade, embroidered silk
		gậm			아랫부분	the lower part
		gặm			갉아먹다. 씹다. 물어뜯다. 조금씩 먹다	to gnaw, to nibble
		gẫm			숙고하다. 깊이 생각하다. 곰곰히 생각하다	to ponder
		gằm			고개를 숙이다. 머리를 숙이다	lower one's head, bow one's head
0227	gan	gan		1	간	a liver
				2	대담한. 용감한	audacious, brave
		gàn		1	고집센	stubborn
				2	~을 하지 못하도록 관여하다	to be involved in not doing something
		gân			근육. 힘줄. 정맥	muscle, tendon, vein (of a leaf)
		gán			전가하다. 할당하다	shift (onto), to assign
		gắn			긴밀하게 하다. 아교를 붙이다	to glue (together), to stick (together), to paste (together), to link, to attach
		gần			가까운	near
		gạn			정수하다. 불순물을 건져내다. (=gạn hỏi)	purify oneself, take out impurities
		gắn			(화가 났을 때) 단호하게 말하다	speak firmly

02 28	ganh	ganh		경쟁하다. 다투다	to envy. to be jealous (of). to compete. to vie (with)
		gánh	1	메다. 짊어지다	to carry (something) on one's shoulder. to shoulder
			2	한번 부담의 양	load (carried at one time on one's shoulder with a shoulder pole)
		gạnh		기식(寄食)하다. 빌붙다	sponge off. mooch off
02 29	gang	găng	1	장갑 (프랑스어 gant)	(clothing) glove
			2	끌어당기다	draw in
		gang		주철. 한 뼘	cast iron. a handspan
		gặng		힐문하다	to ask a question
		gắng		노력하다. (=cố gắng)	to endeavour (to). to strive (to)
02 30	gao	gạo	1	쌀	rice (non-glutinous)
			2	주입식 공부를 하다. (=học gạo)	cram one's studies
		gào		큰 소리로 울다. 비명을 지르다	to scream
		gáo		국자	ladle
02 31	gap	gấp	1	~을 접다. (책을) 덮다	to fold. to close. to shut
			2	긴박한	pressing. urgent. hurry
			3	배(倍). 곱	double, threefold, quadruple...
		gắp	1	꼬챙이. 집게	tadpole. stick. skewer. spit
			2	요리용 젓가락으로 집다	pick up with cooking chopsticks
		gập		접다. 완전히 몸을 구부리다	fold
		gặp		만나다. 우연히 만나다	to meet. meet by chance

02 32	gat	**gắt**	1	강한. 강렬한	(of taste and sunshine) strong or harsh
			2	~를 꾸짖다. 야단치다	to scold. to chide
		gạt		밀어내다	to push aside. to elbow
		gặt		~을 수확하다. ~을 베다	to reap. to harvest
		gật		끄덕이다	to nod (one's head)
02 33	gau	**gầu**	1	비듬	dandruff
			2	저돌적인. 사나운	reckless. wild. fierce
		gâu		(의성어) 개짖는 소리	(onomatopoeia) bark. ruff. arf. woof. au au. bow-wow
		gàu		비듬	dandruff
		gấu		곰	(zoology) bear
		gẫu		일정한 주제없이 이런저런 이야기를 하다	talk about one thing or another without a fixed subject
02 34	gay	**gây**	1	~을 야기하다. ~을 일으키다	to stir up. to rouse. to cause. to create
			2	가시. (=gai)	thorn
		gáy	1	목덜미	the nape of the neck
			2	(닭이) 울다	(of a rooster) to crow
		gay		극히	very. extremely. greatly
		gãy		꺾다. 꺾이다	be broken. be fractured
		gẫy		부러지다	be broken. be fractured
		gậy		막대기. 지팡이	stick. cane. staff
		gảy		현악기 따위를 손톱끝으로 타다	(music) to pluck (a musical instrument). to strum
		gầy		얇은. 여윈	skinny. thin
		gày		얇은. 여윈. (=gầy)	skinny. thin
		gẩy		튀기다. 튕기다. 튕겨 연주하다. (=gảy)	(music) to pluck. (a musical instrumnet) to strum

02 35	ghe	ghe	1	보트	a kind of boat
			2	많은	many, much, a lot
		ghè	1	세게 쳐서 부러뜨리다	to break by hitting
			2	작은 병	a small bottle
		ghẹ	1	(다른 동사 뒤에서) 빌붙다	(behind another verb) sponge off, mooch off
			2	흰딱지를 가진 바다 게의 일종	a type of crab (genus portunus)
		ghé		잠시 들르다	to drop in (on), to stop at, stop by
		ghế		의자	chair (furniture), seat
		ghẻ		의붓엄마	(somewhat derogatory) step-, stepmother
		ghê	1	소름끼치는, 무서운, 끔찍한	horrifying, scary
			2	전율하다, 벌벌떨다, 떨다	to shudder, to shiver, to quiver
			3	소름끼치다, 무서워하다	to be horrified by, to have a horror of
02 36	ghen	ghen		시샘하는, 시기하는	to be jealous of, to envy
		ghèn		(콧물, 눈물 등의) 분비물	rheum (eye discharge)
02 37	ghenh	ghềnh		낙수, 급류, 비탈진 물도랑	falling water, a rapid stream, sloping water ditch
		ghểnh		(장기에서) 말을 움직이다	(chessman) moving the horse
02 38	ghep	ghép		연결시키다, 잇다, 이식하다, 접붙이다	to join, to couple, to graft
02 39	ghet	ghét	1	~를 몹시 싫어하다, 질색하다, 미워하다, 혐오하다	to hate
			2	먼지, 티끌, 몸의 때	dirt, filth
		ghệt		양말대님 (프랑스어 guetre)	gaiter

02 40	ghi	ghi	1	기록하다. 적다. 메모하다	to write something for the record. to write (literary) to remember. to keep
			2	기차 선로를 바꿔주는 전철기 (轉轍機)	a switchboard
		ghì		꽉 묶다. 껴안다	to hold tight
02 41	gi	gỉ	1	녹	rust
			2	녹슬다	rusted
		gì		무엇	what. whatever
		gí		압착하다. 눌러서 펴다	press down. press out
02 42	gia	giá	價(가) 嫁(가) 架(가) 駕(가)	1	콩의 싹. 콩나물	bean sprouts
				2	(손을) 들어올리다	raise one's hand
				3	가격	price
				4	(물건을 올려 두는) 선반	shelf
		già		1	오래된. 늙은	old
				2	연장자. 노인	elder. old person
		giả	假(가) 者(자) 賈(가)	1	인공의. 가짜의	fake. false
				2	~인 체하다. 가장하다	to pretend
		gia	加(가) 駕(가) 家(가)		증대시키다. 보태다	to increase. to add
		giã			통통한. 토실토실한	be chubby
		gịa			쌀을 재는 철로 만든 통 (약 30kg 무게에 해당)	a barrel made of iron to measure rice
02 43	giai	giai	階(계) 佳(가)	1	남자. 남성. (=trai)	boy. male
				2	예쁜. 훌륭한	excellent
		giải	解(해) 邂(해)	1	(심사, 판정하여) 수여하다. (상을) 주다	award sb a prize
				2	(문제를) 풀다	(mathmatics) to solve. to answer

		giái			서클. 모임. (=giới)	meeting. gathering. get-together
		giãi			설명하다. 표명하다	explain. express oneself
		giại			(보통 묘지로 사용되어지는) 부지	a site usually used as a graveyard
02 44	giam	giậm		1	대로 만든 새우잡는 도구	a shrimp-hunting tool made of bamboo
				2	발을 구르다	to stamp (to strike, beat, or press forcibly with the bottom of the foot)
		giam			투옥하다. 수용하다	to detain. to imprison
		giám	監(감) 鑑(감)		통제하다. 감독하다	supervise. keep under control
		giâm			식물을 베다	to do a cutting on a plant
		giăm			끝이 뾰족한 조각(토막)	a pointed piece
		giấm			식초	vinegar
		giẵm			짓밟다	to trampl on
		giảm	減(감)		줄다. 줄이다. 감소시키다	lessen. reduce. decrease
		giầm			찧어 부수다	to crush. to grind
		giầm			(커누) 노	Mekong Delta dialect paddle
		giạm			(결혼을 위해) 선을 보다	look out for a marriage
		giặm			공급하다. 지급하다	to supply. make payment
		giẫm			짓밟다. 무시하다	to step (on). to tread (on). to trample (on)
02 45	gian	gian	奸(간) 姦(간) 間(간)	1	아파트. 방	apartment
				2	부정직한. 불성실한	dishonest
		gián	間(간) 諫(간)	1	(곤충) 바퀴. 투구벌레	a cockroach (type of insect)
				2	간헐적인	intermittent

		giãn		1	느슨해지다. 긴장을 풀다	lax. not tense. physical relaxed
				2	신축성 있는	flexible
		giần		1	체. 조리	sieve. sifter
				2	거르다. 채질하다	filter (out). sift (out)
		giàn			(구조물, 이론 따위의) 뼈대	frame. build. physique. framework. shell. skeleton. outline
		giẫn			세게 내려놓다	lay down hard
		giản	简(간)		간단한. 짧은	simple. short
		giặn			경험많은	experienced
		giận			화내다	to be angry. angry
		giấn			흠뻑 적시다	soak up
02 46	giang	giang	江(강) 肝(간)	1	강	river
				2	메고 나르다	carry with one's back
		giáng	降(강) 絳(강)	1	내리다	to lower. to descend
				2	(음악) 낮은음자리표. (=dấu ~)	(music) flat (symbol that means note is lowered half step) f clef
		giảng			당기다. 잡아당기다	to pull. draw
		giảng	講(강)		설명하다	to explain. to explicate. to lecture
		giẵng			일어서다	stand up
		giạng			옆(가로)으로 넓히다(벌리다)	to spread (out). to stretch (out). to extend
		giăng			달. (=trăng)	the Moon
02 47	gianh	giành		1	쟁취하다. 다투다	to dispute. to fight (for)
				2	대나무로 만든 꾸러미	a package made of bamboo
		giảnh		1	귀를 기울이다	listen carefully (to)

			2	모습	figure. form. image. reflection
		gianh		짚, 억새풀	straw
02 48	giao	giảo	狡(교) 絞(교) 較(교) 咬(교)	1	교수형에 처하다	to hang (a criminal)
				2	교활한	sly. foxy. cunning
		giáo	敎(교) 校(교)	1	작살. 창	lance. spear
				2	가르치다	to teach. to educate
		giao	交(교) 膠(교) 蛟(교) 郊(교)		인도하다. 배달하다. 건네주다. 넘겨주다	to hand over
02 49	giap	giáp		1	갑옷	armor
				2	가까운	close (to). nearby. close by. near
		giập		1	타박상	bruising
				2	부서지다. 깨지다. 멍이 생기다	be bruised
02 50	giat	giật		1	무리하게 당기다. 빼앗다. 낚아채다	to pull forcibly. to snatch
				2	이기다. (돈 등을) 벌다	to win (award, prize). to earn
		giặt			씻다. 세탁하다	to wash (clothes or febric)
		giạt			표류하다. 한쪽으로 밀리다	go adrift
		giắt			찌르다. 꽂다	to stab. to stick. to insert
02 51	giau	giàu			넉넉한	ample. enough
		giâu			뽕나무	mulberry tree
		giàu			넉넉한. 부자인. 풍족한. (=giàu có)	rich. wealthy. abundant
		giậu			울타리	fence. hedge
		giảu			입을 삐죽 내밀다. (=dẩu)	pout one's lips
		giấu			숨기다	to hide

02 52	giay	**giây**	1	초(秒). 순간	second (SI unit of time)
			2	떨어뜨려 더럽히다	soiled by dropping
		giãy		몸부림치다. 투쟁하다	to struggle
		giày		구두	shoe
		giẫy		몸부림치다	to struggle
		giấy		종이	paper (material for writing on)
02 53	gie	**gie**	1	목재를 생산하는 큰 나무의 일종	a kind of large tree that produces wood
			2	쭉 내밀다	stick out. extend. stretch out
		gié		벼이삭	a rice ear
		giẻ		누더기. 걸레	rag. dust cloth
02 54	giec	**giếc**		잉어. (=cá giếc)	a carp
02 55	giem	**gièm**		깔보다. 얕보다. 욕을 하다	look down on. belittle. to cuss
		giếm		숨다	to hide
02 56	gieo	**gieo**		뿌리다. 퍼뜨리다	to sow. to cast
		giẹo	1	비스듬한. 기울어진	oblique. slanted
			2	기울다	incline. tilt. lean
02 57	giet	**giết**		살인하다	to kill. murder. to slaughter (an animal)
02 58	gieu	**giễu**		비웃다. 웃기다	to laugh at. to be funny
02 59	gin	**gìn**		보존하다. 유지하다. gìn giữ의 약 (略)	to keep. to guard
		gin		원형. 원물 (原物)	original

02 60	gio	giỏ	1	바구니	basket
			2	한방울씩 떨어뜨리다	drop by drop
		giỗ	1	제삿날	the day of ancestral ritual
			2	꽃이 피기 시작하다	come into blossom
		gio		(타고 남은) 재. (=tro)	ashes
		giơ		들어올리다	to hold up. to lift
		gió		바람	wind (movement of air)
		giò		가축 또는 새의 정강이. 고기 반죽	leg. meat paste
		giỗ		(개가) 돌진하다	(a dog) makes a rush
		giọ		위협하다	make a threat
		giờ		시(時)	unit for specifying a time in hours
		giở		(책을) 열다. 펴다. 벌리다.	to open (a book)
02 61	gioi	giòi		구더기	(zoology) maggot
		giội		따르다. 쏟다. 붓다	to pour. to dash
		giỏi		목재로 쓰이는 나무	tree for lumber
		giọi		손가락질하다	point a finger at
		giỏi		잘하는	fine. good. skilled. well
		giồi		화장하다. (=giồi phấn)	put on makeup
		giới		원. 세계	world. kingdom. scene
		giơi		날씨	weather
		giỗi		화내다	to get mad. to get angry
02 62	gion	giòn		부서지기 쉬운. 깨지기 쉬운	brittle. fragile. crispy
		gión		손가락 끝으로 가볍게 집다 (잡다)	pinch lightly with fingertips
		giỡn		희롱하다. 장난치다	make a fool of oneself. to joke. to play

		giờn			헤매다. 방황하다	wander (around/about). roam (around/about)
02 63	giong	giong		1	대나무가지	bamboo branch
				2	데리고가다. 나아가다	bring. go forward
		gióng		1	북을 치다	play a drum. to beat. to ring
				2	바구니	basket
		giống		1	종류. 품종. 혈통	kind. race. breed. gender
				2	유사한. ~같은	to be alike. to be similar
		giọng		1	억양	intonation. accent
				2	목소리	(of a singer) vocal. voice
		giông			불행한. 운이 다한	unlucky
		giỏng			귀 기울이다	listen carefully
02 64	giot	giọt		1	물방울	droplet
				2	치다. 내리치다	to pound. to flatten (with a hammer, pestle, etc.) to beat. to thrash. to drub
02 65	giu	giú			숨기다. (=giấu)	to hide. to cover. to conceal
		giũ			흔들다. 떨다. (먼지, 물기를) 털어서 떨어지게하다	to shake off (dust. water)
		giữ			유지하다. 지키다. 지속하다	to keep. to safeguard
02 66	giun	giun			연충 (지렁이, 구더기 등). (발이 없고 꿈틀꿈틀 하는 벌레)	a worm (animal)
02 67	giuong	giương			잡아당기다	pull on
		giường			침대	a bed (piece of furniture)
02 68	giup	giúp			돕다. (=giùm)	to help. to aid
02 69	go	gò		1	언덕	mound. knoll
				2	굽히다	to bend. to curve
		go			씨실. 씨줄	woof. weft

		gõ		두드리다. 두드려 울리다.	to knock. to rap
		gơ		(종자를) 배양하다	cultivate seeds
		gồ		눈에 띄는. 돌출한	conspicuous. protruded
		gỡ		풀다. 해방하다	to disengage. to detach
		gỗ		목재	wood. timber
		gở		나쁜. 불길한	bad. ominous
		gộ		(사슴) 소리치다	(a deer) roars
		gờ		테두리붙임	framing
		gô		묶다	to tie. to tie up. to bind
0270	goa	góa	1	과부(또는 홀아비)의	widowed
			2	사람에게 침을 쏜 후 죽은 벌	a bee that died after being shot at a person
0271	goc	gộc	1	(대나무) 뿌리	bamboo root
			2	큰. 거대한	big. huge. great. gigantic. mammoth
		góc		구석. 모퉁이. 각(角). 일부분	corner. (mathematics) angle
		gốc		기원. 원천. 뿌리	foot (of a tree, etc.). origin. root
0272	goi	gói	1	꾸러미	pack. parcel. bundle
			2	싸다. 포장하다	to wrap around
		gọi	1	부름. 초청. (전화)통화	call. invitation
			2	부르다. 전화하다	to call. make a call
		gởi		보내다	to send. to send in
		gối	1	베개	pillow
			2	무릎	knee
		gội		(머리를) 씻다. 감다	to wash somebody's headhair
		gợi		깨우다. 소생하다. 회복시키다. 자극하다	to arouse. to awake (memories)

		gỏi		생선. 날생선과 야채를 섞어 만든 요리	a salad-like Vietnamese dish consisting of raw vegetables and sometimes also raw fish
02 73	gom	gớm	1	구역질나는. 정말 싫은	loathsome. disgusting
			2	특히. 대단히	especially. very. much
		gom		모으다	to gather together
		gốm		도기. (=đồ gốm)	pottery
		gờm		두려워하다. 싫어하다	be afraid of. to hate
		gồm		포함하다. 구성되다	to comprise. to consist of. to include
02 74	gon	gôn	1	골프	(sports) golf
			2	(축구에서의) 골	goal in soccer or football
		gợn	1	파문	ripple
			2	파도치는. 물결이 이는	wavy. surfacing
		gòn		목화. 솜	cotton
		gọn	1	정돈된. 가지런한	neat and tidy
			2	가지런히 정돈되어 있다. 옷을 단정하게 입다	to be neatly arranged. to dress neatly
02 75	gong	gồng		죄어지다. (=gánh)	to tense up one's body
		gọng		뼈대. 구조. 틀. 테	rim. frame. framework
		gông		(죄수의 목에 씌우는) 칼	cangue
02 76	goong	goòng		채광차	a mining truck
02 77	gop	góp		수집하다. 모으다. 기부하다	to contribute. to donate. to pay jointly with others or on instalment
		gộp		모으다. 합치다	gather. put together
02 78	got	gót		(발. 신발) 뒷꿈치	heel
		gột		씻다	to wash

		gọt		찌꺼기를 걷어내다. 씻어내다	clean up the dregard. wash out
		gọt		깎다. 베다	to peel (by using a knife)
0279	gu	gù	1	등이 굽은. 꼽추의	humpbacked
			2	(비둘기가) 구구 울다	to coo
		gu		취향	taste. set of preferences
		gụ		마호가니 (나무의 한 종류)	mahogany (a kind of tree)
		gừ		(개가) 으르렁거리다	(a dog) growls
0280	guc	gục		머리를 숙이다(인사하다). 엎드려 절하다. (=gục đầu)	to lower (one's head). to bend down
0281	gui	gùi		(등에 메는) 대나무로 만든 바구니. (말등에 걸치는) 용구	basket made of rattan or bamboo, used in moutainous regions to carry things on the back
		gửi		보내다. 맡기다	to send. to leave
0282	gung	gừng		생강	ginger (plant. spice)
0283	guom	gươm 劍(검)		검. 칼. (=kiếm)	sword (=kiếm)
		gượm		멈추다. 잠시 기다리다	to wait a bit. to wait a minute
		gườm		무섭게 째려보다	glare fiercely
0284	guong	gượng	1	억지로 된. 자연스럽지 않은	strained. forced. unnatural
			2	당기다	to pull
		gương		거울	a mirror. an example. a role model
		guồng		얼레	a reel. a bobbin. a spool
0285	ha	hà	1	벌레	worm
			2	입을 벌려 숨을 내뿜다	to exhale. to breathe out (through mouth)

		hạ	下(하) 夏(하)	1	여름	summer
				2	내리다. 아래에 놓다	to lower. to bring down. to take down
		hả		1	(친밀감을 나타내는) 의문사	what? (placed that the end of questions)
				2	(김이 빠져서) 향기와 맛을 잃다	be deflated and lose its fragrance and flavor
		há	呵(가)		입을 크게 벌리다 (열다)	open one's mouth wide
0286	hac	hạc	鶴(학)		학. 두루미. 장수(長壽)를 상징함	(zoology) crane
0287	hach	hách		1	권위적인. 위압적인	authoritative. overpower. overbearing
				2	거만한	proud
		hạch	核(핵)	1	임파선	bubo. lymph node especially an enlarged one. gland
				2	시험하다	put to the test
0288	hai	hài	孩(해)	1	옛날 신발	old shoes
				2	죄를 확정하다	settle a crime
				3	유머러스한	humorous. hilarious
		hai		1	둘. 2	two. 2
				2	두배로. 이중으로	twice as much
		hái		1	낫	a sickle
				2	(꽃, 과일을) 따다. 뜯다. 뽑다	to pick. to pluck
		hại	害(해)	1	손상하다. 손해를 끼치다	to harm. to cause problems to somone
				2	해로운. 유해한. 손해를 입히는	determental. injurious
		hãi	駭(해)		무서워 벌벌 떨다. 두려워하다. (=sợ lắm)	to fear. to be afraid (of)
		hải	海(해)		바다. 대양	sea

02 89	ham	ham		1	애호하다. 매우 좋아하다	be very fond of
				2	욕심많은. 탐욕스러운. 열망하는	greedy
		hàm	含(함) 函(함)	1	턱	jaw
				2	명예직의	honorary
		hăm		1	hai mươi의 줄임말. 스물(20)	short for hai mươi ("twenty (+number)")
				2	가벼운 염증	mild inflammation
		hầm		1	갱도. 참호	tunnel
				2	삶다	to stew. to braise. to simmer
		hâm	歆(흠)	1	끓이다. 뜨겁게 하다. 데우다	to warm up. to reheat
				2	이상한. 별난. 머리가 돈	a bit crazy
		hãm	陷(함)	1	브레이크를 걸다. 제어하다	to brake
				2	(술자리에서 부르는) 노래	a drinking song
		hám		1	탐내다	to covet. to want. to desire. be greedy
				2	무척 바라는	much desired
		hạm	艦(함)		전함	battleship
		hẩm			(쌀. 밥) 변질된	spoiled (rice)
		hằm			움푹패인	hollow
02 90	han	hàn	說(설) 寒(한) 韓(한)	1	납땜하다. 용접하다. 결합하다	to join (metal components) with heat. to solder. to weld
		Hàn	韓(한)	2	한국(韓國)	South Korea
		hãn	罕(한) 汗(한)	1	땀을 흘리다	to sweat
				2	드문. 희귀한	rare
		han		1	(안부를) 묻다	ask after a person
				2	(나무) 가시나무	a thorny tree

		hằn	痕(흔)	1	흔적. 자국	trace. mark
				2	원한을 계속 품다	bear a grudge
		hắn		1	그 (3인칭 대명사). (=hẳn)	(a third-person pronoun) he. him. she. her
				2	상세히 설명하다	explain specifically
		hạn	限(한) 旱(한) 瀚(한)	1	제한. 기한. 한도	limit. due
				2	넓고 큰 모양인	broad and large-shaped
		hẳn		1	확실한. 분명한	certainly. surely
				2	완전히. 영원히	completely. finally
		hán	漢(한)		중국	China
		hẳn			(친밀함 또는 비형식의) 그 (3인칭).	familiar or informal
		hận	恨(한)		앙심. 원한	hatred. resentment
0291	hang	hăng		1	생기있는. 기운찬. 쾌활한	full of voice. pleasant-voiced
				2	코를 찌를 만큼 심한 냄새가 나다	smell bad enough to poke one's nose
		hàng	行(행) 降(강) 航(항) 杭(항) 缸(항)	1	상품. 재화	goods. product. merchandise. freight. cargo
				2	가게. 상점	shop. store
				3	줄	line. row. queue
				4	항복하다. 투항하다	to surrender (to)
		hãng		1	(떨어지는 것을) 잡다. 쥐다. (=hứng)	grasp at the fall. to catch a falling object
				2	흥. 흥미. 영감	interest. inspiration
		hằng	姮(항) 恒(항)	1	하늘나라 선녀. Hằng nga의 약(略)	taoist fairy in heaven
				2	항상. 언제나	always. all the time. at all times
		hang			굴. 우리. 동굴. 궤도	cave. den
		háng			가랑이. 사타구니	groin

		hăng		회사		firm. company
		hẳng		(날씨가) 밝아지다. (=trời hẳng, hửng)		(the weather) brightens
		hạng	項(항) 巷(항)	등급		class. rank. kind. category
		hẵng		(발을) 헛디딘. (중도에 갑자스럽게) 중단된. 부족한		off one's feet. abruptly cut off halfway
		hẵng		~하는 것이 좋다		it is better to do
		hăng		흥하다. 일어나다. 타오르다 (=hừng)		to flourish. prosper. thrive
02 92	hanh	hành	行(행)	1	파. 양파	scallion. spring onion. onion
				2	괴롭히다. 학대하다	to harass. abuse
		hanh	亨(형)		춥고 건조한	cold and dry
		hảnh			빛이 비치다. 해가 나다	be illuminated. the sun comes out
		hạnh	杏(행) 行(행) 幸(행)		살구	apricot
02 93	hao	háo		1	갈망하다. 열망하다	to strongly desire
				2	갈증을 느끼는. 갈증나는	thirsty
		hảo	好(호)	1	(홀로 쓰이지 않음) 좋은. 친절한. 아름다운	good. kind-hearted. beautiful
				2	좋아하다	to like
		hao			소모하다	to greatly consume (energy, etc.)
		hào	豪(호) 濠(호) 壕(호) 鎔(용)		(10센트 은화의 가치가 있는) 동전	hao. one tenth of đồng
		hão			무익한. 허무한. 공허한	no good. empty and out. empty
		hạo	浩(호) 昊(호) 皓(호)		여러 번 실시 해 보다	try it sevral times

0294	hap	hập		1	재빨리 입에 물다	bite quickly
				2	뜨거워서 숨막힐 듯한	stifling with heat
		háp			메마른. 기한이 되기전에 익어서 시들어 버린	dry and dry. withered
		hạp	合(합)		일치하다. 합치하다	to suit (someone). to agree
		hấp	吸(흡)	1	(숨. 연기. 가스 등을) 들이마시다. 흡수하다	to inhale. to absorb
				2	찌다	to steam
0295	hat	hát		1	가극	a dramatic opera
				2	노래부르다	to sing
		hắt			밀쳐내다	to throw. to fling. to push
		hạt			종자(種子)	a small hard piece. a seed, a grain, a nut, etc.
		hắt			쑥 내밀다	stick out
0296	hau	hầu	候(후) 喉(후)	1	첩	concubine
				2	시중들다. 봉사하다	attend to. do volunteer work. service. serve
		hậu	後(후) 厚(후) 后(후)	1	뒤(쪽), 후부	back. behind
				2	뒤의	behind
		hàu			(바다의 식용) 굴	oyster
		háu			지나치게 좋아하다. 밝히다	be too fond of
		hẩu			맛있다	delicious. tasty
0297	he	hè		1	여름	summer
				2	보도. 인도	sidewalk. pavement
		hề		1	도법으로 교화하는 스승	teacher who teaches by morals
				2	익살스러운	comical

		he	1	반응을 보이다	to react
			2	문장 끝 어조사로 상대방의 동의를 구하는 말	words that seek the other's consent by means of an inquiry at the end of a sentence
		hé		반쯤 열다. 조금 열다	open half way of half. open a bit
		hệ	系(계) 係(계)	계(系)	system
		hẹ		골파 (서양파의 한 재배 변종). 부추	garlic chives
		hễ		만약 ~하면	if. whenever. each time
0298	hec	héc		헤르쯔	hertz
0299	hech	hếch		비스듬히 위로 향해 벌어진	obliquely upward
		hệch		너무 크게 벌리다	gape
0300	hem	hem		마른. 여윈	thin
		hẻm	1	샛길. 좁은길. 골목길	narrow place (between two walls, moutains, etc.)
			2	좁은. 협소한	(of an alley) narrow
		hèm		(술의) 지게미	distiller's grains. draff
		hẽm		골목길	alleys
0301	hen	hen		(의학) 천식	(medicine) asthma
		hèn		비겁한	cowardly
		hén		(조사) 문미에 붙어 동의를 구함 (phải không, nhỉ와 같음)	affixed at the end of a sentence to ask for consent
		hến		조개의 일종	a kind of clam
		hẹn		약속하다	to make an appointment to arrange or promise (to meet)
		hẽn		(=hén)	(=hén)

		hên			행운의. (=may mắn)		lucky
03 02	heo	heo			돼지. (=lợn)		a pig
		hẻo		1	운수가 나쁜		unlucky
				2	죽다		fall dead. die
		héo			마른(시든). (=héo gan héo ruột)		(of trees, flowers or fruits) to wither
		hèo			긴 막대. 긴 지팡이		long rod. long cane
03 03	hep	hẹp			폭이 좁은. 제한된		narrow
03 04	het	hét		1	개똥지바퀴(새)의 일종		thrush (bird)
				2	큰 소리로 부르다. 큰 소리로 외치다. 큰 소리로 꾸짖다		to shout. to scream
		hết		1	끝나다. (돈 등이) 다 떨어지다. 다 사용하다		to end. run out of
				2	모두 (관용어구)		all
		hệt			매우 닮은. 똑같은		just like. be the same
03 05	hi	hỉ	喜(희)	1	코를 풀다. (=hỉ mũi)		to blow one's nose
				2	경사(慶事). (=hỷ)		a happy occasion
		hí		1	말의 울음소리		neigh
				2	(말이) 울다		(of a horse) to neigh
		hì		1	웃음소리		laughter
				2	히히 (웃는 모양). (=hì hì)		hehe (a smiling figure)
03 06	hich	hích			신체일부로 쿡 찌르다		poke sb with a piece of one's body
		hịch	檄(격)		격문		a serious sentence
03 07	hiem	hiềm	嫌(혐)	1	의심하다		to doubt
				2	불만족스러운		unsatisfactory
		hiếm			드문. 진귀한 (=hiếm có)		rare
		hiểm	險(험)		험헌		rough. dangerous

03 08	hien	hiến	獻(헌) 憲(헌)	1	헌상(獻上)하다. 기증하다	make a tribute to. make a donation
				2	헌법	constitutional law
		hiện	現(현)	1	나타나다. 떠오르다	rise. appear. come into sight
				2	현재. Hiện giờ의 약(略)	the present
		hiền	賢(현)		상냥한. 온순한. 정숙한	kind. gentle. meek. docile
03 09	hieu	hiếu	孝(효) 好(호)	1	효(孝)	filial piety
				2	좋아하다. 사랑하다	to like
		hiệu	號(호) 校(교) 效(효)	1	상징. 문장(紋章)	symbol. coat of arms
				2	가게. 상점	a shop. a store
		hiểu	曉(효)		이해하다	to understand. to know
03 10	hinh	hình	形(형) 刑(형) 型(형)	1	형벌	pains and penalties
				2	이미지. 사진	image. a figure or silhouette. a photo. a picture
		hình			(코가) 벌렁벌렁하다	have a bulging (nose)
03 11	hit	hít			(코로) 흡입하다. 빨아들이다	to inhale. to breathe in
		hịt			꼭 닮은	like as two peas in a pod
03 12	hiu	hiu		1	우울한. 단정한. 슬픈	melancholic. gloomy. sad
				2	바람이 가벼운. 살랑살랑한	light of wind. soft as a sheet
02 13	ho	hồ	湖(호) 糊(호) 胡(호) 乎(호)	1	풀. 녹말풀	glue
				2	(옷에) 풀을 먹이다. 풀을 먹여 굳어지게 하다	to starch(clothes)
				3	호수	lake
		hờ		1	일시적인. 표면적으로만 하는. 적당히만 하는	transient. in moderation
				2	부주의하게. 건성으로	carelessly. absentmindedly
		hở		1	틈이 있는. 간격이 벌어진	uncovered. half-open

			2	폭로하다	to reveal
	ho		1	기침하다	to cough
			2	천식. 백일해	asthma
	hò		1	큰 소리로 고함치다. 환호하다	to call loudly. to sing out for
			2	옷깃의 가장자리	the edge of a collar
	hộ	護(호) 戶(호)	1	대신해서 도와주다	help on behalf of
			2	집	house
	hố		1	깊은 구멍. 무덤	hole. grave
			2	아무렇게나 하다	do as one pleases
	hổ	虎(호) 琥(호)	1	호랑이	tiger
			2	부끄럽다. 창피하다. (=tủi thẹn)	to be ashamed. embarrassing
	hỗ	互(호) 扈(호)		서로서로	each other
	hơ			불로 말리다. 불로 따뜻하게 하다	to dry or warm up
	họ		1	가족 이름. 성(姓)	onomastics family name, surname
			2	그들	them
	hớ			아직 경험이 없는. 부주의 한	not yet inexperience
	hô		1	외치다. 부르짖다	to scream
			2	(이가) 돌출한. 돌기한. 뻐드렁니의	(of a tooth) protruding
03 14	hoa	hòa	知(지) 禾(화)	1	섞다. 혼합하다	to mix. to blend (with). to dissolve
				2	평화로운. hòa bình의 약(略)	to be at peace. to be harmonious. to harmonize
		hoa	花(화) 華(화)	1	꽃처럼 아름답다	be as beautiful as a flower
			譁(화)			

			2	눈이 흐리다	have dim eyes
			3	꽃	a flower
		họa	和(화) 禍(화) 畫(화)	1	그리다	painting
				2	드물게. họa hoǎn의 약(略)	perhaps. rare. unusual. maybe
		hóa	化(화) 貨(화)	1	변화하다. ~이 되다. 변형시키다	to become. to get. to turn. to grow. to burn
				2	화학(化學). Hóa học의 약(略)	chemistry
		hỏa	火(화)	1	불	fire
				2	화급의. 급속의. (=hỏa tốc)	urgent. rapid
03 15	hoac	hoác		1	크게 열다. 크게 펴다	open wide. spread wide
				2	아주 넓은	as wide as avenue
		hoǎc		1	악취가 나는	foul-smelling
				2	(열악(劣惡)을 강조하는 말) 매우	as bad as a church mouse
		hoặc	或(혹)	1	사람을 혹하게 하다	seduce a person
				2	혹은. 또는	or. either
03 16	hoai	hoài		1	언제나. 항상	ceaselessly. constantly. all the time
				2	무익한. 쓸데없는	to waste. to do in vain
		hoai			부패된. 썩은. 썩는 냄새가 나는	rotten. stinking
		hoại	壞(괴)		파괴하다	destroy
03 17	hoan	hoǎn		1	연기(延期)하다	to delay. to postpone
				2	급하지 않은	in no hurry
		hoàn	丸(환) 還(환) 環(환) 完(완)	1	돌려주다. 반환하다	to return. to give back. to restore
				2	알약. 환약	pill

		hoạn		1	거세(去勢)하다. (=thiến)	to castrate
				2	환관. 내시	eunuch
		hoán	換(환) 喚(환) 煥(환)		정제(精製)하다	to refine
03 18	hoang	hoang	荒(황) 慌(황)	1	황폐한. 방기(放棄)한	uncultivated. uninhabited. virgin
				2	낭비하다	to waste
		hoàng	皇(황) 黃(황) 凰(황) 煌(황)	1	황제(皇帝)	king. emperor. prince
				2	찬란한(huy ~)	glorious
		hoáng	晃(황)	1	당황하다	be confused
				2	눈이 흐린	blurry-eyed
		hoăng			(주로 냄새 등이) 널리 퍼진. 확산된	(smell, etc.) widespread. diffused
		hoẵng			(담황색에 흰 반점이 있는) 사슴	(pale-yellow with white spots) deer
		hoảng	慌(황) 晃(황) 悅(황)		당황하여 쩔쩔매는. 겁에 질린 상태에 있는	flustered with embarrassment. in a state of panic
		hoẵng			문착. 문자크 (작은 사슴)	muntjac
		hoằng	弘(홍)		넓은. 광대한	broad. wide. extensive
03 19	hoanh	hoành	橫(횡) 宏(굉) 衡(형)		칸막이. 병풍. Hoành phi의 약어	partition. folding screen
		hoảnh			완전히 메마른	completely dry
		hoạnh	橫(횡)		횡포(橫暴)하는. 난폭한	rampant. violent. wild as a beetle
03 20	hoat	hoạt	活(활) 滑(활) 猾(활)		활발한. Hoạt bát의 약어	active

03 21	hoc	hóc		1	모투이. 귀퉁이	corner
				2	기계가 걸려 작동되지 않는	machine-inoperative
		học	學(학)	1	학식	learning. (formal) erudition
				2	(언어, 음악 등을) 공부하다. 배우다. (법률, 의학을) 읽다	to study. to learn
		hốc			푹 패인	dented
		hộc	斛(곡)	1	부피를 재는 10liter 정도 되는 용구	a measuring bowl (about 10 liters) for grain volume
				2	(코, 입을 통해) 내뱉다	spit out through (nose, mouth)
03 22	hoi	hổi		1	건조한	dry
				2	실패하다. 그르치다	to fail. ruin. spoil. mar. mess up
		hói		1	(머리 따위가) 벗겨진 (남성형 탈모)	bald (male hair loss)
				2	물도랑. 샛강	a water ditch. creek
		hơi		1	증기. 공기. 가스	gas (state of matter). steam. vapor
				2	약간. 다소. 얼마간	slightly. somewhat. a little
		hồi	回(회) 廻(회)	1	(연극의) 막	time. moment. part of one's life
				2	되살아나다	come back to life
		hội	會(회) 繪(회)	1	모이다. 집합하다. 회합하다	meet. reunite. assemble
				2	협회. 사단. 회사. 클럽	association. division. company. club
		hoi			악취가 나는	smelly
		hỏi			묻다. 물어보다	to ask (request an answer)
		hỡi			(공식적인 강연, 연설에 쓰는) 감탄사	interjection
		hời			(값이) 싼	cheap. inexpensive

		hợi	亥(해)		돼지띠 (12支의 하나)	year of the pig in Chinese zodiac
		hởi			만족하다	satisfied
		hối	悔(회) 誨(회)		후회하다. 뉘우치다	to repent
		hôi			악취가 나는	smelly. foul
03 23	hom	hom		1	박편 (얇은 조각)	a piece of foil. a slice
				2	마른	thin
		hòm		1	상자. 큰 가방	trunk. case. box
				2	잠정적으로 끝나가다. 거의 끝나다	come to an end
		hờm		1	더러운 때. 더러운 먼지	dirty dead skin (cell). dirty dirt
				2	~하려고 준비하다. ~할 참이다	be prepared to do. be about to
		hợm		1	자부심이 강한. 뽐내는	to be haughty. to be arrogant. to give oneself airs
				2	거짓, 사기	false. fraud
		hõm			(눈 따위) 움푹패인. 말라빠진 (뺨 따위)	a skinny face
		hóm			언변있는. 재치있는	eloquent. witty
		hõm			우묵하게 들어간	(be) hollow. dented
		hổm			그 날. hôm ấy의 준말	that day
		hôm			날. 일	day
03 24	hon	hơn		1	뛰어나다. 훌륭하다. 능가하다	excellent. outstanding. remarkable. exceptional
				2	값이 싼	cheap
				3	더욱. 더욱 더	than. more. more than
		hon			(요리) 삶다	(cooking) boiling

		hòn		둥글로 입체적인 것 앞에 붙이는 말		used for small, solid and roudish object, such as rocks,
		hỗn	混(혼)	무례한. 예의를 모르는		rude. rudeness
		hồn	魂(혼)	혼. 영혼. 유령. 정신. (=linh hồn)		soul. spirit. ghost
		hởn		즐거워하다		be delighted (with, by, at). be amused (at). enjoy
		hộn		합계하다		add up
		hờn		삐치다. 토라지다. 원한을 품다		be ticked off. sulk. hold a grudge
		hôn		키스하다. 키스		to kiss
03 25	hong	hồng	紅(홍) 鴻(홍)	1	(과일) 익은 감. 장미	ripe persimmon. rose
				2	장미빛의. 연분홍의	pink
		hổng		1	빈. 속이 빈	(of a hole) empty. hollow
				2	(부정의 의미) ~이 아니다	(the meaning of negation) not ~
		hong		건조하다. 말리다		to dry (in the wind, sun, or near the fire)
		hóng		기다리다		to wait for
		hòng		~하고자 하다		to intend. to aim. to expect
		hống	玩(완) 哄(홍)	울부짖다		give a howl
		họng		목구멍		throat
		hỏng		고장나다		broken. failed. spoiled
		hông		엉덩이. 허리		hip. haunch. side. flank
03 26	hop	hóp		1	낚시대나 모기장용으로 쓰이는 가느다란 대나무	slender bamboo used for fishing or mosquito nets
				2	움푹 패인	hollow. sunken

		hợp	合(합) 洽(흡)	1	적합한. 알맞은. 조화된. 일치된	suitable. consistent
				2	적합하다. 알맞다. 어울리다	appropriate. fit. suitable
		hộp		1	상자. 깡통. 그릇. 주머니	box. can. tin
				2	모양을 부리다	put on shape, form
		hớp		1	빨다. 핥다. 홀짝 빨아먹다	to suck. to lick
				2	기준. 한도	criteria. limit
		họp			모이다. 집합하다. 회의하다	meet. gather. convene
03 27	hot	hốt		1	양손으로 (쓰레기들을) 쓸어담다. 주워 모으다	pick up garbage with both hands. to collect into one place
				2	옛날에 관리가 임금을 알현할 때 가슴에 메달던 패찰	a badge worn by royal officials in the past on their chests
		hớt		1	가위로 자르다. 짧게 깎다. 베다	to cut with scissors. cut short. to cut
				2	치켜 올라간	elevated
		hót			(새가) 지저귀다	(of birds) to sing
		hột			씨. 열매. 종자. (=hạt)	seed. kernel. egg. drop (of liquid)
03 28	hu	hù		1	올빼미류 새	wood owl
				2	몸을 도사리다. 깜짝 놀라게 하다	to scare someone with a surprise
		hủ	腐(부)	1	케케묵은	old-fashioned. narrow-minded
				2	썩다	decay
		hư	虛(허)		부패한. 썩은	corrup. decayed. rotten. spoiled
		hú			고함치다. 울부짖다	to howl
		hũ	缶(부)		항아리. 독	jar

		hừ		노여움. 불만을 나타내기 위해 코에서 내는 소리. 음. 흠	the sound of one's nose to express-dissatisfaction or anger
		hứ		불평. 응석을 나타내기 위해 코에서 내는 소리	a moan of complaiant
		hự		목속에서 짧고 무겁게 내는 소리	a short heavy voice in one's throat
		hử		(친근한 의미) 질문을 강조하는 말. (=hả)	used to reinforce a question
		hụ		(지적. 종. 나팔 따위로) 알리다. 신호하다. (경보를) 발하다	to sound (usually of a siren)
03 29	hua	hua		간장이나 젓갈 속에서 생기는 구더기	maggots arising from soy sauce or salted fish
		hùa		함께 우르르 ~하다	rushing to do together
		hứa	許(허)	약속하다. 계약하다. 보증하다	to promise. to make a promise
03 30	huan	huân	勳(훈) 薰(훈)	1 (불, 연기) 피어오르다	(fire, smoke) rises
				2 공훈	merits. an exploit. distinguished services
		huấn	訓(훈)	1 (홀로 쓰이지 않음) 가르치다. 교육하다	(not used alone) to teach. educate
				2 장학관. huấn đạo의 약(略)	an inspector of schools
03 31	huc	húc	旭(욱) 頊(욱)	(짐승이) ~을 뿔로 받다. ~을 머리로 떠밀다	to gore
		hục		황급히 하다. 서두르다	hurry along. rush. hasten
		hực		불이 활활 타오르다	a fire is blazing
03 32	hue	huệ		(식물) 백합	(plants) lily
03 33	hui	hủi		1 (의학) 나병	leprosy. Hansen's disease
				2 (의학) 나병의	leprosyous
		húi		머리를 짧게 자르다	to cut one's hair short
		hụi		협회. 조합. (=hội)	association. (labor) union

03 34	hum	hũm			웅덩이	a puddle
		hùm			호랑이. (=cọp, hổ)	a tiger
		hụm			한 모금의 양. (=ngụm)	the amount of a sip
		hừm			(조급함이나 위협적인 표시로 쓰이는 말) 어흠!	(a word used as a sign of impatience or intimidation) Mm-hmm
03 35	hung	hung	凶(흉) 匈(흉) 胸(흉)	1	흉악한	brutal. heinous
				2	많이	very. mighty
		hùng	雄(웅) 熊(웅)	1	수컷	male
				2	기세가 강한	strong-spirited
		hứng	興(흥)	1	영감	inspiration
				2	(떨어지는 것을) 잡다. 쥐다. (=hãng)	grasp at the fall. to catch a falling object
		húng			박하(薄荷)의 일종	a kind of mint
		hửng			(날씨가) 밝아지기 시작하다	(the weather) is brightening up
		hừng			흥하다. 일어나다. 타오르다. (=hằng)	to flourish. to prosper. to thrive
		hủng			꺼지다. 함몰하다. 움푹 들어가다	become hollow. become sunken
03 36	huong	hướng	向(향)	1	방향. 방위	direction
				2	향하다. 길을 대다	head for
		hương	香(향)		향내. 향기 (=mùi thơm). 향기로운	fragrant
		huống	況(황)		더구나. 게다가. (=hơn nữa)	besides. moreover
		hưởng	享(향)		누리다. 즐기다	enjoy
		hường			장미빛의. (=hồng)	(color) rose

No					
0337	hup	húp		1	(수프 등을) 마시다	to slurp (a watery dish)
				2	부어오른. 부풀어 오른	swollen
		hụp			물 아래로 가라앉다. 머리를 물속에 넣다	to dive deep. to make one's head lower
0338	hut	hút		1	~을 빨아들이다	to absorb. to suck. to smoke
				2	흔적. 자국. (물)파문	trace. evidence. mark
		hụt		1	불충분한. 모자라는. 결함이 있는	1.inadequate. short of. defective
				2	(목표를) 달성하지 못하다. (겨눈 것을) 놓치다	be missed (a target)
0339	huyen	huyễn	眩(현)	1	틀린. 그릇된. 옳지 못한	wrong
				2	현혹하다. 속이다	be deluded. to deceive
		huyền	玄(현) 絃(현) 弦(현)	1	흑옥(黑玉). 흑옥색. 칠흑	a black jade. black clay
				2	공상의. 망상의	imaginary. reticular
				3	끈. 줄	string
		huyện	縣(현)		현(행정, 사법, 선거 따위를 위해서 구분된 지역. 한국의 군(群)에 해당	district. suburban district
0340	huu	hữu	有(유) 右(우) 友(우)	1	있다. 가지다. 소유하다	to have. to own
				2	오른쪽. 우측	right (direction)
		hưu	休(휴)		쉬다. 정년퇴직하다 (홀로 쓰이지 못함)	to rest
0341	huy	húy			비키다. 피하다	to step aside. to avoid
		hủy		1	궁핍하다	to destory
				2	취소하다. 역행하다	to cancel. reverse
0342	huyet	huyết	血(혈)		혈액. 피	blood
		huyệt	穴(혈)	1	굴. 동굴	cave. tunnel
				2	경락. 침 놓는 자리	an acupoint. a pressure point

03 43	i	i		1	(3인칭) 그. 그사람 (=nó)	that
				2	뚱뚱한	fat
		ì		1	젖은. 축축한	wet. damp
				2	멧돼지의 일종	a kind of boar
		ỉ			움직이지 않는. 부동의	stationary
03 44	ia	ia			대변을 보다. 똥을 싸다	to poop. to defecate
03 45	ich	ích	益(익)	1	이익	benefit. use
				2	유용한. 유익한	useful. helpful. valuable. beneficial. advantageous
		ịch			쿵. 퍽. 툭 (무거운 것이 땅에 떨어질 때 나는 소리와 비슷)	thud
03 46	im	im		1	조용한. 고요한	calm. silent. quiet
				2	조용히 하다	to be quiet. to not talk anymore
		ỉm			입을 다물다. 입밖에 내지 않다. 침묵을 지키다	to hush up
03 47	in	in	印(인)	1	인쇄하다	to print
				2	꼭닮은	as like as two peas
		ìn			돼지	pig
03 48	inh	inh		1	큰 소리를 지르다. 아우성치다	shout loudly. clamor out
				2	귀가 째지듯이	as if one's ears were twitching
		ình		1	눕다	lie down
				2	쭉 펴다	straighten out
		ĩnh			임신하다	get pregnant. pregnancy. be pregnant. conceive
03 49	it	ít			조금. 적은	few. little
		ịt			(개 등이) 으르렁 거리다. (사람이) 딱딱거리다	to snarl. to growl
03 50	iu	iu			습기가 찬. 눅눅한	soft (due to having a high moisture content). soggy

03 51	ke	**ké**		1	덧붙이다. 기대다	add up. lean
				2	산악지방에서 노인을 부르는 말	a word for an old man in the mountains
		kè		1	버팀빗장. 버팀용 보조제방	a brace latch. a supporting embank
				2	바싹 붙어다니다	stick close together
		kẻ		1	사람	pejorative individual. person. man
				2	선을 긋다	to draw a line
		kẹ		1	붙어먹다. 공짜로 먹다. (=ghẹ)	eat for nothing
				2	껍질뿐인	of nothing but skin
		kế	計(계) 繼(계)	1	전략. 군략. 책략	a plot. a scheme. a stratagem
				2	그다음에. 게다가	next to
		kệ		1	선반	a small shelf
				2	무시하다	to ignore. to don't care
		kể			일일히 세다. 열거하다. 말하다	count one by one. to list
		kề			가까이. 근처에	near
		kê			단단히 고정시키다. 버티다	fasten tight. endure
		kẽ			갈라진 틈. 균열. 터진 곳	crevice. crack. seam
03 52	kem	**kem**			아이스크림	cream. ice cream
		kèm			~와 함께 가다. ~에 동반하다	to accompany. to go with
		kềm			집게. (=kiềm)	tongs. pinsers. tweezers. forceps
		kẽm			(화학) 아연. 함석	zinc (element)
		kém		1	보다 적은	less than
				2	약한. 부족한. 나쁜	bad (at doing something)

0352	kenh	kềnh		1	커다란. 대형의	big. large-scale
				2	반듯이 눕다	to lie flat. to sprawl
		kênh		1	수로. 운하	canal
				2	채널	(geography, technology, communication, business) channel
0354	keo	keo		1	풀	glue
				2	엉겨붙다. 응고되다	stick together. become coagulated
		kẹo		1	사탕	candy
				2	인색한	stingy. miserly
		kéo		1	가위	scissors (tool used for cutting)
				2	잡아당기다	to pull
		kèo			서까래	common rafters
		kẻo			~하지 않도록. ~하면 안되므로 ~의 경우에는	for fear that. otherwise in case of
0355	kep	kép			두배의. 이중의	double. twofold
		kẹp		1	집다	to pinch. to clamp. to press (from both sides)
				2	클립	a tool for gripping or pinching. pincers. nippers. clamp. clip
		kếp			(비단이나 명주로 짠) 직조물	a woven fabric
0356	ket	kẹt		1	틈바구니 속에 끼다. 움직이지 않게하다	be stuck. to be stuck. to be busy
				2	벌어진 틈. 물건의 구석	a gap. a corner of a thing
		két			(조류) 앵무새	parrot
		kết	結(결)		엮다. 매듭을 짓다	to plait. to tie in knots
		kẹt			(교통) 막히다. (상황이) 안 풀리다	(traffic is) blocked. things don't go away

03 57	keu	kêu		멀리 떨어져 있는 것을 장대나 막대기로 잡다. 비틀어서 뜯다. 억지로 잡아떼다	catch something far away with a pole or a harness twist open. tear by force
		kêu		소리치다.	to call. to cry
03 58	kha	khá		꽤. 상당히	good. well
		khà		삼킬때 목에서 나는 소리	the sound of one's throat when swallowed
		khả	可(가)	가능한	~able
03 59	khac	khắc	刻(각)	1	파다. 새기다. 조각하다	to carve. to engrave
				2	시각(時刻). 짧은 시각	time. hour. a short time
		khác		다른. 다른 종류의	different. other
		khạc		(피, 침을) 토하다. 뱉다. 헛기침하다	to spit
03 60	khach	khách	客(객)	1	방문객. 손님	visitor. guest
				2	고객	customer
				3	승객	passenger
03 61	khai	khái	慨(개)	1	호랑이. 범. (=cọp)	tiger
				2	분격(분개)하다	be indignant
		khai	開(개)	1	~을 선언하다. 주장하다	to declare. to state. to testify
				2	열리다	to open
03 62	kham	kham		~을 감당하다. 견디다	to be responsible for~. bear up
		khám		1	감옥	jail. prison
				2	조사. 수색	investigation. inquiry (into). search
				3	~을 조사하다. 수색하다. 찾다	to examine carefully (for evidence of crime, etc.) to search. to ransack. to check
		khâm	欽(흠)	공경하다. 공대하다	to respect. treat sb with respect

		khăm		속이다. 놀리다	to deceive. cheat. trick. make fun of
		khẳm		가득 실은	packed to the brim
		khảm	嵌(감)	~을 상감(象嵌)하다	to inlay something
03 63	khan	khắn		1 딱 달라붙은	adhering to
				2 깊이있게. 심오하게. 깊숙이	in depth. profoundly. deep down
		khẩn	懇(간) 墾(간)	1 긴박한. 급박한. 긴급한	urgent
				2 개간하다	to cultivate. reclaim
		khan	看(간)	1 마른. 건조한	dry. dried
				2 보다	to see. to look
		khàn		목이 쉰	hoarse
		khăn		수건. 냅킨. 손수건. 스카프. 터번	towel. napkin. handkerchief. kerchief. turban
		khản		목이 마르다. 목이 잠기다. 목이 쉬다. (=khản cổ)	thirsty. be hoarse. have a hoarse throat
		khẳn		늙어 보이는	old-looking
		khấn		묵념을 올리다	to beg or pray to gods, spirits or ancestors
		khẳn		성미 급한. 성을 잘내는	short-tempered
03 64	khang	khẳng		1 왁스	wax
				2 왁스칠하다	to wax
		khẳng		막대치기 (긴 대나무 막대기로 짧은 대나무 막대기를 쳐서 멀리 날려보내는 아이들의 놀이)	a stick stroke (children's game of hitting short bamboo sticks with long bamboo sticks and sending them far away)
		kháng	抗(항)	저항하다. 항의하다	to resist. make a protest
03 65	khao	khao	念(념)	1 목소리가 쉰	hoarse
				2 노고를 치하하고 위로하다	appreciate and comfort for effort.

		khảo	考(고) 拷(고) 境(경)	1	(독립적으로 쓰이지 않음) 조사하다. 검사하다	investigate. examine
				2	고찰하다. 연구하다	consider. conduct a study. research (into/on)
		kháo			아무런 목적없이 서로 남의 이야기를 하다	talk to each other aimlessly
03 66	khap	khắp		1	모두. 전부의	all over
				2	도처(到處). (=khắp nơi)	everywhere
		khấp			울다	to cry
		khạp			도기주전자	cylinderical pottery with a lid
03 67	khat	khát	渴(갈)		목마른. 갈증나는	thirsty (needing to drink)
		khất	乞(걸)		구걸하다. 빚 갚을 날짜를 연기해 달라고 조르다	beg for. ask for a delay in paying off one's debt
		khật			둔한. 미련한. 어리석은 (=ngốc nghếch)	dense. stupid. foolish
03 68	khau	khâu		1	(과정의) 단계	stage. step (in a process)
				2	꿰매다. 바느질하다	to sew
		khấu	冠(관) 高(고)	1	재갈. 말고삐	gag. bit. reins
				2	공제(控除)하다	to deduct (from)
		khau			물 긷는 커다란 통	a large bucket of water
		kháu			(아기) 귀여운. 예쁜	(baby) cute. pretty
		khẩu	口(구)		입(口)	mouth
03 69	khe	khe			깨진 금. 갈라진 틈	slit. slot. stream. creek
03 70	kheo	khéo		1	능숙한. 교묘한. 솜씨좋은. 훌륭한	be skillful
				2	~하지 않도록	so as not to -
03 71	khep	khép			닫다. 폐쇄하다	to close. close down

03 72	khet	khét			탄 냄새가 나다. 탄내가 나다	smell burnt
03 73	kheu	khều			(과일을) 갈고리로 잡아 당겨 따다	to use hand or other tools to pull something toward oneself
		khều			뽑아내다. 추출하다. 끌어올리다	to extract (with a pointed object) to pull up. to raise. to winkle
03 74	khi	khi		1	때. 시간. 경우	when
				2	~을 얕보다. 깔보다. 경멸하다	look down on. make light of
		khí	氣(기) 器(기) 棄(기)	1	가스. 기체	air. gas
				2	조금. 약간	a little
		khỉ		1	원숭이	monkey
				2	시작하다	to start
03 75	khia	khìa		1	박살내다	smash to pieces of ground
				2	계속적으로	continuously
		khía			얇게 베다.	cut thinly
		khịa			모략하다	conspire against. plot. scheme. set sb up
03 76	khich	khích	激(격) 隙(극)		비웃다. 도발하다	to jeer. to provoke
03 77	khiem	khiếm			부족한. (=thiếu)	insufficient
03 78	khien	khiến	遣(견)		명령하다. 시키다	to cause (someone or something to do something). to make
		khiển			문책(견책)하다	to reprimand. rebuke. reproof. censure
		khiền			때리다. 치다. (=đánh)	to hit
		khiên			원형의 (작은)방패	shield

0379	khieu	khiếu	頃(경)	1	재주. 재능. 소질	gift. talent. instinct
				2	탄원하다. 소송을 제기하다. (=kêu xin)	make a plea. file a lawsuit against
0380	kho	khổ	苦(고)		불행한	miserable. painful
		kho			창고. 보관소	warehouse
		khó			어려운	difficult. tough
		khờ			어리석은	foolish
		khố	庫(고) 敬(경)		미개인 등이 허리에 차는 천	loincloth
		khỏ			두드리다. 두드려 울리다. (=gõ)	to knock. to rap
		khô			마른. 건조한. 물기없는	dried. dry
0381	khoa	khoa	科(과)	1	과(科)	subject of study
				2	시험	examination
				3	움직이다. 흔들다	to move. shake
		khóa		1	자물쇠	lock. padlock
				2	학기. 년도(年度)	school year. academic year. term. course
				3	잠그다. ~을 닫다	to lock. to turn off. to close
		khỏa			휘저어 뒤섞다	to dip and move in water
0382	khoac	khoác		1	(홀로 쓰이지 않음) 쓰다. 입다. 어깨에 걸치다	to drape over one's shoulders
				2	연결하다. 서로 섞다	to link. to interlace
0383	khoai	khoai			고구마. 토란. 감자 따위의 총칭	sweet potato. taro. potato
0384	khoan	khoan	寬(관)	1	송곳. 구멍뚫기	an awl. gimlet. piercing hole
				2	구멍을 뚫다. 꿰뚫다	to drill. get through
		khoán	芬(분)	1	분리되어 나누어진. 부과된	divided into separate parts
				2	증명서. 증서	certificate

		khoản	款(관)	1	항목, 조항	category, clause
				2	후하게 대접하다	treat generously
		khoăn			염려하는, 걱정하는	concerned
		khoăn			좋은, 건강한, 편안한	healthy, comfortable
0385	khoang	khoáng	鑛(광) 曠(광)	1	광석	mineral (dependent word)
				2	광대한, 황량한	extensive, desolate
		khoảng		1	간격, 거리, 범위	interval, distance, range
				2	대략, 약, 대강	about, approximately
		khoang			배밑, 배위 짐칸	ship's bottom, a ship's cargo
		khoãng			움직이다, 배어 나오다	seep out
0386	khoc	khóc	哭(곡)		울다, 눈물을 흘리다	to cry, to weep
		khốc			포악한, 잔인한	fierce, cruel
0387	khoe	khóe		1	구석	corner
				2	속임수	tricks
		khoe			자부하다	to flaunt, to show off, to boast
		khỏe			건강한	healthy
0388	khoi	khối	塊(괴)	1	덩어리	block, mass, piece
				2	충분히 가지다	have enough
		khơi			광활한 바다	the main sea, open sea, high seas
		khoi			도랑을 내다, 물이 흐르도록 길을 내다	make way for the flow of water
		khói			연기	smoke
		khởi			시작하다	to start
		khỏi			(병이) 낫다, 회복하다	to get rid of or be cured from sickness

0389	khom	khom		허리를 굽히다. (=khom lưng)	bend one's back
		khóm		초목이 무성한 곳. 풀숲. 수풀	bush. clump (of trees)
		khọm		늙다. 노쇠하다	be old. grow old. be senile
		khòm		구부러지다	bended
0390	khon	khốn	困(곤)	1 곤란을 당하다	have a hard time
				2 곤궁(困窮)한	in need. poor
		khôn		슬기로운. 지혜로운	wise. smart
0391	khong	khống	控(공)	1 헛된	in vain
				2 공소를 제기하다	bring an indictment against
		khổng		가늘고 긴	thin and long
		không		1 아니. 아니오 (부정을 나타낼 때 쓰임)	not (negates meaning of verb)
				2 빈둥거리는	idly. without doing anything
				3 아무것도 덧붙이지 않고	without anything added
0392	khu	khụ		1 쇠약해지다	become weak
				2 늙은. (=già)	old
		khu	區(구)	구역(區域)	district. area. zone
		khú		썩은 냄새가 나는	stinking
		khử	去(거)	배제하다	to exclude
		khứ	去(거)	가다. 지나가다	go. pass. go by
0393	khuat	khuất	屈(굴)	1 숨기다. 숨다	to be hidden. to be out of sight
				2 결석하다	to be absent
				3 세상을 떠났다. 없어지다	to have passed away. to be gone
0394	khuay	khuấy		휘저어 섞다 (=quấy). 옮겨다니다	to stir up. to stir. to move around
		khuây		편안하게 하다. 경감하다	make comfortable. make light of

0395	khuc	khúc	曲(곡)	1	들국화	camomile, wild chrysanthemum
				2	굽은, 휘어진	curve, bend, be stooped, be crooked
				3	조각, 부분, 부문, 구획, (두툼한) 덩어리, 상당한 량	piece, section, chunk
		khục			뚝뚝 (뼈다귀에서 서로 부딪치는 소리)	the sound of bumping into each other on a bone
0396	khum	khum			구부러진	bent over
0397	khung	khung			테두리	frame
		khùng			화내는. (=nổi khùng)	crazy, mad, insane
		khựng			갑자기 멈추다	to stop suddenly
		khứng			동의하다, 기꺼이 응하다.	to consent, accept, agree
		khủng	恐(공)		공포감을 주다.두려운, 무서운, 끔찍한, 지독한, 거대한, 막대한	fearful, dreadful, enormous
0398	khuoc	khước	却(각)	1	거절하다	to refuse, refusal, rejection, denial, turn down
				2	행운, 축복	lucky chance, luck, good fortune, lucky break, bless
0399	khuon	khuôn			모양, 형태, 패턴, 틀	shape, pattern, mold
0400	khuu	khứu			냄새 맡다	smell something
0401	khuot	khượt			매우 지친	very exhausted
		khướt			매우 피곤한. (=mệt lắm)	very tired
0402	khuy	khuy		1	단추. (=nút)	button, buttonhole
				2	엿보다. (=nghé xem)	have a peek, get a sense (of), watch (out) for
0403	khuya	khuya		1	심야(深夜)	(of night or nightly activities) late
				2	밤늦도록	late at night

04 04	khuyen	**khuyến**	勸(권)	권하다. 충고하다	to encourage. to advise
		khuyển	犬(견)	개. (=con chó)	dog
		khuyên		1 귀걸이	earrings
				2 충고하다	to advise. to recommend. to admonish
04 05	khuyet	**khuyết**	缺(결)	1 결핍된	deficient
				2 결점(缺點). khuyết điểm의 약어	defect. flaw. fault. shortcomings
05 06	khuynh	**khuynh**	傾(경)	기울어진	tilted. incline. slant
		khuỳnh		양손으로 옆구리를 받치다 팔을 들어올렸다 내리다	prop one's sides with both hands. raised one's arm, let down
		khuỷnh		작은 구역. 한 구획	a block. a small area
04 07	ki	**kì**		1 문지르다. 비비다	to rub off. to rub out
				2 기간. 시기	period
		ki		1 제기차기와 비슷한 전통놀이	traditional games similar kick a shuttlecock
				2 인색한	stingy. miserly
				3 볼링핀	bowling pin
		kí	記(기) 旣(기) 寄(기)	1 기록하다	to record, mark, note, jot down. to write
				2 킬로그램. (=ký)	kilogram
		kỉ		작은 탁자	small table
		kĩ		조심하다	careful. thorough
		kị		충돌하다. 두려워하다. 피하다	to clash. to dread. to avoid
04 08	kia	**kia**		1 저쪽에. 저기에	over there
				2 저. 그	that. over there
		kìa		1 저기에. 저쪽에. 건너편에 (약간뒤 먼 곳을 가리킴)	there. over there (farther than "kia" but still visible)

			2	문장앞에 붙어 무엇인가를 기대하고 있을 때 하는 말	words that attach themselves to a sentence and expect something.
04 09	kich	kích	1	규격. 치수. 크기	standard, size
			2	~을 매복 기습하다	to ambush, to attack
		kịch 劇(극)	1	극. 연극	play, drama
			2	딱딱한 것에 부딪치는 소리. 쨍그랑	with a clang
04 10	kiem	kiềm	1	집게. 족집게	tongs, pincers, tweezers
			2	억제하다. 속박하다	keep in check, control, restrict
		kiếm 劍(검)	1	칼	weaponry sword
			2	찾다. 탐구하다	to find
		kiểm 檢(검) 瞼(검)		점검하다. 통제하다. 관리하다	check, keep under control, superintend
		kiệm 儉(검)		절약하다. 검소한	to save, frugal
		kiêm		겸임하다. 동시에 감당하다. (=kiêm nhiệm)	used to join the names of mutiple positions or jobs of the same person
04 11	kien	kiện 件(건) 健(건) 鍵(건)	1	꾸러미	pack
			2	소송하다. 고소하다	take legal action, accusation, charge
		kiến 見(견) 建(건)	1	개미	an ant (insect)
			2	세우다. 건설하다	build up
		kiền 乾(건) 虔(건)	1	8괘의 첫번째인 건(乾)	the first of the eight trigrams
			2	존경하는	respect (for)
		kiên		동요하지 않는	unperturbed
		kiện		고소하다	to sue, to bring legal action (against)

04 12	kieng	kiếng		1	안경	glasses
			2	존경하다	respect (for). regard (for). reverance (for)
		kiềng		1	철로 만든 삼발이	iron tricuspid
			2	기피하다	to avoid. evade. shirk
		kiểng			공(권투따위에서 개시, 종료를 알리는 종)	bell
		kiễng			발끝으로 서다. 까치발로 서다	stand on tiptoe
		kiêng			피하다. 막다. 삼가다	to avoid. to refrain (from). to abstain (from)
04 13	kiet	kiết	結(결) 抉(결) 楗(건)	1	(의학) 적리(赤痢) (이질의 한가지)	one strand of dysentery
				2	빈궁한. 초라한. 가난한	poor. short of money. penniless
		kiệt	傑(걸) 杰(걸)	1	인색한	stingly. miserly. cheap
				2	다 써버리다	run out of
04 14	kiêu	kiểu	矯(교) 嬌(교)	1	양식. 형(型). 모델	model. pattern. design
				2	모조품의	imitation
		kiều	喬(교) 僑(교) 橋(교)	1	신령님을 부르다. 영혼에 구원을 청하다	call a divine spirit
				2	아름다운. 멋있는	beautiful. nice. cool. be stylish. smart. modish
		kiệu			(중국, 인도의) 일인승 가마	palanquin. allium chinense (rakkyo)
		kiếu			거절하다	to refuse. reject
		kiêu			거만한. 오만한. (=kiêu ngạo)	arrogant. proud. haughty
04 15	kin	kín		1	기밀의. 내밀의. 비밀의	secret. private
				2	굳게 숨기다. (=kín đáo)	closed. covered. sealed. enclosed

04 16	kinh	kinh	京(경) 經(경)	1	기도서	a prayer book
				2	무서워하다. 두려워하다	be scared of. be afraid (of)
		kình	鯨(경) 勍(경)	1	고래	whale
				2	대항하다. 겨루다	come up against. have a contest
		kính	鏡(경) 敬(경) 徑(경)	1	유리. 거울. 안경	glass. eyeglasses. mirror
				2	존경하다. 공경하다	to respect. to honor. to revere
04 17	kim	kìm		1	집게. 뺀지	pincers. clamp
				2	집다. 조이다. 억제하다	pick up. tighten. control
		kim			바늘	needle
04 18	kip	kíp		1	긴급한. 급박한	(dated) urgent. pressing
				2	작은 그룹으로 나누다	devide into small groups
		kịp			시간안에 닿다	in time
04 19	kit	kịt		1	아주. 매우	very. much
				2	사람이 구름처럼 많이 모여든 모양	looks like a crowd of people gathered like clouds
04 20	ko	ko			không. 문자할때는 ko, 0, k 등 여러가지로 줄여서 씀	không. when texting, abbreviate it in many ways.
04 21	ky	kỳ	其(기) 期(기) 旗(기) 奇(기) 祈(기) 棋(기) 岐(기)	1	기일. 기한. 기간. (=cờ)	a due date. period (of time). time limit. (fixed) date
				2	비범한. 보통이 아닌. 기이한	extraordinary. eccentric
		ky	箕(기) 畿(기) 奇(기)	1	키	height
				2	검소한. 구두쇠의	frugal. miserly
		ký	記(기) 寄(기) 旣(기)	1	기록계의 서기(書記)	clerk. scribe
				2	보내다. 발송하다	to send
				3	서명하다	to signature

		kỵ	忌(기) 騎(기)	1	상중(喪中). 특히 사후(死後)의 49일간	the period of mourning
				2	두려워하다. 꺼리다. 싫어하다	be afraid (of). be reluctant to. to hate
		kỷ	紀(기) 己(기)	1	일이나 글의 뼈대가 되는 줄거리	a skeleton plot of a job or writing
		kỹ	技(기) 妓(기)		주의깊게. 신중히. 정성들여. 꼼꼼히. 잘	with care. carefully. well
04 22	la	là		1	다리미질 하다	to iron
				2	~이다	It is~
		lả		1	배가 너무 고프거나 햇볕 등으로 지치다	to be too hungry or tired with the sun, etc.
				2	굽다. 휘다	bend. be bent
		la	羅(라)	1	음계상의 "라"음	la of musical scales
				2	소리치다. 고함치다	to cry. to shout
		lạ		1	낯선	strange. unfamiliar
				2	매우	very (much)
		lã			무미(無味)의. 맑은	tasteless
		lá			잎	leaf
04 23	lac	lạc	落(낙) 樂(악) 洛(락) 烙(락)	1	길을 잃다	to lost
				2	땅콩	peanut. groundnut
		lắc		1	강하게 흔들다. 요동하다. 흔들리다	to shake. to wag. to bump
				2	팔찌. 발찌	bracelet. anklet
04 24	lach	lách		1	길을 개척하다	carve out a path
				2	갈대의 일종	a kind of reeds
		lạch			도랑. 개천. 개울	rivulet. canal. creek

04 25	lai	lai	來(래) 萊(래)	1	혼혈의. 잡종의	biracial. crossbred
				2	(다른 종의 식물을) 교배시키다. 접붙이다	to crossbreed
		lái		1	운전하다. 키를 잡다	to control (a vehicle). to drive, to ride, to pilot, etc.
				2	핸들. 운전대	handle
		lài		1	(식물) 자스민	jasmine
				2	기울어진	tilted
		lại	史(사) 賴(뢰) 徠(래)	1	도착하다. 오다	to come
				2	다시. 또	again
		lãi			이자. 소득	(finance) interest
		lải			벼룩	flea
04 26	lam	lăm		1	10단위의 수 이후에 붙는 5 (15, 25, 35,…)	5 after the number of 10 units (15, 25, 35...)
				2	~할 태세를 갖추다 (=lăm lăm)	be ready to do
		lâm	臨(임) 林(림) 淋(림)	1	출석하다. 임하다	to attend. be present (at)
				2	숲. 산림	forest. woods
		lẫm		1	헛간	barn
				2	(바람) 매우 찬. (모습) 매우 경외스러운	cold as a whistle. a most aweinspiring (figure)
		lấm		1	더럽혀진. 오손된	be soiled. be smeared (by mud or dirt)
				2	진흙(탕물)이 달라 붙다	muddy water adheres to
		lắm		1	매우. 대단히	very (placed after the word to intensify)
				2	많은. 다량의	many. much. a lot
		lam	藍(람) 襤(람)		대나무통에 넣어 지은 밥. (=cơm lam)	rice made in a bamboo can
		lãm	覽(람)		전시하다	to exhibit

		làm			~을 하다. 행하다	to do. to make. to work
		lầm			잘못 생각하다. 오해하다. 혼동하다	to make a mistake. to be mistaken
		lẩm			몰래 먹다	eat secretly
		lạm	濫(람)		한계를 넘다	go beyond the limit
04 27	lan	lân	燐(인)	1	(화학) 인광을 함유한. 인을 함유한. 인(燐)의	phosphorus
				2	(신화) 외각수 (말 비슷하여 이마에 뿔이 하나 있는 전설적인 동물, 유니콘)	unicorn (a legendary animal with a horn on its forehead)
		lẳn		1	고체	solid. solid matter
				2	고체의. 견고한	solid
		lẫn		1	혼동하다	to confuse. to mistake (one for another)
				2	잘 잊는. 노망든	to be confused. to be muddled. to be in one's dotage
		lần		1	회(回). 차(次)	time. instance. occurrence
				2	일보일보(一步一步). 점차로	gradually
		lan	蘭(난)	1	난초	orchid
				2	퍼지다. 펴다	to spread. to run
		lạn		1	(노를) 젓다. (핸들) 꺾다	row. pull. paddle. scull. turn (the steering)
				2	빛나는	shining
		lăn			(통 따위가) 굴리다. 구르다. (=lăn vào)	to roll. to wallow
		lán			오두막집. 헛간	a cottage. barn
		làn			손 바구니	hand basket
		lẩn			살짝 가버리다	slip away. hide
		lằn			구김. 주름	fold. wrinkle
		lận			속이다. 기만하다	to cheat. to deceive

		lấn		침식하다. 깎아내다. 잠식하다. 침입하다	to encroach, to invade
		lặn		(물속에) 잠기다. 잠수하다	to dive
04 28	lang	lang	郎(랑) 狼(랑) 玘(기)	1	한방의 (漢方醫)	oriental medical treatment
				2	얼룩이 있다	roan, piebald
		láng		1	광택이 나고 부드러운	smooth, glossy
				2	넘치다	spill over
		lăng	陵(릉)	1	왕릉. 황릉	royal tomb, imperial tomb
				2	내던지다	fling away
		lạng	兩(양) 諒(량)	1	얇은 조각으로 나누다	divide into thin pieces
				2	계량 단위 (보통 100 gram)	hectogram (**100** grams) tael (unit of weight equal to **37.8** grams)
		lẳng		1	(양손으로) 내던지다	throw with both hands
				2	단정치 못한. 외설스러운	slovenly, obscene
		làng			마을	village (a rural habitation of size between a hamlet and a town)
		lặng			조용한. 잔잔한	calm, silent, quiet
		lẵng			바구니	basket
		lắng			(액체를) 저장하다	(of liquid) to settle, to deposit
		lảng			살그머니 나가다	steal out
04 29	lanh	lành		1	원래대로 되다. (상처가) 아물다	go the way it was, a wounds is healed
				2	좋은. 행복한. 온유한	in good condition, intact, kind, mild, gentle, good
		lanh			재빠른. 민첩한	fast, quick
		lãnh	領(령) 嶺(령) 冷(냉)		수령(受領)하다. (=lĩnh)	to receive, to get

		lánh			피하다. 가까이 하지 않다	to avoid. to shun. to evade. to flee (from)
		lảnh			(소리가) 고음이고 듣기 거북한	high-pitched sound that hard to hear
		lạnh			추운	cold (having a low temperature)
04 30	lao	lao	勞(로)	1	투창. 작살	harpoon. javelin. dart
				2	던지다. 돌입하다. (전신의) 힘을 주어 짜내다	to plunge. to dart
		lão	老(노)	1	늙은. 연배(年配)의	old
				2	노인이 자칭(自稱)하는 말	an old man's self-styled remark
		láo			거짓의. 무례한. 태도가 나쁜	to lie. deceive
		Lào			(국가명) 라오스	Laos
04 31	lap	lắp		1	맞추다. 조립하다. 결합하다	to fit. to install
				2	광주리	basket
		láp			과장하다	to exaggerate
		lặp			되풀이하다	to repeat. to iterate
		lấp			막다. 메우다. 폐쇄하다	to fill up. to stop (up)
		lập	立(립)		세우다. ~에 기초를 두다	to set up. to establish
04 32	lat	lắt		1	따다	to pick
				2	작은	small
		lát			잠깐	a moment. short time
		lất		1	하늘하늘 춤추다	dance in the air
				2	흔들흔들하는. 불안정한	swaying. unsettled
		lạt		1	무미건조한. 맛이 싱겁다	bland
				2	나무통에 두르는 테. 대나무 막대기	bamboo string or strip

		lật	1	줍다. (=nhặt)	pick up
			2	발칵 뒤집히다	turn upside down. to over turn
		lặt	1	뒤엎다. 뒤집다(배 따위). (정부를) 전복시키다	turn upside down
			2	험담	gossip
			3	찢어(뜯어) 내다	to pluck off
04 33	lau	lậu	漏(누) 陋(누)	1	임질	(medicine) gonorrhoea
			2	탈세(脫稅)한. 밀수의. 무허가의	contraband. illict. under the table
		lau	1	사립문	a gate made of twigs. a twig gate
			2	닦다. 지우다	to wipe
		láu	1	재치있는. 영리한(아이들에게 쓴다)	witty. smart
			2	교활하다. 간교하다	be crafty
		lầu	1	여러층의 집. 높은 집	multistory house
			2	(암기, 암송 따위가) 유창한 (=làu)	fluent in (hugging, reciting, etc)
		lâu		긴. 오랫동안. 오랫동안 걸쳐서	of time long
		làu		(암기, 암송 따위가) 유창한. 정확한	fluent in (hugging, reciting, etc)
		lẩu		먹기 바로 직전에 뜨거운 국물에 살짝 데쳐서 먹는 음식. 한국의 신선로와 비슷 또는 전골	a food eaten by blanching it lightly in hot soup
		làu		숙달한. 통달한	adept. skilled. versed
04 34	lay	lây	1	1.전염성의. 전파하는(병). 옮기기 쉬운	contagious
			2	~에 감염시키다. 전염시키다. ~에게 영향을 미치다. 퍼뜨리다	(of disease) to spread (from one to another)

		lẫy		1	방아쇠	trigger
				2	(아기가) 자다가 몸을 뒤치다	(a baby) turns in one's sleep
		lay			흔들리다. 흔들다	trembling. not in a stable position
		láy			반복하다. 되풀이하다	to repeat. to reiterate
		lấy			취(取)하다. 잡다. 받다	to take. to seize. to receive. to obtain. to accept
		lạy			무릎꿇다. (=lạy)	get down on one's knees
		lảy			(잎, 책장, 잡초 따위) 잡아뜯다	tear off
		lạy			아부하다. 굽실거리다	to kowtow
		lầy			늪의. 수렁의. 습지의. 진흙투성이의	marshy. muddy
		lẩy			따내다. 벗겨내다. (잎, 깃털 따위를) 잡아뜯다	tear off
04 35	le	lễ	禮(례)	1	축일. 축제일. 예식	festival. festive day. holiday. ceremony
				2	의식에 참가하다	take part in a ceremony
		lẻ		1	나머지 수. 소수점 이하 또는 큰수에 비해 작은 수	the remaining number. below decimal point. a small number for a large number
				2	소량의. 홀로	a small quantity of
		le			상오리 (오리과의 물새)	a duck's water bird
		lè			(혀를) 내밀다. (=lè lưỡi)	to stick (one's tongue) out
		lé			눈크기가 서로 다른. 짝눈인. 사시의	of different eye sizes. cross-eyed
		lẹ			빠른. 민첩한. 날랜. (=nhanh)	fast. quick. swift
		lẽ		1	이유. 동기. 도리(道理). (=vợ lẽ)	reason. ratianale
				2	첩. 둘째 부인	second wife
		lẻ			핀으로 뽑아내다. (=nhể)	draw out with a pin

		lệ	麗(려) 例(례) 隷(례)		풍습. 관례	costom. practice. convention
		lê			풍습. 관례	costom. practice. convention
		lê		1	배나무	pear
				2	질질 끌다. 끌며 걷다	to drag (one's feet)
04 36	lech	lệch		1	굽어서. 꼬부라진. 일그러져 한쪽으로 치우친	curved. crooked. one-sided
				2	벗어난. 일탈한	be deviated. be out of orbit
				3	뱀장어의 일종	a kind of eel
04 37	lem	lem		1	더럽히다. 더러워지다	dirty. get dirty. get filthy. get messy. get soiled
				2	더러워진. 얼룩있는	smudged. soiled
		lém		1	민첩한. 활발한	agile. active
				2	급속히 퍼지다	spread rapidly
		lẹm		1	패인 곳이 있는. 움푹패인. (칼, 톱) 날이 무뎌진	pockmarked. hollowed. dull-drawn
				2	뜨개바늘. 돗바늘	knitting needle
		lềm			빨리 먹어치우다	eat fast
04 38	lep	lép			속이 텅빈. 미숙한. (낟알, 곡물) 여물지 않은	not well-filled. empty. hollow. flat. deflated
04 39	leu	lều			오두막집	tent. cottage
		lếu			(=láo)	(=láo)
		lểu			날카로운	sharp. pointed
04 40	len	len		1	양털. 털실. 모직물	wool
				2	밀치고 들어오다	shove come in
		lèn		1	채우다. 밀어넣다	fill. shove in
				2	산이 연이어 솟아있음	a series of moutains
		lén			몰래. 비밀스럽게	on the quiet. in secret

		lẽn		수줍어하는. 숫기없는. 마음약한	shy. weak-hearted
		lẹn		민첩한. 능란한. (=nhẹn)	nimble. deft
		lẻn		몰래 들어가다. 살그머니 빠져나오다. 잠입하다	steal in. sneak out. break in.
		lên	1	오르다	go up. come up. rise
			2	~위에	to get on
04 41	li	lì	1	평평한	flat
			2	아무렇지도 않은 듯이	casually. lighty
		li	1	밀리미터. (=1/10cm, 1/1,000m)	milimeter (mm)
			2	컵	cup. glass
		lí	1	대중적인 공기	popular air
			2	물리학	physics
			3	이유	reason
		lị		이질 (전염병의 일종)	dysentery (a kind of infection)
04 42	lich	lịch	歷(력) 瀝(력) 曆(력)	달력. 역법	calendar
04 43	liec	liếc	1	곁눈질하다. 힐끗 보다. (=liếc mắt)	to cast a furtive look. to glance furtively. to look sidelong at
			2	갈기갈기 찢다. 날카롭게 하다	to strop. to whet. to sharpen (knife, razor)
04 44	liem	liệm	殮(염)	(시체, 송장에) 수의를 입히다. 수의로 감싸다. 염하다	wash and shroud a corpse
		liễm	干(간)	매달의 지급금	monthly payments
		liềm		낫	a sickle
		liếm		핥다	to lick (to stroke with a tongue)
		liêm		정직한. 청렴한	honest. incorruptible

0445	liet	liệt	列(열) 烈(열) 劣(열)	1	마비된. 불수(중풍)의. 무력한	paralyzed
				2	마비되다	be paralyzed
0446	lieu	liều		1	위험에 내 맡기다. 무릅쓰고 ~을 하다. 모험하다. 결연히 ~하다	to risk. to run the danger (of)
				2	약(藥)의 1회분	dose. dosage (of medicine)
		liệu	料(료) 了(료) 療(료)	1	계산하다	to manage. to calculate
				2	물질의	material
		liễu	了(료) 柳(류)		버드나무	willow (tree)
0447	lien	liên		1	잇따른. 계속되는	continuous. successive
				2	즉시. 바로. 더불어	right off
		liễn	聯(연) 璉(연)		주발. 사발	a bowl
		liến			변설좋은. 수다스러운. 나쁜 농담을 잘하는	talkative. good at bad jokes
		liên		1	연(蓮)꽃	lotus
				2	가입하다. 합병시키다. 단결하다	to join. to associate. to unite
0448	lim	lim			경질재의 나무	hardwood wood
		lìm			고요함. 정적. 평정	silence. quiet(ness). stillness. hush
		lìm			소리없는	silent
		lịm			의식이 몽롱해지다. 소리가 약해져서 잘 들리지 않다	lose consciousness. the sound has become weak and hard to hear
0449	linh	linh	靈(영) 零(영) 玲(영)	1	영혼	soul. spiritual. supernatually powerful
				2	고독한. 유효한. 효험있는. 영험한. 신령한	lonely. in force. valid. bright and profound. divine

		lĩnh	領(령) 嶺(령)	1	옷의 카라	a collar
				2	영도하다. 따르다. 수령하다	go to one's way. follow. receive
		lính			군사. 무사. (하사관 아래에 속하는) 병사	soldier
		lình			송곳	an awl. gimlet
		lỉnh			도망가다. 도주하다	run away
		lịnh	令(령)		순서. 차례. 정렬	sequence. turn. alignment
04 50	lo	lơ		1	숨기다. 감추다. 모르는 체하다. 잘못을 눈감아 주다	to hide. hide out. pretend to not know
				2	자동차의 운전조수. 기차의 표 검사원	the driving assistant of a car. a ticket inspector
		lố		1	1다스. 1타(打). 12개. (=tá)	a dozen
				2	바보같은. 이상한	stupid
		lồ		1	알몸의. 나체의	naked. nude. in the nude
				2	도랑	ditches
		lờ		1	어량(魚梁 : 대나무 따위로 물살을 한 곳으로 흐르게 하여 그곳에 통발을 치고 물고기를 잡는 장치)	a device that allows the current to flow through a single place with bamboo and so on, and then hits and catches fish
				2	멍한. 침울한. 희미한	dazed. minute and elaborate. dimly hearted
		lọ		1	그을림. 매연. 검댕	soot. exhaust
				2	아무 필요가 없는	of no use. unnecessary
		lo		1	불안한. 근심하는. ~에 대해 걱정하는	unstable. worried
				2	걱정하다. 고민하다. 속태우다	to bother. to worry. to attend to
		lộ	路(로) 露(로) 鷺(로)	1	길. 거리. 국도(國道).	road. street
				2	(사실이) 드러나다. 밝혀지다. 들키다. 걸리다	to come out. to be discovered

		lỗ	魯(로) 虜(로) 擄(로)	1	구멍. 굴	hole. tunnel
				2	구멍을 뚫다	drill a hole
		lở		1	부서지다. 가루가 되다. 무너져 내리다	to crack out. be cracked out
				2	습진	eczema
		lớ		1	이 사투리 저 사투리가 뒤섞인. 불분명한	mixed in this dialect. unclear
				2	(흉년) 쌀 기울로 만든 음식	food made from rice husks
		lõ			뚫고 나온. 튀어나온. 뾰족해진. 뼈가 드러난	pierced. popping out. pointed. bare-bones
		lò	爐(로)		난로. 스토브	kiln. furnace. oven. heater
		ló			나타내다. 얼굴을 내밀다. 명백하게 되다	to appear. to heave. to come into sight
		lợ			단맛이 나는	sweet-tasting
		lồ			큰 바구니	a big basket
		lỡ			(기차 따위를) 놓치다. 시간에 대지 못하다	to do something inadvertently. to do by mistake to miss. missed
		lô			부지. 대지	a site (for a building). the earth
04 51	loa	loa		1	확성기. (축음기의 깔대기 모양의) 나팔	megaphone (portable device used to amplify a person's voice). (by extention) speaker. loudspeaker
				2	넓게 퍼지다	spread widely
		lõa	裸(나)	1	나체의. 알몸의. 걸친 것이 없는	in the nude
				2	스며나오다. 배어나오다	seep out. ooze out
		lòa		1	확실히 보이지 않다	dim
				2	어두침침한 시력. 어슴프레한 시각	dim vision. dim view

		lóa		눈부시게 하다. 현혹케하다. 눈이 어지러워지다	to dazzle. to blind. dazzling
04 52	loai	loại	類(류)	1	종류. 종족. 범주	species. kind. type. category. sort
				2	없애다. 제거하다. 삭제하다. 거절하다. 실패하다	to reject. to eliminate. to fail
		loài			생물의 종. 분류. 종별(種別)	(taxonomy) species
04 53	loan	loan	鸞(난)	1	불사조. 난조(鸞鳥)	phoenix
				2	통고하다. 통지하다	give notice
		loạn	亂(난)	1	난. 반란(反亂)	(historical) a rebellion. revolt. uprising
				2	혼란중에 있다. 혼란해지다. 흐트러지다	disordered. chaotic
04 54	loang	loang			(물위에) 넓게 퍼지다	to spread (on a liquid surface)
		loáng		1	번쩍거리다	flash up
				2	순식간에. 일순(一瞬)	in a flash. in a instant. in a twinkling
		loãng			희박한. 묽은. 싱거운. 물을 많이 탄	watery. diluted. weak
04 55	loanh	loanh			일정한 범위내에서 한 장소에서 앞뒤로 움직이다	move back and forth in one place, within a certain range.
04 56	loat	loạt		1	일련. 연쇄. 시리즈. 열(列). 조(組)	series. bunch
				2	일제히 발사하다	fire in unison
		loát	刷(쇄)		인쇄하다	to print
04 57	loc	lóc			벗기다. 제거하다. 살을 빼다 (물을) 거슬러 올라가다	to cut off. to remove the flesh go back. go up
		lộc	祿(녹) 鹿(녹) 碌(녹)		사슴의 일종	a kind of deer
		lọc			여과하다. 깨끗이 하다	to filter. to purify. to cleanse

		lốc	1	회오리바람 (=gió lốc). 소용돌이. 토네이도	a whirlwind. vortex. tornado
			2	블록을 세는 말	counter word block
0458	loe	loe	1	입이 큰	big-mouthed
			2	번쩍이다	flash up
		lóe		(빛. 광선) 번쩍거리다. 번쩍 비치다	flash. glitter. sparkle
		lòe		빛나다	to flesh. to dazzle
0459	loet	loét	1	(상처) 벌려지다. 크게 퍼지다. 커지다	(a wound) spreads wide. grows big
			2	진홍(眞紅)의 (đỏ loét의 경우에 사용)	used in case of bright red
0460	loi	lói	1	(불빛) 깜박이는. 가물가물한	flashing light. dim in the lighted
			2	폭죽	firecracker
		lòi	1	튀어나오다. 싸맨 부분이 쏙 튀어나오다. 내밀다. 나타내다	to protrude. to reveal. to show
			2	귀머거리의	deaf as a beetle
		lối	1	매너. 스타일. 방법. 태도	path. way. track. manner. style. fashion
			2	거만한. 건방진	haughty. cheeky as a mule
		lõi	1	(식물의) 등심. 심지	core
			2	정통하다	get the hang of. be familiar. be well-versed
		lội	1	헤엄치다. 수영하다. (물) 건너다	to swim. to wade through
			2	흙탕물이 있는	muddy
		lỗi	1	꾀가 많은. 잔꾀가 많은	resourceful
			2	단지 혼자서	by oneself
		lọi	1	탈구(脫臼). 뼈의 관절을 뻠	dislocation
			2	남다. 남기다	remain

		lồi	1	돌출한. 튀어나온 (모양의)	be protruded
			2	돌출하다. 튀어나오다	stick out
		loi		세게 때리다. 치다. (=thoi)	hit hard
		lơi		풀리다. 해이해지다. (속도, 힘) 늦추다. 느슨하게 하다	lax. loose. not tight
		lỗi	磊(뢰) 儡(뢰) 寄(기)	과실, 실수, 잘못	mistake. fault. error
		lời		말. 용어. lời văn의 약어. 노래가사	word. lyrics
		lới		묘기. 재주	a feat of art. talent
		lợi		잇몸. 치은	profit. gum (the flesh around the teeth)
		lỡi		(=lễ). 식. 례(禮)	ceremony
		lôi		끌다	to pull. to drag
04 61	lom	lóm	1	몰래(살피다). (=lỏm)	secretly
			2	움푹 들어가다. 꺼지다	sink in. sink down
		lõm	1	움푹한. 오목한. 안으로 굽은	concave
			2	(식물의) 등심. 심지. 싹(움)	(plant) a plant bud
		lỡm	1	얕보고 바보취급하다. 속이다	make a mock of. look down on. to deceive
			2	짓궂게	rudely
		lờm	1	돌출하다. 튀어나오다	stick out. bulge. jut (out)
			2	토하고 싶은	want to throw up
		lòm		신맛이 확 나다	have a strong sour taste
		lơm		(꽃, 잎, 싹) 피어 나오다. (=trổ lá. đâm hoa)	sprout. shoot
		lợm		토해내고 싶어지다. 울렁거리다. 메슥거리다	feel nausea
		lỗm		귓볼 또는 입술에 생긴 궤양(潰瘍)	an ulcer on the earlobes or lips

04 62	lon	lỏm			몰래. 살짝	secretly
		lơn		1	(남녀가) 노닥거리다. 농탕치다	be romantically involved with a man and woman. a man and woman tease
				2	큰 물 항아리. 단지. (=chum)	a large jug of a water. pot
		lọn		1	머리채. 머리 타래	a long tress of hair. string bundle
				2	완전한. (=trọn)	complete full. perfect
		lớn		1	큰. 넓은. (=to lớn)	big (of a great size). large
				2	성장하다. 자라다	to grow. to become big
		lờn		1	너무 버릇없는. 허물없는. 자유분방한(아이)	rude as a judge. candid. (child) free and easy
				2	(문질러) 닳다	wear (out/down)
		lon			음료수 캔	beverage can
		lòn			빠져나가다. 통과시키다. 몰래 들어오다. (=luồn)	get out of. get through. steal in
		lỏn			잠입하다. 스며들다. 숨어들다	break in. permeate. go into hiding
		lồn			(해부) 질(膣). (=âm hộ)	(vulgar. slang) vagina. pussy
		lợn			돼지. (=heo)	pig
		lộn			뒤집다	to turn the inside out. upside down. to reverse. to flip. to overturn. to return
04 63	long	long	龍(용) 隆(융)	1	헐렁헐렁한. 흔들리는. 물렁한	(be) soft. tender
				2	풀다. 늦추다(스프링)	loose
				3	용(龍)	dragon
		lóng		1	마디	joint
				2	맑게하다. (침전물이 완전히 가라앉은 위쪽의) 맑은 웃물을 얻다	clean up. get a clear water

		lộng	弄(농)	1	연안	coastal waters
				2	바람이 세차게 불다	(of wind in an open space) blowing strongly
		lồng		1	우리. 새장. 조롱(鳥籠)	cage
				2	(말) 내닫다. 달아나다	(a horse) runs out. run away
		lọng		1	큰 우산(파라솔). 햇빛막이 우산(양산)	parasol
				2	몰래. 살짝	on the quiet. secretly
		lõng			사슴의 통로	the deer's path in the woods.
		lòng			배. 내장. 심장	heart (emotions or kindness)
		lỗng			버릇없는. 겁없는	ill-mannered. fearless
		lỏng			액체 상태의. 유동성의. 유체 (流體)	liquid
		lông			털. 모피	fur. coat
04 64	lop	lóp			움푹파인	hollow
		lốp			자전거나 오토바이의 바퀴 내부의 고무튜브	tire. tyre
		lớp			급(級). 학급. 학년	a layer. grade. school year. (education) a class
		lợp			덮개를 덮다. 지붕을 얹다 (씌우다)	cover up. put on the roof
		lọp			대나무로 만든 고기 잡는 도구. 어구	a fish catch phrase made of bamboo
04 65	lot	lót		1	(의복 따위에) 안을 대다. 막다. 메우다	to put something under another thing
				2	기저귀	diapers
		lốt		1	허물. (뱀, 매미 등의) 탈피한 껍질. 변한 가죽. 가면. 자국	shed hair (of animals). cast-off skin. slough
				2	가장하다. 위장하다	feign oneself. disguise oneself

		lột			껍질(가죽)을 벗기다. (곤충) 허물을 벗다. (=cởi)	to strip off. to slough
		lợt			(색깔이) 연한. (얼굴) 창백한. (=lạt nhợt)	light in color. pale
		lọt			불어넣다. 집어넣다. 틈새로 들어오다	to fall into
0466	lu	lu		1	독. 항아리	big vase used to contain water
				2	(빛이) 약해지다. 어렴풋한	(the light) become get weak
		lù		1	어슴푸레 밝다	be vagluely bright
				2	밑바닥	bottom
		lũ	屢(루) 縷(루)		무리. (많은 수의) 사람들	group. (a large number of) people
		lú			머리가 둔한. 영리하지 못한	dull witted. unwise
		lư	爐(로)		향로(香爐)	incense burner
		lử			쇠약하다. 기진맥진해지다	fall into decline. be worn out
		lự			~을 염려하다. 걱정하다	be apprehensive of. be worried about
		lừ			(화가 나서) 노려보다. (=lườm)	glare angrily
		lữ	旅(여) 呂(여) 侶(려)		여단(旅團). (=lữ đoàn)	brigade
0467	lua	lựa		1	선택	choice
				2	선택하다. 고르다	to choose (from a number of options)
		lừa		1	당나귀	donkey
				2	속이다. 기만하다	to deceive. play the fool
		lụa		1	명주실. 견사	silk (the finished fabric, not the raw material)
				2	부드러운. 물렁물렁한	soft. soft and soft

		lua			(밥) 빠르게 입에 대고 집어넣다	thrust into one's mouth
		lùa			(바람 등이) 불어오다	(the wind) blows
		lúa			벼. (겉겨가 붙어 있는) 쌀	rice
		lưa			남다. 여분이 생기다	remain. be left (over)
		lứa			(사람. 동물 등의) 무리. 종족 (같은 시기에 성장한 생물을 분류하는 말. 한 배의 (돼지) 새끼)	rank. class. generation
		lửa			불	fire (chemical reaction)
		lữa			자주. 누차. 오랫 동안	often. many times. time after time. for a long time
		lừa			사기치다	to trick. to fool
0468	luan	luân	倫(륜) 輪(륜) 淪(륜)	1	바퀴. 차례	wheel. turn
				2	잠기다. 빠지다. 얽어매다	to sink. tie up
		luận	論(론)	1	논문	thesis
				2	논(論)하다. 논술하다	make an argument. write an essay
0469	luat	luật	律(율)		법률. 규칙	law. rule
0470	luc	lục	六(육) 陸(륙) 綠(록) 錄(록)	1	녹색, 초록	green
				2	찾다. 샅샅이 뒤지다	to rummage. to search with hands
		lúc			짧은 시간. 순간. 찰나	moment. time
		lực	力(력)		힘	(physics) force
0471	lui	lụi		1	찌르다. 꿰뚫다	to stab. get through
				2	종려(棕櫚)나무의 일종	a kind of palm tree
		lủi		1	슬쩍 가버리다. 도피(逃避)하다	slip away. make one's escape
				2	힘이 빠진. 축 늘어진	weak in strength

		lui		물러서다. 후퇴하다. (=lùi)	to step back. to recede. to move backward. to retreat. to (fall, look, think)back.
		lùi		물러서다. 후퇴하다. 철수하다. 되돌아가다. (총이)발사된 후 뒤로 반동하다. (일정을) 연기하다. 잿더미로 굽다	to step back. to recede. to move backward. to retreat. to postpone. to roast in ashes
04 72	lun	lún	1	가라앉다. ~에 빠지다	to subside
			2	비굴한	servile. obsequious. be subsided
		lụn	1	끝까지. 마지막까지	until the end
			2	거의 끝났다	it's almost over
		lũn		복혼합물의. 혼합물과 섞인	compound
		lùn		난장이의. 작은. 낮은	(of a person) short
04 73	lung	lung	1	(생각이) 몹시 힘든	(of thought) very hard
			2	느슨한	loose
		lưng	1	등. 잔등	back (the back of people, animals, or objects)
			2	충분히 채워지지 않은	insufficiently filled
		lựng	1	퍼지다. 감돌다	pervade. diffuse
			2	그윽한. 고혹한	deep. seductive
		lùng		수색(탐색)하다	to search for. to find for
		lũng		계곡. 골짜기	valley
		lừng		울려퍼지다. (=vang lừng)	resound. pervade. diffuse
		lủng		(뚫려서) 구멍이 나다	have a hole. be perforated
		lửng		미완성의. 덜 끝낸. 어중간한	half way. half done
04 74	luoi	lưỡi		혀. 혓바닥	a tongue. (of a nife, sword, etc.) a blade. (of a nife, sword, etc.) a cutting edge
		lười		게으른. 태만한	lazy. slothful

		lưới		그물. 망(網)	net
0475	luoc	lược	略(약)	1	빗	comb
				2	가지치기를 하다. 요약하다	to prune. to abridge
		luộc			데치다. 삶다	to boil
		luốc			재색의	ash-colored
0476	luon	lượn		1	(새) 높이 날다. 비상하다. 선회하다	to soar. to hover. to glide
				2	베트남 소수 민족인 tây족들의 남.녀가 서로 다른 음조로 주고 받는 노래. (=hát lượn)	Vietnamese song in which men and women exchange in different tones
		luồn			빠져나가다. 통과시키다. 몰래 들어오다	to pass through
		lươn			뱀장어	an asian swamp eel
		lườn			옆구리(살)	flank flesh
		luôn			자주. 종종. 대개	always. continually. at once. straight away
0477	luong	luống			무익한. 쓸데없는	futile. useless
		lượng	量(양) 諒(양)	1	용량. 양(量)	quantity
				2	추량(推量)하다	estimate the amount
		luồng			물, 바람, 걷기, 사상(思想)따위 등이 한쪽 방향으로 흐르는 것을 가르키는 말	stream. current. flow (pointing to a flow in one direction)
		lương	凉(량) 梁(양) 糧(양) 良(양)		임금. 급료	pay. earnings
		luỗng			(벌레 등이) 구멍을 내다. 먹어 들어가다. 자르다. 벌채하다	(insects) make a hole. to cut. cut down
		lưỡng	兩(양)		양쪽	both sides
		lường			계량하다	to measure. to gauge

0478	luot	lướt	1	스치다. 스치고 지나가다. 대강 훑고 스치다	to glide. to graze. to pass quickly. to glance through
			2	연약한. 쓰러질 듯한	tender
		lượt	1	양복지 (羅紗)	suit material
			2	여과하다. 거르다	filter out
			3	회(回). 건(件)	time. turn
		luốt		압도하다	get the upper hand. overwhelm. overpower
0479	lup	lúp		돋보기. 확대경. (=kính lúp)	reading glasses. magnifier. magnifying glass
0480	lut	lút	1	푹(깊이, 깊게, 잘, 완전히 등의 의미)	deep. deeply. well. all
		lụt	1	홍수. 범람	flood
			2	(칼날 등) 무뎌진. 둔한	blunt
0481	luu	lưu	流(류) 琉(류) 留(유) 劉(류)	1	멈추다. 머물다	to detain. to keep. (computing) to save
				2	보석류의 하나	one of the jewels
		lựu			석류나무. 석류	pomegranate
0482	luy	lụy	累(누) 淚(누)	1	눈물	tears
				2	곤란하게 하다. 불행에 처하다. 의지하다	to trouble. to be in misfortune. to depend on
		lũy	累(누) 壘(루)		성벽. 성루(城壘)	rampart. wall. hedge
0483	luyen	luyện	練(연) 煉(연) 鍊(연)		단련하다. 연습하다	to train. to drill. to exercise
		luyến	戀(연)		사랑하다. 몹시 동경하다. 매력을 느끼다	(only in compounds) to be fond of

0484	ly	ly	1	유리컵. 작은 잔	cup. glass
			2	아주 조금	very little
			3	설사	diarrhea
			4	통할하다. 관할하다	have jurisdiction over
		lỳ	1	목석같은. (=lì)	wood-like
			2	항상	always
		lý	里(리) 理(리) 李(리) 履(이)	이유. 근거. 이성	reason. basis. rationality
		lỵ		이질 (전염병의 일종)	dysentery (a kind of infection)
0485	ma	mà	1	그런데. (=không과 동반할때)	but
			2	그리고. 그러나	and. but
		ma	魔(마) 麻(마)	1	마귀	goast (spirit appearing after death)
			2	장례의	funeral
		mã	馬(마) 瑪(마) 能(능)	1	외모	one's outward looks
			2	열등한, 질이 낮은	inferior
			3	코드 (code)	code (short symbol). code (computer instructions)
		mạ	罵(매)	1	종묘(씨). 벼 모	rice seedlings
			2	도금하다	to plating
		mả		1	무덤	tomb. grave
			2	절묘한. 능숙한	exquisite. skillful
		má			볼. 뺨	(anatomy) cheek
0486	mac	mặc	默(묵) 墨(묵)	1	(옷) 입다	to wear. to put on
			2	먹. 잉크	china ink. ink stick. ink

		mạc	莫(막), 幕(막), 漠(막), 膜(막)	1	(영화의) 자막	subtitle
				2	모사하다	copy out
		mắc		1	옷걸이. (=mắc áo)	a hanger
				2	매달리다. 몰두하다	to hang. to hook. to catch. to fall into
		mác			삼일월도(칼의 종류). (=mã khắc)	scimitar
0487	mach	mạch	脈(맥), 貊(맥), 陌(맥)	1	맥박	pulse
				2	단숨에. 일거에. (=một mạch)	at a gulp. at a single stroke
		mách			고자질하다	to sneak. tell. tales
0488	mai	mai	梅(매), 枚(매), 埋(매)	1	아침	morning
				2	아침의	morning
				3	내일	tomorrow
		mái		1	지붕	roof
				2	창백한. 병색의	pale. morbid
		mãi	買(매)	1	사다	to buy
				2	계속	continuously
		mại	賣(매)	1	팔다	to sell
				2	눈꼽	sleep
		mài			(칼 따위를) 갈다	to grind (to remove material by rubbing with an abrasive surface)
		mải			몰두하다. 열중하다. (=mải miết, mải mê)	get one's act together. get into a passion
0489	mam	mám		1	[방언] (물고기가) 미끼를 물다	[dialect] take the bait
				2	[방언] 사이가 긴밀한	[dialect] close to each other

		mắm	1	새우. 생산 등을 소금에 절인 젓갈국물	Vietnamese salted, fermented fish
			2	입술을 깨물다. 이를 악물다	bite one's lips. clench one's teeth
		mâm		쟁반(큰접시)	food tray
		măm		물다. 빨다	(onomatopoeia, colloquial, of a baby) to eat
		mắm		확신하다 (chắc mắm 이라고도 함)	to be sure
		mầm		싹. 발아. 병원균	bud. germ. pathogen
		mẫm		토실토실한	chubby
0490	man	man	蠻(만) 瞞(만) 漫(만)	1	만(萬)	ten thousand
				2	속이다	to deseive. cheat. trick
		mãn	滿(만)	1	고양이. (=con mèo)	cat
				2	가득한. 충만한. 만성적인. (=thỏa mãn)	full to the brim. chronic
		mản		1	작은 알갱이	small grain
				2	소심한	timid
		mắn		1	빨리 열매가 열리다	be quick to bear fruit
				2	행운	lucky chance
		mần		1	일하다. (=làm)	to do. to work
				2	부스럼	boil. abscess. carbuncle
		màn			커튼. 막. 모기장	curtain. screen. mosquito net
		mân	珉(민) 蚊(문) 旻(민)		손끝으로 살며시 건드리다	touch gently with one's fingertips
		mẫn			더듬다. 만지작거리다	feel one's way around. grope (around). fiddle about
		mặn			소금기 있는	salted. salty

		mạn	漫(만) 慢(만) 丹(단)		지구(지역)	region, area
		mận			자두(나무)	plum, wax apple
		mãn			(스커트 속에 입는) 페티코트	petticoat
		mǎn			접골하다	graft a bone
		mẫn	敏(민) 憫(민) 閔(민) 愍(민)		통찰력 있는, 정신이 맑은	discerning, lucid
		mẩn			매혹되다	be enchanted
04 91	mang	mang	忙(망) 茫(망) 芒(망)	1	아가미	gill(s)
				2	운반하다	to carry
		mảng		1	대나무, 뗏목	bamboo, raft
				2	~에 열중한	keep on, be absorbed in, be intent on
		máng		1	홈통 (지붕의 물받이)	gutter
				2	구유, 여물통	manger, trough
		măng		1	죽순	bamboo shoot
				2	아주 어린	as young as a lamb
		màng		1	(얇은) 막	membrane, film, coat
				2	(부정적 문장에서만 사용) 고려하다	often in negative sentences to take interest in (something), to be concerned (with)
		mạng	命(명)	1	일생, 생명	lifetime, life
				2	꿰매다, 옷을 수선하여 깁다	sew (up), mend clothes
				3	인터넷	the internet, (computing) network
		mừng		1	축하하다	to congratulate
				2	행복한, (=mừng)	happy
		mắng			꾸짖다, 혼내다	to scold, to chide

0492	manh	mảnh		1	파편. 조각	piece. bit. fragment
				2	아주 약한. 가느다란	weak as a mule. thin. frail
		manh	萌(맹) 盲(맹)	1	조각(1편)	piece
				2	얇은	thin
		mành		1	대나무 발	bamboo nets
				2	가는. 끊어지기 쉬운	slender. thin. fragile
		mãnh	猛(맹)	1	미혼인 채로 죽은 남자	a man who died in single
				2	용맹한	valiant
		mánh			책략. (=mánh khóe. mánh lới)	trick. stratagem
		mạnh	孟(맹) 命(명)		건강한. 강한. 센	strong
0493	map	mập		1	살찐 (=mập mạp). 통통한	fat. obese. stout. plump
				2	상어	shark
0494	mat	mắt		1	눈(目)	an eye
				2	(값) 비싼. (=đắt)	expensive
		mật	蜜(밀) 密(밀)	1	꿀	honey (of bees)
				2	비밀의	secret
		mạt	末(말)	1	새의 진드기(이)	certain species of mites and louses
				2	초라한. 가난한	extremely poor. be in deep poverty
		mát			신선한. 시원한	cool
		mất		1	잃다	to lose something.
				2	죽다	to die
				3	시간이 걸리다	to take (time)
		mặt			얼굴	a face

0495	mau	**mầu**		1	신비한	miracle. mysterious
				2	색깔	color
		mậu	戊(무)	1	10간 중 戊(무)	the fifth Heavenly Stem
				2	틀리다. 오류를 저지르다	to be wrong
		mau			빠른	fast. quick. quickly
		mâu			모순	contradiction
		máu			피	blood
		màu			색	colour. color
		mấu			마디	joint
		mẩu			조각	piece. bit
		mẫu	母(모)		모델. 모형. 양식. 견본. (=kiểu mẫu)	model. pattern. sample
0496	may	**may**		1	행운	lucky
				2	꿰매다. 깁다	to sew
		mày		1	눈썹	eyebrows
				2	(임금이 신하에게 호칭할 때) 너. 경	(singular, informal, familiar or derogatory) you
		máy		1	기계	machine. engine
				2	움직이다. 씰룩거리다	to move. to twitch
		mẩy		1	신체. (=mình mẩy. thân thể)	body
				2	열매가 알찬	fruitful
		mấy		1	얼마. 얼마나 (몇)	how much. how many
				2	2 이상이지만, 그다지 많지 않은 수 (약 10미만)	some. an indefinite quantity greater than one
		mạy		1	작은 대나무의 일종	a kind of small bamboo
				2	어렴풋이	dimly
		mây			구름	cloud

		mậy		(방언. 구어로 문장끝에 사용) 당신. 너	(dialect. spoken language) you. (used at the end of sentence)
		mầy		당신(아랫사람)	you (one's inferiors)
		mảy		극미량	microscopic quantity
0497	me	mé	1	방향	direction
			2	자르다	to cut
		mế	1	노파	an old woman
			2	무의식의	unconscious
		mẻ	1	파편. 조각	fragment. chip. piece (of)
			2	떨어져 나가다. 빠지다	chiped
		me		엄마 (어머니의 유아어). (=mẹ)	mom
		mè		참깨	sesame
		mệ		할머니	grandma
		mẽ		외모	one's outward looks
		mề		새의 모래주머니	gizzard (of a bird)
		mẹ		어머니	mother. mom
		mễ		(탁자 등을 받치는) 가대	trestle
		mê		아주 좋아하다. 동경하다. 숭배하다	to like. yearn for. worship
0498	mem	mem		(아기에게 주기위해) 밥을 잘게 씹다	chew the rice finely (for the baby)
		mèm		몹시. 아주. 무척	very
		mềm		부드러운	soft. flaccid. tender. flexible
		mẻm		아주 확실한. (chắc~)	quite certain
0499	men	men	1	효모균	yeast
			2	접근하다	gain access to

		mền	1	이불	blanket
			2	3중의, 세겹의	three fold, treble, triple
		mén		작은, 어린(이의)	small, juvenile (of a louse)
		mến		애호하다	to love, to like, to be fond of
0500	meo	meo	1	곰팡이	mold, mildew
			2	굶주린	starved
			3	고양이 울음소리	meow, miaow
		méo	1	찡그리다	distorted, twisted
			2	비뚤어진	crooked
		mèo		고양이	cat
		mẻo		조금	a little
		mẹo		술책	ruse, trick, stratagem, tip
0501	met	mét	1	가죽 숫돌, 혁지(革砥)로 갈다	leather whetstone
			2	창백한	pale
			3	미터	meter (unit of measure)
		mẹt		키(평평한 바구니)	flat basket
		mệt		피곤한, 피로한, 지친	tired, fatiqued, weary
0502	menh	mệnh	命(명)	운명. (=số mệnh)	destiny, fate, luck
0503	mi	mi	眉(미)	1	속눈썹	eyelashes
				2	당신(아랫사람). (=mầy)	you (one's junior)
		mí		눈꺼풀	eyelid
		mì	麥(맥)	1	밀, 소맥	wheat
				2	국수	noodles, noodle soup
		mị	媚(미)	매끈매끈한	smooth and smooth
		mĩ	美(미)	1	mĩ miều 아름다운	beautiful
				2	미국, 미국인	The United States, American

		mỉ	密(미)		tỉ mỉ 미세한. 세밀한. 자세히	minute and minute. detailed. in detail
05 04	mia	mía			사탕수수	sugar cane
		mìa			욕하다	speak ill of
05 05	mien	miễn	免(면) 勉(면) 娩(만)	1	면제하다	to exempt (from)
				2	다만 ~한다면. 다만 ~할 뿐인	if only~. but only
		miến	麵(면)		당면	cellophane noodles
		miện	冕(면)		왕관	an imperial crown
		miền			지구	region. district
		Miên			캄보디아. 캄보디아인(人)	Cambodia. Cambodian
05 06	mieng	miếng			조각	piece. crumb
		miểng			폐유리. 조각	wasted glass
		miệng			입(口)	a mouth. a member of a family
05 07	miet	miết		1	열심히 문지르다. (=xiết)	rub hard
				2	단숨에	at a gulp
		miệt	蔑(멸)	1	멸시하다. (=miệt thị)	look down on. scorn. contempt. disdain
				2	지역	area. region. district. zone
05 08	mieu	miếu	臺(대)		사당	shrine
		miếu	廟(묘)		묘(신전)	temple. shrine
		miều			아름다운. Mĩ~	beautiful
05 09	mim	mím			단단히 죄다. (=mím môi)	to tighten (lips)
		mĩm			mũm~ . 토실토실한	chubby. tubby. plump
		mỉm			입술을 꼭 다물다	to press one's lips together
05 10	min	mìn			윗사람이 아랫사람을 향해 자칭하는 말. 나	I. me
		mìn			지뢰. 다이너마이트	mine. dynamite

05 11	minh	mịn			부드러운. 섬세한	soft. delicate. detail
		minh	明(명) 盟(맹)	1	맹세	swear. vow. pledge
				2	밝은	bright. clear. alliance
		mình			몸. 자기자신. 나(어린아이들이 쓰는 말)	body. I. me. one (person pronoun)
		mịnh			운명. 숙명. (=mệnh)	fate. destiny. luck
05 12	mit	mít		1	빵나무 (잭푸르트 나무)	jackfruit (tree)
				2	무지의. 밀폐되어 있는	(chiefly in compounds) be hermetically closed
		mịt			tối~. 매우 어두운	very dark
05 13	mo	mo		1	(식물) 불엽포	certain plants
				2	뻔뻔스러운	impudent
		mò		1	손으로 더듬다. 느끼다	feel with one's hand. feel by hand
				2	닭에 붙는 이의 일종	a kind of insect attached to a chicken
		mơ		1	살구	apricot
				2	꿈꾸다(공상하다)	to dream
		mở		1	열다. (=tháo)	to open. to be open (a door, lid, path, source code)
				2	열려진	open
		mộ	墓(모) 慕(모) 募(모)	1	묘(무덤)	tomb. grave
				2	사모하다	have a fondness
		mỡ		1	지방(기름)	oil. grease
				2	윤택한. 부드러운	smooth
		mớ		1	한무더기. 한벌. 한짝	one set. pair
				2	잠꼬대를 하다	to have bad dreams. nightmares
		mó			접촉하다. 손대다	touch upon

		mõ		불교의 목어		wooden fish. temple block
		mờ		흐린		dim. vague. unclear. blurred
		mỗ		아무개		just referring to someone
		mỏ		주둥이		(of a bird or a platypus) beak. (of a person) mouth
		mổ		메스를 가하다		to cut open
		mồ		무덤		tomb. grave
		mợ		숙모		maternal aunt-in-law. mother's brother's wife
		mô		흙무더기		mound
05 14	moc	móc		1	갈고리	hook. crochet. clasp
				2	(고리로) 걸다	to hook
		mốc		1	곰팡이	mould. mildew
				2	곰팡이가 난	mouldy
		mộc	木(목)	1	나무	tree
				2	가공하지 않은	unprocessed
		mọc			(식물 등이) 성장하다. 자라다	(of a plant) to shoot out of the soil (of hair, nails, teeth, feathers or claws) to start to grow (of the sun) to rise
05 15	moi	mọi		1	모든	every. all
				2	모이족(베트남 중부의 산악에 사는 종족)	mọi tribe
				3	노예	slave
		mới		1	새로운	new (recently made or created)
				2	단지. 비로소	just. at last
		moi			파헤치다	to drag out something
		mơi			내일. (=mai)	tomorrow
		mòi			징조	signs

		mỗi	每(매)		각각의. 모든	each
		mội			원천(源泉)	source. root. origin. wellspring
		mồi			먹이. 미끼	a prey. bait
		mỏi			지친	weary. tired
		mời			초청하다. 청하다	to invite. to ask
		mối			흰개미	termite
		mòi			청어	herring
		môi		1	입술	lip
				2	수프를 뜨는 국자	dipper. ladle
05 16	mom	mõm		1	주둥이. (동물의) 코. 입부분	a muzzle (part of animal's head)
				2	너무익은. 부패한	rotten
		mờm		1	동물의 어깻살	animal shoulder flesh
				2	시도하다. (=ướm thử)	try
		móm			이가 빠진	be toothless
		mồm			입 (=miệng)	(anatomy, rather informal) a mouth
		mớm			입으로 먹여주다	to feed with premasticated food
		mỏm			튀어나온(곳)	a bulging (spot)
05 17	mon	mòn			닮다	have a similarity
		món			아이템. 항목. 요리	dish (food item)
		mơn			쓰다듬다	to pet. to stroke
		mớn			선적 용량	shipping capacity
		mọn			적은. 작은	a little. small
		môn			교과. 학과. 과목	subject. discipline
		mòn			낡다. 헌. 무디다. 해지다	be out of date. old

05 18	mong	**mống**		1	짧은 무지개	a short rainbow
				2	누구나	anyone
		mòng		1	말파리	horsefly
				2	기대하다	to anticipate
		mộng	夢(몽)	1	새싹	sprout
				2	거세되다	be castrated
		mong	望(망)		희망하다. 바라다. (=mong đợi, mong chờ)	to except, to wish for something
		móng			손톱. 발톱	nail, claw
		mỏng			얇은	thin, slender, slim
		mọng			수분이 많은	succulent, juicy
		mồng			한달의 초순 10일간 (=mùng)	used in front of numerals from **1** to **10** to denote one of the first ten days of a month.
		mông			엉덩이	buttock, bottom
05 19	mot	**một**		1	하나. 1	one, **1**
				2	제1의	primary
		mót			줍다	pick up
		mốt		1	모레	day after tomorrow
				2	패션. 트렌드	fashion, trend
		mọt			(곤충) 나무좀	weevil
05 20	mu	**mù**		1	안개	fog, mist
				2	무턱대고 ~하다	to do something without anyhow
				3	눈 먼 (볼 수 없음)	blind (unable to see)
		mu		1	갑각	carapace
				2	불룩한	bulging, fat

		mụ	1	(나쁜 의미) 노파	(derogatory) an old woman
			2	기력이 쇠약해지다. 기억력이 저하되다	lose one's memory
		mũ		모자	hat. cap. helmet
		mủ		고름	pus
05 21	mua	mưa	1	비가 내리다	to rain
			2	비	rain
		mứa	1	남기다	leave. save
			2	잉여의	surplus
		mua		사다	to buy. to purchase
		múa		춤추다	to dance (ritually, with fan or sword)
		mùa		계절	season
		mửa		(음식 등을) 토하다	to vomit
05 22	muc	mục	1	항목	item
			2	썩은	rotten. decaying. decayed
		mực	1	오징어	a squid (sea animal)
			2	잉크. (오징어의) 먹물	ink (coloured fluid used for writing) ink (dark fluid ejected by squid, etc.)
			3	검다	black
		múc		담아올리다. 푸다	to scoop or ladle (as soup or water) into a bowl
		mức		수준. 정도	degree. extend. level
05 23	mui	mui		(차, 배의) 덮개. 지붕	covering proof (for car, boat, etc.). hood
		mùi	未(미) 味(미)	1	냄새	smell. odor. scent
				2	(노래, 악기소리 등이) 정감있는. 단아한	affectionate. elegant
		mũi		코	nose

		múi		과육(果肉)	usually of a fruit segment
		mụi		남은 (여분의)	remaining (extra)
05 24	mun	mun		재	ashes
		mùn		부스러기	dust. particle
		mụn		여드름	acne. pimple
05 25	mung	mừng	1	축하하다	to rejoice. to congraturate
			2	기쁜. 행복한	glad. happy
		mùng	1	한달의 초순 10일간. (=mồng)	used in front of numerals from **1** to **10** to denote one of the first ten days of a month
			2	모기장	a mosquito net
		mủng		작은 대바구니	a small bamboo basket
		mửng		방식. 방법	method
05 26	muoi	muồi	1	(과일 등이) 잘 익은	ripe (fruit)
			2	(과일 등이) 익다	(fruit) ripen well
		muối	1	소금	salt
			2	(소금, 설탕 또는 식초 용액에 음식을 보존하기 위해) 절이다	(to preserve food in a salt, sugar or vinegar solution) to pickle
		muội	妹(매) 昧(매)	1	희미한	dimly-hearted
				2	그으름. 검댕	soot
		mươi		열. 10	ten. **10**
		muỗi		모기	mosquito
		mười		열. 10	ten. **10**
		muôi		국자	a ladle. soup ladle
05 27	muon	muốn		원하다. 희망하다. 소망하다	to want
		muộn		늦은. 늦다	late. tardy
		mướn		세주다. 빌려주다	to hire. to rent

		mượn		빌리다	to borrow
		muôn		일만. 10,000	ten thousand
05 28	muong	mương	1	도랑. 배수로	ditch. trench
			2	도랑에 빠지게 하다	fall into a ditch
		muỗng		깔때기. (=phễu)	funnel
		muỗng		숟가락. 스푼	spoon
		mường		므엉족 (북부 베트남 소수민족중의 하나)	mường tribe
05 29	mut	mút	1	말단. 끝. 극단	termianal stage. end. extreme
			2	빨다. 흡수하다	to suck (at/on). to absorb. absorption
		mụt		여드름. 종기	acne. pimple
		mứt	1	잼	jam
			2	설탕을 넣어 보존한 과일	fruit preserved with sugar
05 30	muu	mưu	謨(모) 1	계획. 기획. 모의. 계략. 음모	scheme. plot. conspiracy
			2	고려하다	to consider. allow for
05 31	my	Mỹ		미국. 미주	The United States. America
05 32	na	nà	1	문장끝에 붙이는 말로 nào와 같은 의미	the same meaning as nào at the end of a sentence
			2	강하게. 세게	strongly
		ná	1	석궁	crossbow
			2	약아빠진. 교활한	sly. foxy. cunning
		nả	1	짧은 기간의 시간. 적은 양	a short period of time. a small quantity
			2	문장끝에 쓰이는 의문사와 같은 강조어구	an emphatic phrase, such as an interrogative verb, used at the end of a sentence.
		na	那(나)	천도 복숭아. (=mãng cầu)	sugar apple

		nã	拿(나)		체포하다. 잡다	make an arrest
		nạ			가면	mask
05 33	nac	nác			물. (=nước)	water
		nạc			기름기없는 살코기. 기름기가 없는	lean (meat)
		nấc			계단. 사다리의 가로대	step. stair. grade. notch. degree
		nặc	穹(궁)		냄새가 나다. 발생하다	reeking of. smelling strongly of. pervaded with
05 34	nach	nách		1	겨드랑이	armpit
				2	겨드랑이에 끼고 가다	go under one's arm
05 35	nai	nai		1	사슴	a sambar deer
				2	단단히 묶다	tie sth tightly
		nài		1	말이나 코끼리를 사육하는 사람	a breeder of horses and elephants
				2	계속 졸라대다. 요청하다. 빌다	to beg
		nại	耐(내)	1	(소금생산) 염전	salt field. salt pond
				2	염려하다. 마음에 두다. 주저하다	to be concerned. worry (about). to hesitate
		nái			동물들의 암컷	female (certain animals only, suchas pigs)
		nải			작은 가방	a small bag
05 36	nam	nắm		1	쥐다. 잡다	to hold
				2	한줌. 한움큼	a handful
		nạm		1	한주먹	a fistful
				2	새겨넣다	to engrave
		nam	男(남) 南(남) 溝(구)	1	남쪽	south
				2	남자	man. male

		năm		1	다섯. 5		five. 5
				2	년(年). 해		year
		nám			탄. 햇볕에 그을린		burnt. sunburned
		nầm			돼지와 소의 가슴 고기. 안심. (=thịt nầm)		tenderloin
		nậm			목이 긴 유리병. (=nắm)		a long-necked glass bottle
		nằm			눕다. 자다. 놓여있다		to lie (be in a horizontal position on a surface)
		nắm			목이 긴 유리병. (=nậm)		a long-necked glass bottle
		nấm			버섯		mushroom
05 37	nan	nan	難(난)	1	어려움		difficulty
				2	어려운		difficult
		nản		1	낙담한. 낙심한		depressed. disappointed
				2	낙담하다. (=nản chí, nản lòng)		to be discouraged. to lost heart. disappointment to recoil from difficulties
		nân			통통한. 살찐		chubby. fat
		nàn			위험. 재난. (=nạn)		accident. danger. calamity. disaster. peril
		nán			오래 머무르다		to linger. to stay on
		nắn			(손으로) 만지다		to change. to modify something's shape
		nặn			모형을 만들다		to make a shape out of clay or similar material
		nạn	難(난)		위험. 재난		accident. danger. calamity. disaster. peril
05 38	nang	năng	能(능)	1	종종. 자주		frequently. often
				2	능력. 성능		performance. ability
		nạng		1	목발. 버팀목. 지팡이		crutch
				2	밀어내다. 몰아내다		to push. to push off

		nang	囊(낭)		주머니. 배낭. (피부의) 모낭	pocket. backpack. follicle
		nâng			들어올리다	to raise. to lift
		nàng			그녀. 당신. 아가씨. 부인이라는 뜻의 호칭	lady. dame. young woman. she. her
		náng			약용식물의 일종	crinum asiaticum. poison lily. spider lily
		nựng			(마음을) 달래다. (=nựng)	to soothe
		nắng			양지바른. 햇볕이 잘드는	sunny. sunshine
		nẵng			훔치다	to steal
		nặng			거대한. 무거운. 부피가 큰	heavy
		nắng			충동적인. 성욕이 넘치는. (성기) 발기하는. (=nứng)	impulsive. sexually active. erection
05 39	nanh	nanh			송곳니	eye tooth. fang
		nạnh			시기하는. 질투하는	envious. be jealous of. envy
		nánh			옆으로 비키다. 피하다. 벗어나다	to move to the side. to avoid. get out of
		nành			đậu~ 콩	soybean
05 40	nao	nao	軀(구) 鞠(국)	1	시어(時語)에서 의문사로 쓰이는 말. (=nào)	a word used as a questionable subject in a poem
				2	걱정하는. 불안한	anxious
		nào		1	어느(것). 어떤(것)	which
				2	문두, 문미에 붙어 화제를 바꾸기 위한 경우 또는 주의를 환기시키기 위한 뜻을 지닌 단어	a word intended to change the subject or to call attention
		não	腦(뇌) 惱(뇌)	1	뇌	brain. cerebrum
				2	고민의. 슬픈	agonizing. sad
		náo	國(국)	1	소란스러운	tumultuous
				2	시끄럽게 하다	to make noise

		nạo	1	후벼내다	to grate, to squeeze, to scrape
			2	깎는 도구, 깎는 칼	a cutting tool, a cutting knife
05 41	nap	nắp		겉표지, 표지, 뚜껑	lid, cover
		nạp	納(납) 1	제출하다. (=nộp)	hand in
			2	총알을 장전하다. 배터리를 충전하다	to load (bullets), to charge (battery)
		nấp		숨다. 몸을 숨기다. (=núp)	hide oneself
05 42	nat	nát	1	구겨진, 으스러진	crushed, crumbled
			2	협박하다. 겁을 주다	to intimidate, to cow
		nạt		협박하다. 큰 소리로 윽박지르다	to threaten, to intimidate
05 43	nau	nâu		갈색	brown (having a brown color)
		náu		숨다. 은신하다	to hide oneself away
		nẫu		너무 익은	overcooked
		nấu		요리하다. 밥을 짓다	to cook, to boil
05 44	nay	nay		지금, 현재	now
		nãy		조금전 (단독으로 쓰이지 않음)	then, at that time
		này		이(것, 곳)	this, here
		nảy		싹트다. 나기 시작하다	to sprout
		nấy		그	that it
		nạy		~을 지레로 들어올리다. ~을 억지로 열다	to pry something open, to pry, to prize, to prise
		nầy		이(것, 분), 여기. (=này)	this, here
		nẩy		(=nãy)	(=nãy)

05 45	ne	né		1	휙 몸을 틀다. 벗어나다. 피하다	to dodge. to avoid
				2	누에가 고치를 틀도록 깔아주는 용구	a tool for silkworms to spin cocoons
		nẻ		1	(채찍 등으로) 때리다	whip (with a whip, etc.)
				2	금이간. 살갗이 튼	(of a surface) cracked. fissured
		nề		1	지주(支柱). 받침대. 쐐기	pillar. support. prop. wedge
				2	몸이 부어오르다	swell up
		nệ			고집하다. 집착하다. 주장하다	insist. persist. stick to. obsess over
		nể			남의 마음을 상하지 않도록 하다. 존중하다. 존경하다	to respect. to admire
		nè			꺼리다	be reluctant to. to avoid
		nè			이(것, 곳). (=này)	this. here
05 46	nem	nem			넴 (베트남식 튀김 만두)	spring roll
		ném			던지다. 가볍게 치다. 집어던지다. 내던지다. 던져버리다	to throw. fling. cast. chuck
		nệm			매트리스	mattress
		nếm			(음식, 음료수 등을) 맛보다. 시음하다	to taste
		nêm			쐐기. 쐐기를 박다	wedge. to wedge
05 47	nen	nén			제지하다. 제한하다. 억제하다. 보류하다	to press. to control. to restrain
		nền		1	토대. 기초	foundation. basis. background
				2	(색상) 품위있게 어울리는	(color) harmonize (with). match
		nến			(양)초	candle. taper. wax
		nện			찌르다. 찧다. 때리다	to beat. to hit. to strike

		nên	1	그러므로. 따라서. 그래서	therefore. so
			2	~하지 않으면 안된다	should. ought to
05 48	neo	neo	1	닻을 내리다	drop anchor
			2	부족한. 결핍한	insufficient. deficient
		néo		(로프를) 죄다. 단단히 조이다	tighten (a rope)
		nẻo		길. 방법. 방향	road. method. direction
05 49	nep	nếp	1	주름(살). 접은 금. 머리를 땋다	fold. crease. plait
			2	집. 건물	house. buiding
			3	버릇이 들다	habit
		nép		쭈그리다. 웅크리다	clouch down. squat (down). curl up
		nẹp		테. (옷) 끝단	rim
05 50	net	nét	1	인상. 용모. 형태. (글자) 획	a line. a stroke. (of a human body part) a curve
			2	(음성 또는 형태가) 분명한. 맑은	clear (in speech or form)
		nẹt		협박하다. 위협하다. (=đánh. de dọa)	to threaten. to intimidate
		nết		행위. 행동. 품행	act. action. conduct. behavior
05 51	neu	nếu		만약	if (supposing that)
		nêu	1	장대. 기둥 : 음력설에 집앞에 대나무 기둥을 높이 세우는 베트남 풍습	long bamboo pole traditionally erected during the Vietnamese luner new year
			2	(문제, 질문 따위를) 제의하다. 떠올리다	to raise (question, suggestion, etc.). to bring up to set
05 52	nga	Nga	娥(아) 峨(아) 名(명) 鵝(아)	1	러시아(사회주의 연방 공화국)	Russia. The Russian Federation
				2	읊조리다. (=ngâm nga)	to recite
				3	달	moon

		ngà		1	(코끼리의 엄니) 상아	ivory
				2	상아색의	(color) ivory
		ngã	我(아)		넘어지다. 굴러떨어지다	to fall. to tumble down
		ngả		1	길(방향). 노정	way. direction. direction along a road or path
				2	(몸, 물건, 의견 따위가) 기울어지다. 가라앉다	to lean. to incline
05 53	ngac	ngạc	姆(모)	1	악어	crocodile
				2	대합조개	clams
				3	막히다	be blocked
		ngấc			머리를 들다	raise one's head
		ngắc			말이 막히다. 사업이 곤궁에 처하다	be at s loss for words. one's business is in trouble
05 54	ngach	ngách			지류. 옆길	tributary stream. branch (of). a side road
		ngạch	額(액)		문지방	the threshold
05 55	ngai	ngai			왕좌	throne
		ngái		1	나무의 일종. 감기치료약을 만드는데 쓰인다	a kind of tree used to make cold medicine
				2	냄새가 나는. 설익은	having a unpleasant smell
		ngại		1	걱정하는. 두려운	worried. hesitant. fearful
				2	걱정하다. 고민하다. 속태우다	to fear. to be afraid
		ngài			귀하 (상대방을 존경해서 하는 말)	Mr. Sir
		ngãi			정당함. 공정함	righteousness. faithfulness
05 56	ngam	ngăm		1	위협하다. 협박하다. (=hăm(dọa))	to threaten. to intimidate
				2	황갈색의	yellowish-brown
		ngầm		1	비밀의	secret. underground
				2	몰래. 살짝	on the quiet

		ngâm	吟(음)		읊다	to soak. to steep
		ngàm			(건축) 열장이음	dovetailing. a dovetail (joint). a fantail
		ngám			딱맞는. 적합한	to fit. to be just right
		ngẫm			사고하다. 숙고하다	to think deeply. to muse. to meditate
		ngắm			주시하다	to be attentive to something. to watch. to view
		ngấm			잠기다. 침투하다	sink. penetrate into. pass through
		ngậm			입을 다물다. 입에 물다	to hold inside one's mouth
05 57	ngan	ngàn		1	절제하다	exercise moderation. self-control. restraint
				2	이만큼. 저만큼	this much. as much as that
		ngăn		1	서랍	drawer
				2	단락을 짓다. 칸막이하다. 가르다	to stop or prevent someone to do something
		ngán		1	혐오감이 나다. 싫어지다	be bored of a food or dish
				2	싫증난. 피곤한	having boredom in doing something
		ngân	銀(은)	1	여운을 남기다. 진동하다	leave an afterglow
				2	은(銀)	silver
		ngẩn		1	망연하다. 아연하다	lose one's head. be struck dumb
				2	아직 덜 찬. (=lưng)	be not yet filled
		ngan			집오리의 일종	muscovy duck
		ngàn			(숫자) 천. (=nghìn)	thousand
		ngắn			짧은	short. brief
		ngấn	痕(흔)		상처자국. 자취. 종적	the mark of a wound. trace. whereabouts

		ngạn	岸(안) 諺(언)	강안. 강가	a riverside. a riverbank
05 58	ngang	ngang		1	가로의. 횡단하는	horizontal. level
				2	~와 동등하다	be equal to
		ngãng		1	몰래 빼내다. 살금살금 피하다	sneak out. sneak off
				2	넓은	broad. wide
		ngáng		1	막다	keep out
				2	(대나무) 마디	a joint
		ngắng			좁은	narrow
		ngẳng			세우다. 쳐들다. 머리를 쳐들다. (=ngửng)	raise one's head
		ngẵng			가늘고 긴	slender and long
05 59	nganh	ngảnh		1	뒤돌아 보다. (=ngoảnh)	to turn one's head. to turn around
				2	바다로 툭 튀어나온 육지. 갑. 곶	a cape shooting out into the sea
		ngạnh	硬(경) 梗(경) 居(거)	1	낚시바늘 끝. 갈고리. (철조망) 가시	hook
				2	고집센. 완고한	stubborn as a mule
		ngành			작은 가지. 분야. 업종. 업계	branch
05 60	ngao	ngao		1	(동물) 집지키는 개. (어패류) 조개의 일종	watch dog. a kind of shellfish
				2	흥얼거리다. 콧노래하다. 어슬렁거리다	to hum. hum a tune. hang about
		ngào		1	바짝 조리다	cook hard
				2	잼	jam
		ngạo		1	우롱하다. 경멸하다. 놀리다	to show contempt of others. to be arrogant
				2	교만한. (=ngạo đời)	arrogant. haughtiness. pride. conceit. arrogance

05 61	ngap	**ngập**	1	침수하다. 넘치다	to flood. to overflow
			2	홍수의. 침수된	be flooded
		ngáp		하품을 하다	to yawn
05 62	ngat	**ngật**	1	(머리가) 어지럽다	have a dizzy head
			2	정신이 어릿어릿한. 어지러울 정도로 높은	in a dithering spirit. dizzy high
		ngất	1	높게 솟은 것. (=cao ngất)	very high or tall
			2	실신하다. 정신을 잃다. 기절하다. (=ngất đi)	to faint (to lose consciousness)
		ngạt	1	숨막히는. 답답한. 압박하는. (=ngạt hơi)	stifling. stuffy. suffocating. pressing
			2	꺽쇠. 쥠쇠. 집게. (=~kéo)	tangs. pincers
		ngắt	1	(꽃 잎등을) 따다.	to pick
			2	날카롭게 방해하다	to sharply interrupt
		ngặt	1	엄중한. 엄격한	stern and stern. strict. rigid
			2	(울음) 막히다	be choked (with tears)
		ngát		향기가 나는. (=thơm ngát)	fragrent
05 63	ngau	**ngâu**	1	들소	bison. buffalo
			2	갑작스러운	out of the blue. sudden
		ngấu	1	발효된. 잘익은. 잘 우려낸	fermented. well-done
			2	(음식물을) 빨리 씹다	chew food quickly
		ngàu		진흙의. 진흙투성이의. (색깔) 흐린	muddy. cloudy in color
		ngàu		흐리다. (=ngầu ngầu)	muddy. cloudy. turbid. of eyes blood shot
		ngẫu	偶(우)	우연히. 뜻밖의	by chance
		ngậu		시끄럽게 하다. (=ngậu xị)	to make noise

0564	ngay	ngây	1	천진난만한. 순진한. 소박한	looking stupit. looking naïve. catatonic
			2	망연하다. 멍하고 있다	lose one's head. (be) vacant. blank
		ngấy	1	(식물) 싫어지다. 혐오감 느끼다	grow weary of. feel repugnance
			2	(식물) 오얏나무의 일종	(plants) a kind of plum tree
		ngay		곧. 즉시로. 직접	as soon as. direct. straight
		ngày		날. 일(日). 주간	day. date. daytime
		ngáy		코를 골다	to snore
		ngầy		귀찮게 하다	to bother somone
		ngậy		영양분이 많고 맛있는	nutritious and tasty
0565	nghe	nghe	1	듣다. (귀가) 들리다.	to hear
			2	듣다. 귀를 기울이다	to listen
		nghé	1	물소 새끼	a baby water buffalo
			2	엿보다. (=nghé xem)	have a peek. peep (into/through)
		nghè	1	신을 모시는 신전	temple of the gods
			2	윤이 나도록 방망이질하다. 반듯하게 펴다	straighten out
		nghề	1	직업. 생업	profession. occupation (=nghệ)
			2	정통한	well-informed. well-versed
			3	재주. 기량	talent. skill
		nghễ		경멸적인. 거만한. (=ngạo nghễ)	contemptuous. haughty
		nghệ		(생강과에 속하는 식물) 심황. 심황 뿌리	turmeric
		nghẻ		불쾌하게 하다. 화나게 하다. (=bể nghẻ)	make somebody unpleasant. ruffle a person's feathers

05 66	ngheo	nghẹo		1	방향을 틀다. 옆길로 새다	change one's course. leak into a side street
				2	굽은. 뒤틀린. (=ngoẹo)	curved. warped. twisted
		nghèo			가난한. 궁핍한	poor
		nghẽo			약한 말(馬). 시원찮은 말(馬)	a weak horse.
		nghẻo			죽다. (=ngoẻo)	fall dead. die
05 67	nghet	nghẹt		1	질식해 죽은. 목이 메인	suffocated to death
				2	꽉 조르다	tighten one's grip on
05 68	ngheu	nghều			키가 크고 마른	tall and thin
		nghêu			조개	shellfish. clam
05 69	nghi	nghi	疑(의) 宜(의) 儀(의)	1	의심하다. (=nghi là)	to doubt. to suspect
				2	외양. 모습. 의례	appearance. formality. ritual. ceremony
		nghỉ		1	쉬다. 묵다	to take a break. to get to temporarily leave work
				2	(방언) 그여자. 그남자	(dialect) the woman. the man
		nghĩ	擬(의)		생각하다. 사색하다	to think. to contemplate
		nghì			시종 변하지 않는 정의. (=nghĩa)	ever-changing definition
		nghị	議(의) 誼(의) 蟻(의)		상의하다. 호의하다	to discuss. to deliberate
05 70	nghia	nghĩa	義(의)		의미. 뜻. 가치	a meaning. a sense. morality
05 71	nghich	nghịch	逆(역)	1	장난의	to play with. to toy with. to twiddle with
				2	반항하다. 반대의	opposite. contrary. hostile. rebellious. to rebel

05 72	nghiem	nghiệm	驗(험)	1	확인하다	to consider
				2	(약) 효험이 있는	(medicine) effective
		nghiêm			엄격한. 엄한. 호된	strict. grave. stern
05 73	nghien	nghiến		1	삐걱거리다	to squeak
				2	이를 갈거나 악물다	to grind or clench (one's teeth)
		nghiền			분말로 만들다. 으깨다.	to grind
		nghiện			중독이 되다	to be addicted to
05 74	nghieng	nghiêng			비스듬한. 기울어진	tilted. leaning. oblique. lopsided
05 75	nghiep	nghiệp	業(업)		사업. 직업	trade. profession.
05 76	nghin	nghìn			천(千). (=ngàn)	thousand
		nghìn			짧은 거리	a short distance
05 77	ngo	ngó		1	보다. 쳐다보다	to see. to look at
				2	나무의 싹	the bud of a tree
		ngỏ		1	열린	open. left open. unlocked
				2	열다. 공개하다	to open. to openly express
		ngộ	梧(오) 誤(오) 遇(우)	1	약간 이상한. 기묘한. 진기한	queer. quaint
				2	미치다. 발광하다. (=dại)	go mad. go completely
		ngò			(음식) 향료의 일종. 고수	cilantro (coriander leaf)
		ngõ			(골목)길. 골목	lane. alley. bystreet
		ngơ			무시하다	to ignore
		ngỏ			건방진	saucy-faced
		ngờ			의심하다. (=ngờ ngợ)	to doubt. to suspect. to be suspicious (of)
		ngọ	午(오)		십이지의 오	(archaic) noon
		ngớ			망연하다. 제정신을 잃다	lose one's marbles. take leave of one's senses

		ngố		멍청한	doltish, dull-headed
		ngỡ		생각하다. 상상하다	to think that, to believe that
		ngờ		의심하다	to doubt, to suspect, to be suspicious (of)
		ngô		옥수수	corn, maize
0578	ngoac	ngoặc		괄호를 붙이다	put parentheses on
		ngoắc		걸다. 매다. 낚다. (=mắc vào)	hang (on a hook), hook
		ngoạc		크게 열다	open wide
		ngoác		(=ngoạc)	(=ngoạc)
0579	ngoai	ngoài	1	밖. 외면. 외부	outside, exterior
			2	이외. 이 문제에 더하여. ~은 별도로 하고	besides
		ngoái	1	작년. (=năm ngoái)	last year
			2	고개를 돌리다	to turn (one's head) round
		ngoại	外(외) 1	어머니쪽의. 외가의	related to the mother's side of the family
			2	지나다. 넘다	pass by
			3	바깥 (외관)	outside
		ngoải	1	그 밖	other than that
			2	그 밖에서	that place outside, out there, outside
0580	ngoan	ngoan		품행이 좋은. 착한. 단정한. 유순한	good, well-behaved, submissive
		ngoạn	玩(완)	유람하다. 관람하다	have a pleasure trip, to watch
0581	ngoanh	ngoảnh		뒤돌아 보다	to turn one's head, to turn around
0582	ngoay	ngoáy		후비다	to pick, pierce
		ngoảy		화가나서 샐쭉하여 돌아서다. 외면하다. (=ngoay ngoảy)	turn away in anger

0583	ngoc	**ngóc**		1	머리를 들다	to raise one's head
				2	(=ngách). 지류. 옆길	(=ngách). tributary stream. branch (of). a side road
		ngốc			어리석은. 무지한. (=ngốc nghếch)	stupid. naive. foolish
		ngọc	玉(옥)		옥. 보석	a gem. a precious stone
0584	ngoi	**ngoi**			떠오르다	to emerge. to rise up (from a surface)
		ngõi			기대하다	to expect
		ngơi			쉬다. 휴식하다	to rest. to knock off
		ngòi			개천	canal
		ngói			기와	tile. turtle dove
		ngồi			앉다	to sit
		ngời			빛나다	shining. beaming. radiant
		ngợi			칭찬하다	to praise
		ngỡi			(=nghĩa)	(=nghĩa)
		ngôi			지위. 계급	throne. Indicates nouns for structures, buildings, markets, graves and stars
0585	ngon	**ngon**			맛있는	delicious. tasty. succulent
		ngón			손가락. (=ngón tay)	a digit (finger or toe)
		ngộn			(일이) 넘치는. 푸짐하게 많은	full (of work). plentiful
		ngọn			선단	the top. tip. extremely end (of a tree)
		ngốn			너무 빨리 소비하다	to be crammed. to engorge
0586	ngong	**ngong**			마음을 졸이며 기다리다	wait with nervousnessfully
		ngổng		1	높다	high
				2	키가 커서 삐쭉솟다	be tall and sprung up

		ngỗng	1	줄기	stem
			2	높이 튀어 나온	high-spirited
		ngóng		희망하다. 대망하다	to hope for
		ngõng		축	axis
		ngòng		홀쭉한. 호리호리한	slim. slender. thin.
		ngỗng		거위	goose
		ngọng		언어 장애의. 더듬거리는	speech-impaired. stammering
		ngổng		늘리다	increase. expand. add to. extend
		ngông		낭비하는. 사치하는	wasteful. extravagant
0587	ngot	ngót	1	감퇴하다	drop out. decline. weaken. deteriorate
			2	대강. 대략 ~정도	roughly. approximately
		ngọt		(맛) 달다. 감미롭다	sweet
		ngột		질식되다. (=ngạt)	be suffocated
		ngớt		약해지다	to weaken. to abate. to subside
		ngốt		숨이 막히다	be suffocated
0588	ngu	ngù	1	(모자, 옷) 깃털. 비단실 등의 장식용 방울술	tassel
			2	질주하다	make a dash
		ngự	御(어) 禦(어)	1	어 (황제에 대한 존칭)	royal
				2	임금님이 옥좌에 앉다	a king sits on the throne
		ngu	愚(우) 隅(우) 虞(우) 娛(오)		미련한. 어리석은	stupid. idiotic. moronic
		ngũ	五(오) 伍(오)		다섯	five. 5

		ngữ	御(어) 語(어)		언어	language. word
		ngụ	寓(우)		임시 거처하다. 머무르다	stay for a while
		ngủ			잠자다	to sleep
05 89	nguc	**ngúc**			(머리) 들다. (=ngóc)	raise one's head
		ngực			가슴. 흉부	a chest
		ngục	獄(옥)		감옥. 교도소	prison
05 90	ngung	**ngưng**			그만두다. 그치다. 중단하다. 멈추다	to stop. to desist
		ngùng			흔들거리다. 동요하다. 주저하다	be in a flap. unrest. agitation
		ngửng			머리를 쳐들다. 우러러보다. (=ngẩng)	look up to
		ngừng			그만두다. 정지하다. 멈추다. 세우다	to stop. to desist
05 91	nguoi	**ngươi**		1	아랫사람에게 사용하는 2인칭. 너. 자네. 등	you
				2	눈동자	pupil (the hole in the middle of the iris of the eye)
		nguội		1	찬	cold
				2	차게하다. 식히다	(of foods) be cooled off
		người		1	사람. 타인. 사람들. (=con người)	a human. a man. a person. an individual. a people
				2	존경하는 인물의 3인칭 (이 경우에는 대문자로 쓴다) Người	a person of respect (3rd person) you. he. him
05 92	nguy	**nguy**	僞(위) 魏(위)	1	가짜의. 잘못된. 괴뢰의	fake. wrong. puppet
				2	위(國名)	Wei Dynasty
		nguy	危(위) 譯(역)		위험한. 위험이 많은	dangerous

0593	nguyen	**nguyền**		약속하다. 맹세하다	promise, swear, pledge, vow
		nguyện	願(원)	서원하다	make a vow
		nguyễn		원(國名)	Nguyễn Dynasty
		nguyên		흠 없는. 온전한. 그대로인	original, intact, brand new, entire, unbroken
0594	nguyet	**nguyệt**	月(월)	(천문) 달. (=tháng, mặt trăng). 월	Moon, month
0595	nha	**nha**	衙(아) 牙(아) 芽(아) 鴉(아) 臆(억)	1 (관청의) 부문. 국. 과	the branch of a government office
				2 (=nhé)	alternative spelling of "nhé"
		nhá		씹다	to chew, to masticate
		nhã	雅(아)	우아한. 정숙한	elegant, graceful, refined
		nhà		집. 가정	a house, a home, a dwelling, a family, a spouse
		nhả		서슴지 않고 말하다. 내뱉듯이 말하다	to stop holding in mouth, to spit out, to stop biting
0596	nhac	**nhác**		1 힐끗 보다. (=mắt nhìn qua)	take a glance at
				2 게으른. 어리석은	lazy, idle
		nhạc	樂(락, 악)	음악	music
		nhắc		들다. 들어올리다. (=nhắc đến). 재촉하다. 상기시키다	to lift, to raise, to prompt, to remind
		nhấc		들어올리다	to lift, to raise
0597	nhai	**nhái**		1 개구리. 청개구리	small frog, tree frog
				2 흉내내다. (=nhại)	to imitate, to mimic
		nhai		(잘게) 씹다	to chew, to masticate, to ruminate
		nhãi		개구장이. 어린애. (=nhãi con, nhãi ranh, nhãi nhép)	punk kid, a child
		nhại		말을 흉내내다	to imitate, to mimic

		nhài		자스민	jasmine
0598	nham	nhắm	1	겨냥하다	to aim (at). to fall (on). in order to
			2	올바른. 공정한	correct. fair
		nhám		꺼칠꺼칠한. 잘 미끄러지지 않는	(of a surface) rough. harsh
		nhàm		성가신	annoying. bothersome. troublesome. tiresome
		nhâm	壬(임)	십간(十干)의 임(壬)	the ninth Heavenly Stem
		nhăm		(숫자) 오(五). 20이상의 5를 나타내는 말 (lăm의 변형음)	dialect spelling of lăm. a word that represents five of twenty or more (25, 35 ~)
		nhậm	任(임)	받아들이다. 떠맡다. (=nhận)	accept. charge oneself with
		nhầm		실수하다. 잘못 알다. (=lầm)	to mistake. to get something wrong
		nhắm		(눈을) 감다. 겨냥하다. 홀짝홀짝 마시다	to close (eyes). to aim. to sip
		nhảm		진실이 아닌. 허위의	untrue
		nhẩm		머리속으로 생각하다	think in one's head
		nhấm		갉아먹다	to gnaw at. to nibble
		nhậm		(눈이) 충혈되다	be bloodshot (eye)
0599	nhan	nhẫn	忍(인) 刃(인)	1	반지	ring (round piece of (precious) metal worn around the finger)
				2	약간 쓴	be slightly bitter
		nhân	因(인) 仁(인) 人(인)	1	사람. (=người)	people. person. human. man
				2	늘리다. 곱하다	multiply by
		nhan	顏(안)		얼굴	face
		nhãn	眼(안)	1	용안 (식물)	(plant) longan
				2	라벨. 상표	label. trademark

		nhăn			주름이 있다	be wrinkled
		nhàn	閑(한)間(간)		한가한. (몸이) 편한	leisurely. idle. free
		nhãn			많은	many
		nhặn			정중한	courteous. polite. respectful
		nhạn			제비	swallow
		nhẵn		1	매끄러운. 심지어. 평평한	smooth. even. flat
				2	완전히 없어지다. 만반의. 매우 친숙하다	all gone. all finished. to be very fimiliar
		nhắn			전해주다. 전갈을 보내다. 문자를 보내다	to send word. to leave a message
		nhấn			꽉 누르다	to press. to stress. to emphasise. (=nhận)
		nhận	認(인)	1	받다	to get. to receive
				2	동의하다. 인정하다	to agree. to accept. to acknowledge
		nhằn			(앞니로) 먹다	to eat (with front teeth)
0600	nhang	nháng		1	빛나는. 번쩍이는. (=nhoáng)	shining. flashing
				2	일순간에. 금방. 금새	in an instant. soon
		nhằng		1	휘감기다. 뒤엉키다	wind round. be wound (around). be coiled around get tangled up
				2	엉터리같은	nonsense
		nhặng		1	청파리	flies in the Calliphoridae family
				2	건방진. 거드름피우는. 어지러운. 헝클어진	saucy-faced. pompous. disheveled
		nhang			향. (=hương)	the scent
		nhãng			깜박 잊다	get over one's head
		nhăng			엉터리같은. 닥치는 대로의	nonsense

		nhẳng		예의를 모르는. 뻔뻔스러운. 소란스럽게 하는	ill-mannered. shameless
		nhẳng		단단한. 굳은. 깡마른. 날씬한	hard as a rock. skinny. slim
06 01	nhanh	nhánh	1	(나무) 가지. 지점(Branch)	branch of a plant
			2	나누어진. 가지친	divided
		nhảnh	1	입을 조금 벌리다	open one's mouth a little
			2	겉치레의. 꾸민듯한	ostentatious. dressed up
		nhanh		빠른	fast. quick. quickly
		nhành		나뭇가지. (=nhánh. ngành)	branch
06 02	nhao	nhao	1	뛰다. 동요하고 있다. 소란스럽다	to jump. to be in a stir. to be uproarious
			2	시끄럽다. 격동하다. 소란스러워지다	to be noisy. to be turbulent. to become uproarious
		nhão	1	썩어서 녹다	rot and melt
			2	(근육 따위가) 축 늘어진. 연약한. 부푼	flaccid
		nhạo	1	술단지	a pot of liquor
			2	조롱하다. 비웃다	laugh at. mock. jeer at
		nháo		서두르는	in a hurry
		nhào		뛰어들다. 돌진하다. 처박다	jump in. make a dash. ram
06 03	nhap	nháp	1	꺼칠꺼칠한	rough-and-trap
			2	초안을 쓰다	write a draft
		nhập 入(입)	1	넣다. 입력하다	to enter. to join
			2	수입	income. earnings. revenue
		nhắp		혀끝으로 핥아보다. 맛을 보다	taste the food
		nhấp	1	담그다. 적시다 (컴퓨터 마우스) 클릭하다	to dip into water. to moisten to click (a computer mouth)
			2	자르다. 베다. 찌르다	cut. thrust poke

06 04	nhat	**nhất**		1	하나. 첫째	the most. the first
				2	최초의. 제일의	the first
		nhật **Nhật**	日(일)	1	태양	sun. day
				2	일본	Japan
				3	일본의	Japanese
		nhặt			줍다. 주워모으다	to pick something up (usually from the ground)
		nhạt			(맛이) 엷은. 싱거운	(of flavor) tasteless or bland. (of color) light. pale
		nhắt			조그만	teeny. tiny
06 05	nhau	**nhau**		1	서로. 함께	each other. mutually. one another
				2	태반(胎盤)	placenta. afterbirth
		nhâu		1	빨리. 신속히	quick. quickly. swiftly. promptly. with dispatch
				2	마시다	to drink
		nhâu			모으다	gather
		nhàu			구김이 있는. 주름이 있는	be wrinkled
		nhầu			구겨진. 주름이 있는. (=nhàu)	crumpled. be wrinkled
		nhẩu			활발한	active
06 06	nhay	**nhay**			갉아먹다	gnaw at
		nhảy		1	뛰다. 뛰어오르다	to jump. to leap. to dive
				2	뛰기	running
				3	춤추다	to dance
		nhạy		1	민감한. 예민한. (=nhạy lửa)	sensitive
				2	곧 반응하다	react promptly
		nháy			눈을 깜박이다. 눈짓(윙크)하다	to wink
		nhây			질질끌다	drag on

		nhầy		끈적이는. 달라붙는. (=nhầy nhầy)		sticky. adhering
		nhẫy		기름기가 돌아 빛나다		be oily and shiny
		nhẩy		춤추다. (=nhảy)		to dance
		nhậy		(의복이나 책 등에 붙는) 좀. 곰팡이		a snuff, fungus, etc. attached to clothing or books
06 07	nhe	nhẽ		1	논거. 이유	the basis of an argument. reason
				2	제2위의. 두번째의	second
		nhe			이를 보이다. (=nhe răng)	to bear. to show
		nhè			노리다	be after. aim (at/ for)
		nhé			문장 끝에 붙여 권유 또는 제의할 때 쓰는 말	a word used at the end of a sentence to make a recommendation or offer.
		nhẹ			가벼운. 부드러운	light. (of wind) gentle
		nhả			꺼내다. 도려내다. (=lể)	pull it out. cut out
06 08	nhi	nhì		1	둘째	second
				2	둘째의	second
		nhĩ	耳(이)		귀. (=tai)	ear
		nhị	二(이)		둘. 2	two
		nhỉ			문장 끝에 붙여 강조하는 말	word at the end of a sentence to emphasize
		nhí			젊은. 연소한. 어린	very young. little
		nhi		1	그리고. 그리고 나서. 그럼에도 불구하고. 그러나	and. and then. and yet. but
				2	어린아이	child
06 09	nhich	nhích			조금 움직이다	to inch
06 10	nhien	nhiễn			잘 반죽된. (=nhuyễn)	well-kneaded

06 11	nhiem	**nhiệm**	任(임)	1	숨겨진	hidden
				2	맡기다	leave (sth to sb)
		nhiễm	染(염)		감염되다. 감염시키다	be infected
06 12	nhiet	**nhiệt**	熱(열)		열. (=nóng)	heat. thermal
06 13	nhieu	**nhiều**		1	많은. 다수의	many. a lot
				2	많이	much
		nhiễu		1	괴롭히다. 성가시게 굴다	to pester. to trouble
				2	바탕이 쪼글쪼글한 비단 (측면사)	silk with a crumpled base
06 14	nhim	**nhím**			고슴도치	hedgehog
06 15	nhin	**nhìn**			보다. 보이다	to look at
		nhín			절약하다. 비축하다	save. stock up
		nhịn			삼가다. 참다. 억제하다	to endure. to bear. to refrain
06 16	nhip	**nhịp**		1	박자. 리듬	rhythm. rate. beat
				2	두드리다. 치다	knock (at/on). beat. rap (on/at). tap (on)
		nhíp			펜치. 족집게	tweezers
06 17	nho	**nhỡ**		1	중간 크기의. 중형의	medium-sized
				2	놓치다. 잃어버리다	to miss
		nhờ		1	~에 의지하다. ~에 기대다. 부탁하다	to have recourse to. to ask. to rely on. to depend on
				2	~덕분에. ~덕택에. ~에 힘입어	thanks to. owing to
		nhợ		1	끈. 줄	string. cord. line
				2	단맛이 나는	sweet-tasting
		nhọ		1	더러워진	dirty
				2	(지위나 명예를) 더럽히다. 욕보이다. 손상시키다	tarnish (of status or honor). be a disgrace. damage

		nhỏ	1	작은. 잘은. 젊은	small. little. child
			2	떨어뜨리다	to drop
		nho		포도	grape
		nhơ		더러운. 비열한. (=dơ)	dirty. filthy
		nhó		눈을 깜박이다. 윙크하다	blink one's eyes. give a wink
		nhổ		뽑다. 쥐어뜯다. (생선 따위의 뼈에서) 살을 발라내다	to spit. to pluck (weed, grass, feathers, hair…)
		nhớ		생각해내다. 기억하다. 보고싶다. 그리워하다	to remember
06 18	nhoc	**nhóc**	1	어린아이	kid. child. brat
			2	뚱뚱보(아이를 놀릴 때 쓰는 말)	fat guts (words used to make fun of a child)
		nhọc	1	몸이 나른한. 피곤한	langguid. tired
			2	피곤하다	to tire. tiring
06 19	nhoe	**nhóe**	1	비명을 지르다. (=nhoe nhóe)	give a scream
			2	번지는. 스며드는	spreading. permeating
		nhòe	1	스며들다. 번지다	seep into. spread out
			2	얼룩진. (=loang lổ). 번진	smeared. smudged. to be smeared. to blur
			3	아낌없이	lavishly
06 20	nhoi	**nhoi**		끌어올리다. (위로) 스며올라가다. (=nhoai. ngoi)	pull up. to emerge. seep out
		nhói		쿡쿡 쑤시는. (고통이) 심한. (=đau nhói)	stinging pain
		nhối		쿡쿡 쑤시는	stinging pain
		nhởi		뛰놀다	to frolic. gambol
		nhồi		~으로 가득채우다. (=nhồi sọ. nhồi nhét)	to stuff (with). to fill (with). to cram (with)
		nhơi		(소. 물소) 먹다 (되새김질)	to chew the cud

06 21	nhom	**nhóm**	1	불을 피우다	to make a fire, to start a fire
			2	집단. 그룹. 일행	group
		nhom		여윈. 가느다란. 병약한. (=gầy ốm)	thin, sickly
		nhòm		들여다보다. 살펴보다. (=dòm)	to see, to peek
		nhớm		시작하다	to start
		nhổm		일어나다. (=nhỏm)	get up, stand up, rise, sit up
		nhỏm		일어나다	get up, stand up, rise, sit up
		nhờm		겁나다. 무서워하다	be frightened
		nhôm		알루미늄	aluminium
06 22	nhon	**nhón**	1	요약하다	to sum up
			2	발끝으로 걷다	to tiptoe
			3	조금. 약간	a little
		nhõn		아주 조금	just a little
		nhòn		줄이다	to reduce
		nhờn		매끄러운. 기름기 있는	greasy, oily
		nhộn		어수선해지다. 복작거리다	troublesome, noisy
		nhỡn		장난치다. 잘 놀다	make a fool of oneself, have a good time
		nhớn		큰. (=lớn)	big
		nhọn		날카로운. 뾰족한	pointed
06 23	nhot	**nhớt**	1	끈끈한	slimy
			2	자동차 기름. 모빌유(油)	car oil
		nhột	1	간지러운	feeling ticklish
			2	간지럽히다	tickle
		nhót		비벼서 끊다	rub off

		nhốt			가두다. 감금하다. 우리에 넣어두다	to confine
		nhợt			색이 바랜. 창백한. (=lợt)	faded. pale
		nhọt			종기. 진액. 진물	a boil. true riquid. discharge
06 24	nhu	như	如(여)	1	닮다. 비슷하다	have a similarity
				2	2.~처럼. ~같게	like. as
		nhừ		1	삶은. 연한. 부드러운	boiled. soft
				2	녹초가 되다. 진이 빠지다	be worn out. be exhausted
		nhử		1	눈곱. (=ghèn)	eye discharge
				2	먹이를 주다. 유혹하다	to feed. to tempt
		nhu	需(수) 構(구) 軀(구)		부드럽고 온화한. (=mềm)	soft and gentle
		nhũ	乳(유)		금색 페인트	gold paint
		nhú			싹이 돋다. 드러나다. 나타나다	bud. sprout. come up
		nhủ			충고하다. 상담하다. 논하다. 권유하다	to message. to advise. to tell (an idea)
		nhứ			(미끼로) 유인하다. 꾀다	lure (with bait)
06 25	nhua	nhúa			더러운	dirty
		nhựa			(나무 따위의) 진. (담배) 진. 수지	resin. gum. sap. plastic
06 26	nhuan	nhuần		1	스며들다	seep into
				2	윤(閏)의. 윤년의	leap-year
		nhuận	閏(윤) 潤(윤)		윤달의. 윤년의. (=nhuần)	leap month's. leap-year
06 27	nhuc	nhục	肉(육)	1	창피를 당하다. 부끄럽게 여기다. 불명예스럽다	be humiliated. to consider embarrassing
				2	(동물의) 살. 고기. 근육. (=thịt)	flesh. meat. muscle
		nhức			쑤시다. 통증을 느끼다	ache. throb (with). be sore. feel pain

06 28	nhun	nhún		아래 위로 움직이다	move up and down
		nhũn		공손한. 온화한. (=mềm)	very soft
		nhủn		부드럽게 하다	soften
06 29	nhung	những	1	(접두어) 명사앞에 붙여 복수를 나타내는 말	(prefix) plural marker
			2	(접두어) ~까지	(prefix) until
		nhưng	1	그러나	but. though. however. nevertheless
			2	면제하다	give a exemption
		nhung		벨벳. 우단	velvet
		nhũng		부패하게 하다. 어지럽히다	corrupt. make a mess of
		nhúng		담그다	to dip. to immerse
		nhửng		줄어들다. 조용해지다	decrease. quiet down
06 30	nhuom	nhuốm		물들이다	to dye. to color
		nhuộm		물들이다. 염색하다	to dye. to color
06 31	nhut	nhụt	1	끝이 무딘	blunt at the end
			2	의기소침하다. 기운이 없어지다. 약하게하다. (=nhụt chí)	be depressed. lose one's energy
		nhựt		해. 태양. (=nhật)	the sun
		nhứt		하나. 첫째. (=nhất)	first
06 32	nhuyen	nhuyễn	軟(연)	잘 반죽된. 부드러운. 연한	well-kneaded
06 33	ni	nỉ		양털. 모직	wool of sheep. woolen cloth
		ni		여승. 비구니. (=ni cô, ni sư)	a woman buddhist monk
06 34	nia	nia		(크고 평평한) 바구니	a (large flat) basket
		nĩa		(식사용)포크	fork

06 35	niem	niệm	念(념)	기억하다. 읽다. 말하다	to remember. to read. to say
		niềm		감정. 느낌. 감정을 나타내는 명사앞에 붙이는 종별사	feeling. sentiment
		niêm		봉인하다. 밀봉하다	seal up.
06 36	nien	niền		테. (수레의) 가장자리	rim. frame
		niên	年(년)	년(해)	year
06 37	nieu	niếu		요소(尿素)	urea
		niêu		작은 냄비. 토기 항아리	earthenware pot
06 38	nin	nín		말을 멈추다. 말을 억지로 참다. 모욕을 참다	to hold back (crying, breathing, etc.). to stop. to shut up
06 39	ninh	ninh	寧(녕) 舊(구) 苟(구)	요리하다. (약한 불로) 오랫동안 끓이다.	to cook. boil for a long time (on)
		nịnh		아첨하다. 아양떨다. 비위맞추다	to flatter. to fawn (upon)
06 40	nit	nít		1 술을 넣는 작은 병	a small bottle of wine
				2 갈라지다	split up
		nịt		1 벨트	belt
				2 조이다. 매다	to belt (one's belly). to fit tightly
06 41	niu	níu		잡다. 붙들다	take hold of. hold on to
06 42	no	no		1 너무 많이 먹은. 포식한. 배가 부른	full (of a stomach)
				2 포식하다. (=ăn no). 실컷 먹다	eat one's fill
		nơ		1 목과 머리에 두르는 비단장식. 나비 넥타이	silk ornaments worn around the neck and head. bowtie
				2 갖고 가다. (동물이) 입에 물고 가다	take away. the animal is going to put it its mouth

		nỏ		1	큰 활, 석궁	crossbow
				2	마른, 건조한	dry, dried
		nỡ		1	까불다. 장난치다. 들떠서 떠들다	fool around, make a noise with excitement
				2	한꺼번에. 집중적으로	all at once
		nợ		1	빚. 채무	debt
				2	빚을 지다	to owe
		nó			그	he, him, she, her, it
		nố			부분. 일당. 무리	group, crowd, party
		nộ	怒(노)		화내다. 성내다. (=giận)	to get mad, get angry
		nọ			지난. 이전	before
		nở			(꽃이) 피다	(of flowers) to blossom
		nớ			그 (=ấy)	that
		nổ			(포탄. 총. 보일러. 감정 따위가) 폭발하다. 터지다	to explode, to pop, to burst
		nỡ			참다. 견디다	to bear, to endure
06 43	noan	noãn			달걀. 알. (=trứng)	egg
06 44	noc	nốc		1	꿀꺽 삼켜버리다. 마시다	to gulp
				2	배	small boat
		nóc			용마루 꼭대기. (동물의) 등. 등마루. 사물의 가장 높은 곳	rooftop, ridge (of a roof), top part (of some object)
		nọc		1	독. 독액	venom
				2	말뚝 박다. 큰 말뚝을 박다	drive in a stake
06 45	noi	nổi		1	(기름이) 뜨다. 표류하다. (물위에) 떠다니다	to float, to over float
				2	뜨는	floating
		nòi		1	인종. 혈통	race, ethnicity, a lineage
				2	혈통의. 순종의	of pedigree, purebred

		nội	內(내)	1	안. 내부	inside. internal
				2	국내의	domestic
		noi			따르다. 본받다	to follow
		nói			말하다. 이야기하다. 지껄이다. 담화하다	to speak. to talk. to say. to tell
		nơi			장소. 곳. (=chỗ)	place
		nới			(나사를) 풀다. (벨트, 너트를) 느슨하게 하다	to loosen. to slacken
		nồi			항아리. 독. 남비. 솥	pot
		nỗi			사정. 심경	feeling (usually negative)
		nổi			생활이 편하게 되다. 일어나다. (싹이) 돋아나다	make one's life easier. sprout up
		nối			결합하다. 연결하다. 묶다. 매다	to join. to add. to unite. to connect
		nôi			요람. 유아용 침대	a cradle (oscillating bed for a baby)
06 46	nom	nom			보다. 주시하다	to look at. to look after
		nơm		1	낚시제구. 어롱(魚籠)의 일종	fishing tools
				2	nơm으로 고기를 잡다. (=đi ~cá)	catch a fish with nơm
		nồm		1	동남(東南)에서 습기를 몰고 불어오는 바람 (=gió nồm)	a wind blowing moisture from the southeast
				2	습기가 있는	damp
		nòm			섶나무. 불이 붙은 나무. 불쏘시개	a firecracker
		nộm			종이 인형	paper doll
		nỡm			친밀한 의미의 꾸짖는 말	an intimate scolding
		Nôm			중국어원에서 이어져온 베트남 문자	Vietnamese alphabet from the Chinese Language Institute.

06 47	non	non	1	젊은. 미숙한. 갓태어난	young. tender. green. new. mild
			2	~보다 조금 덜한	a little less than~
		nõn	1	새싹. 어린가지	sprout. a young branch
			2	부드럽다	soft. smooth
		nón		논 (월남식 삿갓모자)	Vietnamese conical hat
		nọn		한줌의. 한움큼의	a handful of
		nôn		토하다. 게우다. 구토하다. (=ói. nôn mửa)	to throw up. to vomit
06 48	nong	nong	1	크고 납작한 바구니. 큰 키 (箕)	winnowing basket
			2	넓히다. 크게하다	to make bigger or larger
		nõng	1	대형의 키(箕). 큰 대바구니	a large winnow. a large basket
			2	들어올리다. 쳐들다	lift. take up
		nồng	1	더운. (냄새, 색깔 따위가) 강렬한. 진한	warm. ardent. strong. pungent. hot. torrid
			2	진한 감정을 느끼다	have a deep feeling
		nòng		총렬. 총의 포신	gun barrel. core
		nóng		더운. 뜨거운. 타는듯한	hot (temperature)
		nổng		흙무더기. 둔덕	a heap of earth. a low hill. a (small) mound
		nọng		(동물 따위의) 목	neck
		nông		농경기의. 농업. (=nông nghiệp)	agricultural. the farming industry
06 49	nop	nớp	1	두려운. 무서운	afraid (of)
			2	두려워 하다	frighten
		nóp		거적 또는 대를 엮어 만든 모기를 쫓는 임시 오두막집	a temporary cottage made of bamboo
		nộp		내다	to hand in. to pay (taxes, fine, etc.)

06 50	nu	nữ	女(녀)	1 여성	female. woman
				2 부인의. 여성의	feminine
		nư		화냄. 성냄. (=cơn giận)	anger. rage
		nụ		꽃눈	flower bud
06 51	nua	nua		나이든	old age
		nửa		절반. 1/2	half. 1/2
		nữa		더. 더 많은. 여분의	more. further
		nứa		대나무의 일종	neohouzeaua (a genus of medium-sized tropical bamboo)
06 52	nuc	nực		1 더운. 염열(炎熱)의	(of weather) hot
				2 (냄새) 퍼지다	(smell) diffuse
		nục		1 살찐. 뚱뚱한. (=béo nục)	fat
				2 (과일) 너무 익다	(fruit) overripe
		núc		단단히 묶다(죄다)	tie tightly
		nức		테두리를 하다	to frame
06 53	num	núm		1 튀어나온 둥근 머리모양의 것. 젖꼭지	teat
				2 잡다. 쥐다	to catch. hold
06 54	nung	nung		(빨갛게) 굽다	to burn at high temperatures
		núng		약해지다	weaken. become. weak
		nưng		올리다. (=nâng)	to raise. lift. put up
		nũng		응석부리다. 어리광부리다	be naughty. be childish
		nứng		(성적으로) 충동적인. 발기상태의	(sexually) impulsive. erectile
		nựng		(아기를) 소중히 키우다. 응석부리게 하다. 달래다	raise a child dearly. make naughty

06 55	nui	**núi**			산	a mountain
		nùi			(불을 붙이거나 봉을 박기 위한) 짚과 누더기 조각. 휴지조각 뭉치	straw. ragged piece. a bundle of scraps of paper
06 56	nuoi	**nuôi**			(임종직전에) 눈을 감지 않으려고 애쓰다	try not to close one's eyes (before one's death)
		nuôi		1	기르다. 키우다. 먹여살리다	to feed and raise. to rear
				2	양자로 삼다	adopt
06 57	nuoc	**nuộc**		1	(실을) 끈	twisted thread
				2	여러겹으로 묶다	tie up in layers
		nước			물. 물결	water. liquid. fluid
		nược			돌고래. 참돌고래	dolphin
06 58	nuong	**nương**	娘(낭)	1	계단식 밭. 고지의 계단식 논	stepped field. terraced rice paddy in highland
				2	의지하다	turn to. lean (on/against). look to (sb for help)
		nướng			(불에) 굽다. 익히다	to roast. to grill
		nuông			제멋대로 하게 하다	give a person his own way
06 59	nuot	**nuột**			무늬가 없는	patternless
		nuốt		1	삼키다	to swallow
				2	확인하다. 통제하다	to check. to control
06 60	nup	**núp**			피난(대피)하다	take refuge. to evacuate
06 61	nut	**nút**		1	(병) 마개	stopper. cap. (of a machine) button. button. key
				2	~에 마개를 끼우다	put a stopper on
		nứt		1	(피부 등이) 찢어지다. 터지다. 금이가다. (=nứt nẻ)	to crack open. to split open
				2	금이 간. 찢어진	be cracked open

06 62	o	o		1	숙모. 백모	paternal aunt. father's sister
				2	여자의 비위를 맞추다	curry favor with a woman
		ơ		1	단지. 항아리. 독	pot. crock. jar
				2	놀람을 나타내는 감탄사	an exclamation of surprise
		ó		1	독수리	buzzard. hawk
				2	큰 소리로 외치다	shout out
		ố	惡(악)	1	증오하다. 싫어하다. 혐오하다	to hate
				2	얼룩진. (=loang lổ)	spotted. stained
		ợ		1	(연기 따위를) 내뿜다	to burp
				2	트림	burp. belch
		ở		1	살다. 거주하다	to live. to stay
				2	~에. ~에서	at. in
		ồ		1	오! (놀람을 나타내는 말)	oh! (an exclamation of surprise)
				2	돌진하다. 밀려들다	make a dash. crowd in
		ớ			부르는 말. (=ớ này)	a calling word
		ổ			보금자리. 둥지	nest
		ờ			희미한 기억이 되살아 났을 때 내는 소리	yeah
		ô		1	우산. 양산	umbrella. parasol
				2	구분. 구획	division. section
06 63	oan	oan	寃(원)		사실이 아닌. 거짓의	untrue. false
		oán	怨(원)	1	원망하다. 원한을 품다	blame. bear a grudge
				2	원한	grudge (against). resentment
		oăn			내려앉다. 처지다. 휘다	to bend (down due to having to endure a great force). to curve. to be bent

0664	oc	óc			뇌. 지능. 두뇌	brain
		ộc			솟구쳐 나오다. 넘쳐 나오다	spring up. overflow up
		ọc			토하다	to throw up. to vomit
		ốc	握(악)	1	우렁	refers to certain mollusks with hard, typically spiral, shells.
				2	너트 (볼트에 조립하는)	a nut (that fits on a bolt)
0665	oi	ối		1	양막. 태아를 둘러싸는 막	amniotic fluid
				2	놀람이나 공포시에 하는 소리	an expression of surprise
		oi		1	숨막히는. 몹시 더운. (=oi ả. oi bức)	hot and oppressive. sultry
				2	죽다	fall dead. die
		ơi			부르는 말	hey. hello
		ói			토하다	throw up
		ỏi			시끄러운	loud. noisy
		ới			호격조사. (=ơi)	hey. hello
		ổi			(과일) 구아바	guava
		ọi			헛기침하다	cough in vain
		ôi			(음식이) 신선하지 않은. 고약한 냄새가 나는	tainted (meat). putrid (flesh)
0666	om	om		1	(일 등을) 길게 끌다	take long (work, etc.)
				2	시끄러운	loud. noisy
		õm		1	아픈. 질병이 있는	ill. sick
				2	병이나다. (=mắc bệnh)	get sick
		ôm			포옹. 껴안다. 포옹하다	a hug. to hug. to embrace
		ớm			응달에서 자라 발육이 나쁜	ill-developed from obscurity
		ỏm			시끄러운. (=ồm tỏi)	loud. noisy

0667	on	ồn		1	소음. (=ồn ào)	noise
				2	시끄러운. 소란한	loud. noisy
		ơn	恩(은)		호의. 은혜. (=ân)	favour/favor
		ổn	穩(온)		온화한. 안정된	settled. steady
		ộn			함부로	without permission
		ớn			냉기를 느끼다. 오싹하다.	get the shivers
		ôn			복습하다	to review. to revise
0668	oanh	oanh	鴦(앙) 螢(영)	1	원앙새	a mandarin duck
				2	울리다	make sb cry
0669	ong	óng		1	윤이나다	be glossy
				2	반들반들 빛나는	shiny and shiny
		ong			벌	bee
		ỏng			(어린아이가 질병으로) 배가 나오다	a child's belly is swollen (with disease)
		ống			파이프. 관	tube. pipe. duct
		ông		1	노인. 할아버지	grandfather. grandpa
				2	선생님 (상대를 높여 부르는 말)	Sir. Mr. you (to address an older man)
0670	ot	ót		1	목덜미. 목 뒤. (=gáy)	nape
				2	작은 꾸러미를 단단히 묶다	tie up a small package tightly
		ợt			장난같은	mischievous
		ớt			고추	chili pepper. pepper in general
0671	oxy	oxy			산소	oxygen
0672	pha	pha		1	(자동차의) 라이트	(a car) light
				2	(차. 커피 등 마실 것을) 끓이다. 타다. 섞다	to boil. to mix (tea, coffee, etc.)

		phà		1	나룻배. 연락선	ferry
				2	(연기를) 내뿜다. 숨을 내뱉다	to blow air out
		phá	破(파)	1	갯벌. 만	lagoon
				2	깨다. 부수다. 허물어 뜨리다	to destroy. to demolish
		phả			(증기. 연기) 내뿜다. 냄새를 풍기다	to give off (smoke, etc.). to reek of
0673	phac	phác			밑그림을 그리다. 스케치하다	to sketch. to outline
		phắc			조용한. 적적한. (=im phắc)	quiet. lonely
0674	phach	phách	拍(박) 魄(백)	1	방법. 정신	a way. a manner. a soul. a spirit
				2	오만한. 거만한	proud. snobby. snooty
		phạch			크고 넓고 가벼운 것이 날리는 소리. 철썩! 꽝! (=phạch phạch)	the soud of something loud, wide and light blowing
0675	phai	phải		1	옳은	right. correct. obverse
				2	(동사앞에 붙여서) ~해야만 한다. (=bị)	have to
		phái	派(파)	1	대표로 보내다. 위임하다	to dispatch
				2	파. 파벌. 가지	(chiefly martial arts) a school. a sect
		phai			(색이) 바래다. (=phai màu)	(of colours) to fade
0676	pham	phạm	犯(범)	1	범하다. 어기다	to violate. to offend. to commit
				2	범인	suspect. culprit. criminal
		phàm	凡(범)	1	평범한. 보통의. 조잡한. 무례한. 속물	ordinary. coarse. rude. philistine
				2	게걸스럽게 먹다. 조악하게 말하다	eat greedily. speak in a crudely
		phẩm	品(품)		안료. 염료	dye. ink

06 77	phan	phân	分(분)	1	비료. 거름	fertilizer. manure. (feces. stool. excrement)
				2	나누다. 분배하다. 분리하다. 설명하다	divide. distribute out. separate
		phán	反(반)		판단하다	to judge
		phẫn	憤(분)	1	뚜껑	lid. cover. cap. top
				2	화를 내다. 분개하다	lose his temper. be indignant
		phản	反(반)	1	(교도소 따위의) 판자침대	board bed
				2	반대하다. 배신하다	to betray. anti-. to be disloyal to
		phăn			추적 조사하다	make a follow-up investigation
		phấn	粉(분)		쵸오크. 분필. 분말	chalk. powder
		phạn	飯(반) 梵(범)		범어(梵語)	sanscrit
		phần	分(분)	1	부분. 몫	part. portion. share. season
				2	대변. 똥. (=cứt)	feces. stool. excrement
		phẩn			부분. 할당. 배당. 몫	proportion. allocation. dividend. share
06 78	phang	phang		1	몽둥이로 세게 때리다	beat sb hard with a club
				2	몽둥이의 일격	a club blow
		phăng		1	즉시. 즉각	immediately. instantly. promptly. at once. right away
				2	조용한	quiet
		phàng			잔인한. 지독한. (=phũ phàng (잔인한)	cruel. terrible
		phẳng			평탄한. 고른. 평평한	level. flat. even
06 79	phanh	phanh		1	크게 벌리다. 열다	open wide
				2	브레이크. 제동기	brake (of a vehicle, etc.)

06 80	phao	phao		1	부표. 구명대	a buoy
				2	헛소문을 내다	make a false rumor
		phào		1	순식간에 지나가다. 불다	go by in a flash. blow
				2	(미장이의) 천정에 달아 사용하는 발판	a platform used on the ceiling
		pháo	砲(포)		폭죽	firecracker
06 81	phap	pháp			법. 법률. 법칙	rule. law. standard. method
		Pháp			프랑스 (공화국)	France
		phập			날카로운 도구로 강하고 깊게 절단하는 소리	the sound of a strong, deep cutting with a sharp instrument.
06 82	phat	phát	發(발)	1	(총. 화살) 한발. 한방	a shot
				2	분배하다. 발행하다. 배달하다	to distribute. to dispense. to issue. to deliver
				3	(풀 등을) 베어내다. 제거하다	to slash grass or weeds
		Phật	佛(불)		부처. 석가모니	Buddha
		phắt			즉시. 당장	right off. right now
		phất			휘날리다. 흔들리다. 움직이다	flutter about. shaking. move
		phạt	罰(벌)		벌하다. 벌금을 과하다	to punish. to fine
06 83	phau	phẫu	剖(부)	1	유리로된 입이 넓은 병	a glass-mouthed bottle
				2	해부하다. 수술하다	to dissect. operate (on)
		phau			새하얀	spotless. immaculate
06 84	phay	phay		1	식칼. 칼	a kichen knife. knife
				2	(칼) 분쇄하다	crush up
		phẩy		1	부드럽게 부채질하다	to gentle fan
				2	콤마(,)	comma
		phây			통통한. 토실토실한. (가슴이) 풍만한	plump and healthy. buxom
		Phây			페이스북	face book

		phảy		조용히 움직이다. 가볍게 흔들다	move quietly. shake lightly
0685	phe	phe		진영. 파(派). (=phe phái)	faction. side. sect. camp
		phè		매우. 몹시. 심히.	excessively
		phệ		지나치게 살찐. 뚱뚱한	excessively fat
		phế	廢(폐)	폐지하다. 폐기하다. (=bỏ phế)	abandon. remove from office. throw away
		phê		비평하다. 평가하다	to comment. to give remarks or comments
0686	phen	phen		횟수(번). 회(回). 도(度)	time. degree
		phèn		명반. (=phèn chua)	alum
		phẽn		회초리로 때리다	beat with a whip
		phện		마구 때리다	give a person a good thrashing
		phên		대나무 칸막이	bamboo partition
0687	phep	phép	1	법칙. 관습	rule. custom. usage. method. permission.
			2	허가. 인가	permission. authorisation
			3	마법의 힘	magical power
0688	phi	phỉ	1	만족한. 흡족한	satisfied
			2	서로 욕하다	speak ill of each other
		phi	飛(비)	(말이) 질주하다. 전속력으로 달리다	(of horse) to gallop. to flee. to travel very quickly
		phị	肥(비)	살이찐. 통통한	(of face, cheeks) chubby. bloated
		phì		1	뚱뚱한. 살찐	fat
			2	내뿜다	let out
		phí	費(비)	1	낭비하는. 헛되이 쓰는	to waste. to squander. to spend
			2	비용	expenses. cost. charge

06 89	phia	**phía**			방향. 쪽	side. way. direction
		phịa			꾸며내다	make up
06 90	phich	**phích**			보온병	thermos
		phịch			무거운 것이 떨어지는 소리. 쿵. 퍽. 툭	thud
06 91	phien	**phiến**	片(편)	1	(돌의) 석판. 얇은 조각. (=tấm mỏng)	slab. block. sheet
				2	부추기다. 선동하다	stir up
		phiền		1	방해하다. 폐를 끼치다. 귀찮게 하다	to disturb. to bother
				2	복잡한	complex. complicated
				3	슬픈. 속상한	sad. depressed. upset. melancholy
		phiện			아편 (Á phiện. thuốc phiện)	opium
		phiên		1	(의무적인) 차례. 순서	turn. time. session
				2	번역	translation
06 92	phieu	**phiếu**	票(표) 慓(표)	1	표. 투표용지	ticket. vote. ballot. ballot paper
				2	표백하다	to bleach
06 93	phim	**phim**			필름	film
		phím			(비파, 거문고 따위의) 줄굄목	bridge (a device for supporting a string of string instrument)
06 94	phinh	**phĩnh**			부풀다. 붓다. 배부르다(임심하다)	to swell. swell (up). puff up. get pregnant
		phình			부풀다. 팽창하다	to swell up. to become bigger (due to having too much inside). to bulge
		phỉnh			아첨하다. 아부하다	to flatter. fawn (on/over). butter up
		phính			부푼. 불룩한	be swollen. bulish

0695	pho	phò	扶(부)	1	돕다. 부조하다. (=giúp)	to help
				2	매춘부. 창녀	prostitute
		phó	副(부) 材(재)	1	직인(職人)	(official) seal
				2	위탁하다. 부탁하다	consign to. ask
		pho			책이나 어떤 형상의 각 부분이 완전히 갖춰진 한 세트를 이룬 것.	set
		phơ			순백의	pure white
		phờ			피곤해서 녹초가 된	tired out
		phố			거리	street
		phổ		1	악보를 만들다. 가사를 넣다. 멜러디를 넣다	write a score. add lyrics. add a melody
				2	분광. 스펙트럼	spectrum
		phở			쇠고기 또는 닭고기를 곁들여 놓는 베트남의 쌀국수	pho (a soup made with bánh phở noodles, usually served with beef, pork, or chicken)
		phô			~를 과시하다. ~를 돋보이게 하다	show off. make stand out
0696	phoi	phoi			(금속. 목재) 깎아내다	shavings
		phơi			(불이나 태양빛에) 말리다. 건조시키다	to dry in the sun
		phòi			빼내다. 터뜨리다	to come out
		phổi	肺(폐)		폐. 허파	lung
		phới			휘날리다	flutter about
		phôi			형성 시작 단계의 생물의 신체. 태아	embryo. fetus
0697	phon	phởn			들떠서 떠들다. 날뛰다	be excited
		phồn			무리. 조(組)	group. crowd. party. bunch. shift
		phôn			전화하다. 전화기	to telephone. telephone. phone

0698	phong	**phong**	封(봉) 楓(풍)	1	작은 꾸러미	a small package
				2	봉하다	to wrap. to package
		phỏng		1	~에 탄. ~에 덴. 열상	scald
				2	약. 대강	about. roughly
		phòng	房(방) 防(방)	1	방	large room. chamber
				2	막다. 예방하다	keep out. prevent
		phỗng		1	도자기인형	a porcelain doll
				2	집어들다. 빼앗다	pick up. take away
		phóng	放(방)		던지다. 발사하다. 쏘다	to throw. to launch. shoot
		phồng			부풀어오르다. 불룩해지다	swell up. become convex
		phộng			~을 부풀리다. 물집이 생기다	to enlarge. get blisters
		phộng			땅콩	peanut
		phông			배경. 무대장면	background. font
0699	phu	**phụ**	負(부) 附(부) 父(부)	1	배반하다	to betray
			婦(부) 輔(보)	2	아버지	father
				3	돕다	to aid. to help. to assist
		phú			(재능 따위를) 부여하다. 기부하다	grant to. to endow
		phù		1	부적(符籍)	amulet. talisman. charm
				2	돕다. 부조하다. (=phò)	to aid. to help. to assist
		phủ	俯(부)	1	관저. 주택	palace. residence
				2	덮다	to cover
		phu			남편	husband
		phũ			매우 거칠게. 매우 사납게. 잔인하게	with great violence. cruelly

07 00	phuc	phúc	福(복)	1	복. 행운	good fortune. good luck. happiness. bliss. felicity
				2	다행스러운. 복이 있는	lucky. fortunate
		phức	馥(복)		향기가 풍기는	fragrant
		phục	伏(복) 服(복)	1	감탄하다. 존경하다.	to admire. to esteem
				2	매복하고 기다리다	wait in embush
				3	참고 견디다	to bear. to endure
07 01	phung	phụng	奉(봉) 鳳(봉)	1	~에 굴복하다. 복종하다	give in. submit. yield. surrender. obedience. obey
				2	불사조. (=phượng)	phoneix
		phủng		1	꿰뚫린. 관통한	penetrated
				2	관통하다. 침투하다. 빠지다	penetrate through
		phùng			부풀게하다. 팽창하다. (=phồng)	to enlarge
		phúng			죽은 자에게 제물을 바치다	offer sacrifices to the dead
		phừng			갑자기 나타나다. 순간적으로 움직이다. (=phong)	pop up. move at a moment's notice
07 02	phut	phụt		1	(물이) 솟아나오다	(water) gushes out
				2	갑자기	all of a sudden. suddenly. all at once
		phút			순간. 분(分)	minute (time)
		phứt			결행하다. 주저하지 않고 하다	go through with. effect. carry out. have no hesitation in doing
		phựt			실이나 끈이 잘리는 소리 (의성어)	(onomatopoeia) the sound of a string being cut off.
07 03	phuoc	phước			행복. 행운. (=phúc)	good fortune. good luck. happiness
07 04	phuong	phương	方(방) 芳(방)	1	방향	way. direction. means. method
				2	방해하다. 막다	disturbance. interrupt. block

		phường	坊(방)	1	무리. 한패	group. crowd. party. bunch.
				2	동네. 마을	ward (of a city, town or district)
		phượng	鳳(봉)		봉황새. (=chim phượng)	phoneix
07 05	qua	quả	果(과)		과일. (=trái)	fruit
		qua		1	~를 가로지르다. 횡단하다	across. through. by
				2	전날에. 지난번에	last. the past
		quá	過(과)	1	(한계나 정도를) 초과하다. 넘다	to exceed
				2	매우. 몹시	very. excessive
		quà			(=quà cáp). 선물	present. gift
		quạ			까마귀	crow
07 06	quach	quách		1	~해 버리다. (=cho xong)	to do something
				2	석관. 관(棺)의 외부	sarcophagus. outer coffin
07 07	quai	quai		1	손잡이. 자루	handle. grip. shaft. haft
				2	주먹으로 때리다	hit with one's fist
		quái	怪(괴)	1	괴물. 장애물	monster. obstacle
				2	기이한. 기괴한	eccentric. grotesque. odd
		quài			손을 펴다	open one's hands
07 08	quan	quăn		1	오그라들다	shrivel up
				2	꼬부라진. 꼬인	crooked. curly
		quắn		1	주름지다. 곱슬곱슬해지다. (머리) 파마하다	be wrinkled. get curly. get a perm
				2	곱슬곱슬한. 구부러진	(of hair) curly
		quần	裙(군)	1	바지	pants
				2	피로하게 하다. 지치게 하다.	tire out

		quấn	1	(식물) 감다. 휘감다	to wind. to twine
			2	(식물) 회전성의. 휘감기는	winding
		quản	管(관)	1	우려하다. 꺼리다	to worry. be reluctant to
			2	관리하다. 제어하다	to manage. to control
		quặn		1	뒤틀리듯 아프다	be in a warping pain
			2	깔대기. (=phễu)	a funnel
		quan			관리. 공무원	an official
		quân	軍(군) 均(균)		군대. 부대	troops. army
		quàn			(시체를) 일시적으로 안치하다	temporarily lay (a corpse) in state
		quán	館(관)		임시로 지은 오두막집. 식당. 상점. 집	inn. restaurant. store. house
		quẩn			빙글빙글돌며 운동하다. 움직이다	work out round and round
		quẫn	窘(군)		궁핍하다	be in need
		quằn			구부러지다. 기울어지다	bend over. crook. warp. be bent. lean down. slant
		quận	郡(군)		지역. 행정구역	district
0709	quang	quang	光(광)	1	하늘의	heavenly
				2	빛	light
				3	맑은. 분명한. 확실한	clear
		quàng		1	서두르다	to hurry up
				2	터무니없는. 무의미한. 불합리	nonsensical. absurd
		quáng		1	눈 부시다. (=quáng mắt)	be blinding
				2	눈먼. 장님의	blind
		quăng		1	던지다. 팽개치다	to throw (horizontally, forcefully, and far). to cast. to fling. to hurl
				2	모기애벌레. 유충	mosquito insect

		quãng		거리 또는 시간의 일부분을 나타내는 말	space. distance. interval
		quẳng		내던지다. 버리다. (=vứt bỏ)	throw away. fling away
		quảng		넓은	broad. wide. extensive
		quẩng		정신없이 날뛰다. (=quẩng mỡ)	run like astray
		quặng		광석	ore
		quầng		(태양과 달의) 무리	a flock (of sun and moon)
07 10	quanh	quanh	1	주위. 주변	around. round
			2	주위의. 가까이의	around. surrounding. attendant
		quánh	1	후라이 팬	frying pan
			2	끈질기다. 끈기있다	persistent. persevering. tenacious. dogged
		quành		돌다. 회전하다	to whirl. to reverse. to turn back
		quạnh		고립된. 적막한. 황량한. (=quạnh quẽ)	isolated. deserted
07 11	quat	quạt	1	부채. 선풍기	fan (hand-held or electrical device)
			2	날개치다	to fan (to blow air on by means of a fan)
		quất	1	중국 귤. 금귤	kumquat
			2	채찍으로 치다	to lash. to whip
		quặt	1	비틀어 구부리다	twist and bend
			2	병약한. 계속 허약한	sickly
		quát		고함치다. 소리치다	give a shout. shout
		quắt		주름이 지다. 위축하다. 줄어들다	get wrinkled. shrink from. grow less
		quật	堀(굴)	파내다. 발굴하다	to dig up. to disinter

07 12	quay	quay		1	팽이	a top
				2	돌리다. 향하다	to turn. to revolve. to swivel. to whirl. to reverse. to turn back
		quẩy		1	한짐	a pack of load
				2	어깨에 메다. (=quảy)	to carry with a shoulder pole
		quảy		1	한짐 (지금의 50Kg)	a pack of load (50Kg)
				2	어깨에 메다	to carry with a shoulder pole
		quày			(빙글) 돌리다. 돌아오다	to spin. come back
		quây			둘러싸다. 휘감다	to enclose. to surround. to encircle
		quẫy			(물고기가 꼬리를) 세게 움직이다. 사방으로 요동치다	to move in different directions to try to get out of a place
		quầy			진열케이스	showcase. low cabinet in a shop or store for displaying goods
		quấy			반죽하다. 천천히 섞다	to stir
		quậy			방해하다. 괴롭히다. 짓궂게 하다	to disturb. to harass. to be mischievous
07 13	que	que			작은 가지. 막대기	small stick
		què			마비된	be crippled
		quế	桂(계)		계수나무. 육계나무. 계피	cinnamon
		quệ			쇠약한. 고갈된	frail. weak. depleted
		quẻ	卦(괘)		괘. 점. 예언	divinatory sign or symbol. lot. forecast (of the future)
		quê		1	고향. 시골	a birth place. a hometown. countryside. the country
				2	부끄러운. 수줍은	shy. bashful

07 14	quen	quen		1	알다. 친하게 지내다	get to know
				2	친한. 익숙한	familiar
		quền		1	가치없는. 빈약한	worthless
				2	약간. 조금. 겨우	slightly. a little bit
		quén			끌어올리다. 걷어올리다	lift up. roll up
		quẹn			색이 바랜. 햇볕에 그을린	faded. sunburned
		quến			착 달라붙다	stick fast
		quện			달라붙다. (=quến)	stick (to). cling (to). adhere (to)
		quên			잊다. 방치하다. 남겨두다	to forget
07 15	quoc	quốc	國(국)		국가. 나라. (=nước)	nation. state. country
07 16	quy	quý	癸(계) 季(계) 貴(귀)	1	10간(干)의 계(癸)	the tenth Heavenly Stem
				2	소중히 여기다	to treasure. to hold dear
		quỷ	鬼(귀)	1	귀신. 마귀	demon. devil. monster. ogre
				2	간사한. 교활한	cunning
		quỳ		1	해바라기	sunflower
				2	무릎굻다	kneel on one's needs
		quỹ	機(기)		금고. 펀드	fund. treasury. bank
		quỵ			무릎꿇다. 붕괴하다. (=quì)	kneel on one's needs. break down
		quý			아끼다. 아깝다	save. what a waste
		quy			전환하다. 합치다. 개종하다	to bring together. to convert
07 17	quyen	quyến		1	비단	glossy black silk gauze
				2	사랑하다. 좋아하다	love. like
		quyển	卷(권)		권(卷). 책	of documents and stories, usually long ones

		quyền	權(권) 拳(권) 圈(권)	권리. 권한	a right. power. (chiefly martial arts) a punch
		quyện	卷(권)	붙이다. 들러붙다. 부착되다	stick to. adhere to
		quyên		모으다. 모집하다	to collect. to recruit
07 18	quyet	**quyết**	決(결)	1	결정하다. 결심하다	to decide. to determine
				2	반드시. 결코	necessarily. never
		quyệt		교활한	cunning. deceitful
07 19	quynh	**quýnh**	窘(영) 去(거)	당황하다. 허둥대다	beside oneself (with joy, fear, etc.). out of one's wits
07 20	ra	**ra**		1	나오다. ("~로 나오다"의 경우 "ra+지명"의 형식을 취한다) ra sân 뜰로 나오다	go to out. to leave
				2	(어느 지점에서 어느 지점) 까지	(from point) to point
		rạ		1	볏짚. 그루터기	rice straw. stump
				2	다음에 태어난	next born
		rà		문지르다. 비비다	to rub
		rã		녹다. 부패하다	to dissolve. to decay. to decompose
		rá		쌀 씻을 때 쓰는 바가지	bamboo basket
07 21	rac	**rắc**		1	흩뿌리다	scatter spread
				2	금. 깨진 틈	crack. broken gap
		rạc		1	감옥	prison
				2	초라해진. 여윈	shabby. thin
		rác		먼지. 쓰레기	trash. garbage. rubbish
		rặc		썰물이 되다 (조수가 빠지다)	be time for edd tide
07 22	rach	**rạch**		1	개천. 도랑. 수로	small irrigation canal. ditch. arroyo
				2	자르다. 깎다. 쪼개다. 분열하다	to slit. to slash. to split. to devide

		rách			찢어진	be torn
07 23	ram	ram		1	불에 굽다. 튀기다	roast over a fire. fry up
				2	연(連) (종이의 수량을 나타내는 단위로 양지는 **480**매, 신문은 **500**매)	as a unit of quantity of paper, **480** papers and **500** newspapers
		râm		1	그림자의. 응달의	shady
				2	시끄러운	loud. noisy
				3	어두워지다	get dark
		rầm		1	기둥. 대들보	beam (in a house)
				2	세게 울리다. 울려퍼지다	ring hard. to resound
		rám			햇볕에 탄	sunburned
		răm			(버들) 여귀의 일종	willow
		rậm			무성한. 밀집한	dense
		rặm			근질거리다. 근질근질하다	tickle. itch. be itchy
		rắm			방귀. (=rắm rít)	fart
		rấm			숙성시키다. 익숙하다	ripen. familiar
		rạm			(동물) 게의 일종	a kind of crab
		rằm			보름. 달(月)의 15일	**15**th day of lunar calendar, the day of full moon
		rẩm			느끼다	feel. find. sense. experience
07 24	ran	ran			울려 퍼지다	to resound. to spread widely
		rạn		1	균열이 생기다	having cracks
				2	암초	rock reef
		rần		1	시끌시끌한	noisy
				2	시끌벅적	noisy
		rắn		1	뱀	snake. serpent
				2	딱딱한. 단단한	hard. solid
		rân			울려 퍼지다. 번지다. (=ran)	to resound. to spread widely

		rán		기름으로 튀기다	to fry
		rǎn		논하다	to discuss
		ràn		(가축의) 외양간. 마구간	stable (enclosure for cows/kine or horses)
		rằn		잡색의. 줄무늬의	multicolored. striped
		rặn		(출산하기 위해) 힘주다	to try to force something out of one's body with difficulty through lower orifices.
		rằn		불평하다. (=cằn rằn)	to complain
		rận		이(곤충). 기생충	body louse (pediculus hamanus)
		rán		노력하다. 애쓰다. 고심하다	make an effort. try. put one's minding
07 25	rang	ráng	1	(하늘 빛깔이) 변색하다	evening-glow (in the sky)
			2	빗자루 재료로 쓰이는 나무	a tree used as a broomstick material
		rang		볶다	to roast. pop
		ràng		묶다. 죄다. 고정하다	to tie. tighten. fix in
		răng		이. 치아	tooth
		rặng		줄. 행	row (of standing object)
		rằng		주문(主文)을 보충하기 위한 접속사	that. to speak
		rạng		밝아지다	to dawn. be lighted
07 26	ranh	ranh	1	이가 난 채 태어난 아이	a child born with teeth
			2	건달의. 짖궂은	mischievous
		rành	1	명료한	clear. plain. evident. obvious
			2	완전히 알다. 능통하다. 능란하다	to know cleary. to be acquainted (with)

		rảnh		1	한가한. 유유자적한	having to much time on one's hands and nothing productive
				2	자유롭게 되다	free. unoccupied. unbusy
		rãnh			도랑. 수로	a ditch. a waterway
07 27	rap	rập		1	복사하다. 본뜨다	to copy closely
				2	(작은 새와 쥐를 잡는) 망	a net (for catching small birds and mice)
		rạp		1	천막. 천막친 오두막	temporary shed. outbuilding. tent
				2	머리를 숙이다. 몸을 구부리다	to bend. to stoop. to bend down
		ráp		1	모으다. 소집하다. 조립하다	to fit. to assemble. to join together
				2	거칠거칠한. 껄껄한. (=nháp)	tough
		rấp		1	(장애물로) 길을 막다	to block up with thorny branches. to cover up
				2	긴급한	urgent
		rắp			이제 막 ~하려고 하다. (=rắp tâm. sắp sửa)	to be about to. to be on the point of
07 28	rat	rát		1	쓰린. 따끔따끔 쑤시는	be hurt like when peeled skin being touched
				2	심하게. 격렬히. 쉬임없이	badly. in a rage. without a break
		rặt		1	아무것도 섞지 않다	do not mix anything
				2	순수한	pure
		rặt			지극히. 매우. 아주	very (placed before the word to intensify)
		rạt			한쪽 방향으로 몸을 기대다. 비켜서다	lean in one direction. step aside
07 29	rau	rau			야채. 채소	greens. vegetables

		ráu		조르다. 치근거리다	to pester. nag. press. badger
		râu		수염	(of a human) beard. (of a animal) whiskers
		rầu		슬픈 (=buồn rầu). 우울한.	gloomy. melancholy. grieved. sad
07 30	ray	ray		레일 (đường ray)	rail
		rầy	1	꾸짖다. 나무라다. (=quở mắng)	to chide. to rebuke. to scold
			2	레일. (=ray)	rail
		rây	1	체	sieve
			2	(체로) 치다. 거르다	to sieve. to sift
		rẫy	1	화전(燒畑)	mountain field (obtained by deforestation, tree burning and replanting)
			2	포기하다. 아내를 돌보지 않다	to abandon. to repudiate. to renounce (one's wife)
		ráy		팀파니. 드럼	timpani. drum
		rãy		거절하다. 기각하다	to refuse. to dismiss. to reject
		ràý		지금. 오늘날. 현재	now. today. this time
		rảy		뿌리다. 끼얹다. (=rẩy)	to sprinkle
		rẩy		살짝 흩뿌리다	sprinkle lightly
07 31	re	re	1	용솟음치다. 샘솟다	shoot out. spring up. surge up. well up
			2	빨리	quick
		ré	1	밝게 비추다	shine brightly
			2	(개, 짐승 따위가) 짖다. 으르렁거리다	bark (at). howl. bay
		rệ	1	가장자리. (=vệ)	edge. side
			2	차의 한쪽 바퀴가 미끄러지다	one wheel of a car slips

		rẻ	1	부채꼴의 것	fan-shaped thing
			2	값싼. 낮은 가격의	cheap. inexpensive
		rè		목이 쉰. 목이 잠긴	hoarse
		rẽ		뿌리	root
		rể		신랑	a groom (man about to be married)
		rế		냄비 받침. (뜨거운 것을 받치는) 대바구니	a bamboo basket used as a pad for hot pots
		rẽ		꺾어지다. 돌아가다. 나누다. 쪼개다	to turn (to another path). to split (into branches)
		rê		끌다	to drag (on the ground). to spread out. to lay out
07 32	ret	rét	1	차가운. 추운	very cold. cold
			2	추위에 떨다	to shiver (from cold)
			3	말라리아	malaria
		rết		(동물) 지네. (=rít)	a centipede
		rệt		분명한. 명확한	clear as day
07 33	reu	rệu		변질된. 흐물흐물한	the fruit is ripe and mushy
		rểu		산보하다. 산책하다. 어슬렁거리다	take a walk. hang about
		rều		(강물 등 위에 뜬) 나뭇잎. 톱밥. 풀잎	(floating on a river, etc.) sawdust. leaf
		rêu		이끼	moss. lichen
07 34	ri	ri	1	참새의 일종. (=chim ri)	a kind of sparrow
			2	이처럼	like this
		rí	1	여자 영매사(靈媒師). 여자 주술사	a woman sorcerer
			2	극소의	infinites
		rì	1	짙은. 너무 느린	dark. too slow
			2	바싹 끌어 당기다	pull close

		rỉ		새다. 스며들다. 배어나오다	to leak. to drip
		rị		(다시) 끌어 들이다. 꼭 틀어막다. 딱 달라붙다	draw (back) in. block up. stick like a limpet
07 35	rieng	riêng	1	생강과의 일종. 맵고 향기로운 맛이 나며 양념 만드는데 사용.	a kind of ginger. spicy and fragrant, and used to make seasoning.
			2	신랄하게 꾸짖다. 책망하다	scold harshly. to reproach
		riêng	1	자신의. 개인의. 사적인	private. personal
			2	~에 관하여. ~를 제외하고	as to. as regards. except for
07 36	rieu	riễu		조소하다. 비웃다	to laugh at
		riểu		창피한 일. 부끄러운 일	a shameful thing
		riêu		베트남 음식의 한 종류로 생선과 게를 우려 만든 시큼한 국물	sour crab or fish soup
07 37	rinh	rinh	1	두 손으로 운반하다	to carry (something with both hands)
			2	시끄러운	noisily. loudly
		rình	1	관찰하다. 감시하다	to ambush. to spy. to lurk
			2	꽤. 상당히. 아주	quite. rather. fairly. pretty. considerably. very. so. extremely
07 38	riu	ríu		교차하여 얽히다. 얽힌	entangled. tangled
		rìu		도끼. 큰 도끼	axe
07 39	ro	rợ	1	가는 끈(줄)	a thin string(line)
			2	야만인	a barbarian
		ró	1	골풀 광주리. 고기잡는 도구	basket. a fishing tool
			2	살짝 훔치다. (=lấy cắp)	to steal
		rơ	1	손가락을 굽혀 유아의 혀를 문질러 주다	rub an infant's tongue with one's fingers
			2	헐거워진. 이가 꽉 맞지 않는	loose

		rò	1	물이 새다	water leaks
			2	어린 가지	a young branch
		rõ	1	선명한. 분명한	(of view) clear
			2	명확한. 명료한	distinct
		rớ	1	손 그물 (낚시용)	small net for fishing
			2	우연히 잡다	catch by accident
		rổ		광주리. 바구니	basket
		rờ		만지다. 감촉하다	to touch
		rỏ		흘리다. 떨어뜨리다	to drop
		rồ		실성한. 정신나간	out of one's mind
		rọ		대로 짠 바구니 (동물운반용 대바구니)	a basket made of bamboo (for animal transport)
		rở		입덧 (신 것을 먹고 싶어하는 임산부의)	morning sickness (of pregnant women who want to eat something sour)
		rỗ		(얼굴에) 천연두 자국이 있는. 곰보인. (=rỗ hoa)	with smallpox marks on one's face
		rỡ		빛나는. (=rực rỡ, sáng sủa)	billiant. sparkling
		rộ		풍부하게. 다량으로	in abundance. in large quantities
07 40	roi	rõi	1	계통. 혈통	lineage
			2	뒤를 밟다. 미행하다	follow in one's heels
		rối	1	흐트러진. 얽힌	tangled. ravelled. entangled
			2	뒤죽박죽인. 혼란스러운. 무질서한	jumbled. confused. disorderly
		rồi	1	이미	already
			2	아무것도 하지 않는. 한가한	free
		rời	1	떨어진. 분리된. 흐트러진	separate. in disarray
			2	그만두다. 취소하다	to break off. to break loose. to leave

		roi		장대. 회초리	whip. rod
		rơi		떨어지다. 내려앉다. 추락하다	to fall. to drop. to come down
		rói		밝고 신선해 보이는	bright and fresh
		rọi		(햇빛이) 들어오다. 비추다	to beam. to illuminate. to shine. to focus (light)
		rỗi		한가한. 유유자적한	free (unoccupied. not busy)
		rỗi		고깃배	a fish ship
		rỏi		단단한	hard as a rock
		rợi		우울한	gloomy
07 41	rom	rơm		볏짚	straw (dried stalks considered collectively)
		ròm		빈약한. 앙상한. (=ốm ròm)	skinny
		rờm		귀에 너무 익은	too familiar to hear
		rớm		(눈물을) 흘리다. 젖다. (=rướm)	to be wet with (tears, etc.). to be moist with
		rọm		송충이. 털벌레	pine caterpillars
		rởm		우스꽝스러운. 괴상한	grotesque. ludicrous. ridiculous
		rộm		일제히 생기다	appear in unison
		rôm		땀띠	prickly heat. heat rash
07 42	ron	rộn	1	번잡한	busy. chaotic. crowed. congested. jammed
			2	야단법석을 떨다	noisy. disorderly
		rốn	1	배꼽	navel. a belly button
			2	끝내버리다. 질질끌다	finish off. drag on
		rơn		몹시. 매우	very (much)
		rón		발끝으로 걷다. (=rón bước)	walk on tiptoe
		ròn		부러지기(부서지기) 쉬운 (=giòn)	brittle

		rọn		날카로운. 뾰족한. (=nhọn)	sharp. pointed
		rởn		무서워하다. 겁내다. 소름이 돋다	be scared of. fear. be afraid (of)
		rỡn		농담하다	make a joke. tell a joke. make a crack
		rỏn		정찰하다. 순찰하다. (=đi rỏn)	make a reconnaissance. to patrol
		rợn		두려움에 몸을 떨다. (=rợn rợn)	having such a fear that one's body starts shivering
0743	rong	rong	1	해초류	seaweedlike algae. seaweed
			2	배회하다. 어슬렁거리다	wander about. loiter about
		ròng	1	순수	pure
			2	(파도가) 흘러가다. (물)결을 이루어 흐르다	flow in waves
		rộng	1	넓은. 광대한. 헐렁한	broad. wide. extensive. ample
			2	광범위하게	broadly
		róng		말뚝	a stake
		rỗng		빈. 공허한. 내용이 없는	hollow. empty
		rồng		용(龍)	dragon
		rống		(소. 코끼리. 호랑이 등이) 울다	(of animals) to roar
		rỏng		무거운 물체가 물에 떨어질 때 나는 소리. 첨벙	splashing
		rông		방목의	usually of animals, including livestocks be controlless. be out of control
0744	rot	rọt	1	창자	a bowel
			2	(물) 새어나가다	get out of. leak. escape
		rốt	1	최후의	last
			2	가두다. 우리속에 가두다	lock up. shut (sb) up (in)
		rót		붓다. 따르다. 쏟다	to pour. to fill up

		rột		물집 등이 아물다. 시들다. (=dột)	heal (up). close (up). wither away
		rớt		떨어지다. 격추하다	to drop. to fall
07 45	ru	ru	1	자장가를 부르다	to put (a baby) to sleep. to sing/lull (a baby) to sleep.
			2	문장끝에 붙어 의문을 나타내는 말	a question at the end of a sentence
		rú	1	숲. 산림. (=rừng)	forest. woods
			2	큰 소리를 내다. 고함치다	to shout. yell. scream
		rũ		(힘이 다해) 지치다	an act of being exhausted and tilted down because of no energy or after hard works
		rủ		요청하다. 초대하다	to ask (someone to do something with you). to invite
		rư		(=ru)	(=ru)
07 46	rua	rua		묘성(昴星)	name of the constellation
		rùa		거북이	turtle
		rũa		(고기가) 부패하다. (=rữa)	to be rotten
		rửa		씻다. 닦다. (굴욕 따위를) 씻어버리다	to wash. to clean
		rữa		(꽃 등이) 시들다. 부패시키다. (과일)너무 익다	to decompose
		rựa		덤불을 베는 낫의 일종	machete
		rứa		똑같은. 그와같은	like that. such
		rủa		~에게 욕하다. 악담하다. 저주하다	to curse
07 47	rui	rui		운이 없다	be unlucky
		rủi	1	흉(凶). 흉운(凶運). 불행	ill luck. mishap
			2	불행한	unlucky. unfortunate
		rụi		말라 비틀어지다	become dry and twist

07 48	ruc	rúc	1	기다. 기어 들어오다	crawl, creep, crawl in
			2	길게 울거나 전화를 걸다	to make a long cry or call
		rục		푹 찐. 푹 익힌	thick as a pancake, well-cooked
		rực		빛나다. 밝다. (= sáng rực)	bright, glowing, flaring up brightly, shining bright
		rức		지끈지끈 아프다. 쑤시다. (=nhức)	have a sharp pain, ache, throb (with), be sore
07 49	run	run	1	(무릎, 손) 떨림. (목소리, 땅) 떨림	tremor
			2	(추위, 근심 등으로) 떨다. (전등이) 깜박이다. (목소리) 떨다	to tremble, to shiver (due to cold)
		rún		배꼽, 중심. (=rốn)	navel, belly button, center, the middle
		rủn		녹초가 되다	be exhausted
		rùn		후퇴하다. 되돌아가다	to pull back, to take back
07 50	rung	rùng	1	어망(漁網)	a fishing net
			2	떨리다. 미동하다	tremble, move in motion
		rừng	1	숲. 산림	forest, woods, jungle
			2	사나운. 야생의	fierce, wild
		rung		(나무 등이) 흔들려 움직이다	to put in motion, to shake, to agitate, to ring (bell)
		rúng		쇠약하게 하다. 상하게 하다	debilitate, injure
		rụng		떨어지다	to fall, to drop
07 51	ruoc	rước	1	맞이하다. 접대하다	to greet, entertain
			2	공손한 말	polite words
		ruốc		작은 게의 일종	a kind of small crab
07 52	ruoi	ruỗi	1	펴다	spread out
			2	대들보. (=ruỗi nhà)	cross-beam

		ruồi		파리	(zoology) fly
		rươi		해안가의 땅에서 생기는 작은 벌레	ragworm. clam worm
		ruổi		뒤쫓다. 질주하다	chase after. make a gallop
		ruối		울타리용으로 심는 나무	fence-planting wood
		rưới		뿌리다. 끼얹다	to sprinkle
		rưỡi		절반. 반 (100이상 숫자의 반수를 나타낸다)	alternative form of rưởi
		rượi		상쾌한. 산뜻한	refreshing. fresh and fresh
		rưởi		어느 단위의 반	after a number or noun and a half. half past
07 53	ruong	ruỗng		(벌레가 먹어서) 구멍난. 속이 빈	(by eating a bug) punctured. empty in the inside
		ruồng		절연하다. 관계를 끊다	break off a relationship
		rương		트렁크. 상자	trunk. box
		ruộng		논	field (an area of open land used for growing crops)
		rường		대들보	cross-beam
		rướng		눈을 크게 뜨다. (=nhướng)	open one's eyes wide
07 54	ruot	rượt	1	추적하다. 뒤쫓다	to chase. trace. track down
			2	말쑥한. 단정한	neat and tidy
		ruột		장(腸). 창자	intestine. gut. entrails. inner tube. biologically related
07 55	ruou	rượu		술. 포도주	non-beer alcoholic beverage
07 56	rut	rút		뽑다. 뽑아내다. 빼내다. 꺼내다	to pull out or pull back. to withdraw
		rứt		쥐어짜다. 잡아뽑다. 잡아당겨 찢다. 끊다	squeeze out. pluck out. tear by pulling.
		rụt		움츠리다. 뒤로 당기다	to pull back. to take back

0757	sa	sả		1	레몬글라스	lemongrass
				2	(고기, 야채) 잘게 썰다	to cut into pieces, to chop up
		sa	紗(사) 沙(사) 砂(사) 裟(사)	1	모래	sand
				2	떨어지다, 내리다	fall, drop down, prolapse
		sã		1	늘어뜨리다	hang down
				2	갈기갈기 찢긴	torn to shreds
		sá		1	길, 도로	road, street
				2	마음을 쓰다	have one's mind on
		sà			(새가) 스쳐 날아가다, 급강하하다	(a bird) flips away, take a dive
		sạ			벼의 무작위 파종 농법	random sowing of rice
0758	sac	sắc	色(색) 勅(칙)	1	예리한, 날카로운	sharp
				2	색	color
				3	칙령(왕의 법령)	an imperial decree
		sác			염수 식물의 일종	a kind of saline plant
		sặc			숨막히다, 목이메다, 질식하다, 내뿜다	to cough or sneeze to choking
		sạc		1	충전하다, 재충전하다	to charge, to recharge
				2	꾸짖다, 야단치다	to scold
0759	sach	sạch		1	깨끗한, 청결한	clean
				2	완전히	completely
		sách			책	book
0760	sai	sai		1	틀린, 잘못된	be incorrect
				2	명령하다	to order, to send
		sài		1	아이들 피부병의 총칭	a general term for children's skin desease
				2	(돈) 쓰다	to spend money

		sái	1	불길한		ominous. inauspicious
			2	뿌리다		to sprinkle
		sải	1	(양 손 또는 두 팔을) 펼친 길이		arm span
			2	(수영) 한 번 손발을 놀리기		a once-in-a-swimming trick
		sãi		불교의 승려		monks
0761	sam	sam		삼채. (=rau sam)		an egg-shaped vegetable with thick leaves
		sàm	1	고자질하다. 모함하다		tell tales. tell on
			2	무질서한. 무례한		disorderly. rude
		sầm	1	강하게 부딪혔을 때 나는 소리 (의성어)		the sound of a strong bump
			2	갑자기 어두워지다. 우울해지다. (=tối sầm)		suddenly darken. become depressed
		sâm		(식물) 인삼		ginseng
		săm		(타이어) 내부 튜브. (=ruột xe)		an inner tube
		sẫm		(색이) 어두운. 짙은. (=thẫm)		(of colors) deep. dark-shaded
		sậm		(색이) 어두운. 짙은. (=sẫm)		(of colors) deep. dark-shaded
		sạm		햇볕에 그을은. 검게 탄		sunburned. tanned
		sắm		준비하다. 구입하다		to buy (something special)
		sẩm		어두워지기 시작하는. 어스레한		beginning to darken. dusky
		sặm		색이 짙은. (색깔이) 어두운		dark in color
		sấm		천둥		(weather) thunder
0762	san	sán	1	가까이 가다		get near
			2	촌충. 회충		tapeworm
		săn	1	~을 쫓아가다. 사냥하다		to hunt. to hunt down
			2	흐름이 급한		water runs hard

		sấn		1	돌입하다. 강제로 들어가다. 쇄도하다	force one's way into, rush upon
				2	단숨에. 즉시	at a burst, at a breath, by one effort, right off
		sẵn		1	준비하다	ready, prepared
				2	이미(벌써) 있는	already in existence
		sẩn		1	습진이 생기다	get eczema
				2	굵기가 다른 실. 울퉁불퉁한(粗絲)	bumpy thread
		sạn		1	자갈. 조약돌. 모래알	gravel, pebble, a grain of sand
				2	(비유적으로) 경험하다	experience
		sắn		1	카사버속의 식물	cassava, topioca
				2	힘든. 고된	hard, though, arduous
		san			평평하게 하다. (=san cho đều)	level the ground, flatten
		sàn			높은 바닥. 층. 마루. (=sàn gác)	floor
		sân			안마당. 안뜰	yard, courtyard, ground
		sần			거칠은. 까칠까칠한	rough
		sản	産(산)		출산하다. 산출하다	to produce, to create, to generate
0763	sang	sang		1	건너다. 지나다	to go over, to come over, to cross, to transfer
				2	귀족적인. 풍족한. 유복한	aristocratic, plentiful, well-off
		sàng		1	키 (곡식을 고르는 도구)	winnowing basket
				2	키질하다. 키로 치다. 거르다	to winnow, to sift, to strain
		sáng		1	아침. 새벽	morning
				2	빛나는. 찬란한	bright
		sảng		1	헛소리를 하는. 제정신을 잃은	out of one's mind

			2	정신 착란이 되다. 실수하다	become delusional. to make a mistake
		săng		궤짝. 관	(wooden) box. coffin
		sâng		향엽식물의 일종	a kind of plant
		sắng		(냄새 등이) 퍼지다. 큰 소리로 웃다. (=cười sằng sặc)	smell spread. laugh aloud
		sẵng		스프용 야채의 일종. (=rau sẵng)	a kind of vegetable for soup
07 64	sanh	sanh	1	(한 쌍의) 짝짝이. 캐스터네츠	(instrument) castanets
			2	태어나다. (=sinh)	to be born
		sành	1	(유약을 바른) 토기	glazed terra cotta
			2	~에 숙련된. 정통한	skilled. well-informed
		sánh	1	비교하다	to compare
			2	끈기가 있는. 끈적끈적한	sticky
		sảnh	1	(호텔 등의) 로비. (건물의) 홀	lobby. hall
			2	정청 (큰 집의 입구 가까이에 있는 객실로된 방). 관저	a room close to the entrance of a large house. official residence
05 65	sao	sao	1	별 모양의 것	a star (luminous celestial body)
			2	어째서. 어떻게	why
		sáo	1	검은 새	blackbird
			2	플루트. 피리	flute
		sảo	1	대나무 격자 바구니	bamboo lattice basket
			2	조산하다. (=sảo thai)	have a premature birth
		sào		장대. 대나무 장대	pole. stick
		sạo		말을 퍼뜨리다. 소문내다. 소곤거리다. 거짓말하다	make a rumor. to lie

0766	sap	sắp	1	(근접 미래 조동사 역할) 막 ~ 하려 하다	future marker about to. be about to
			2	떼. 무리	group. party. bunch
		sấp	1	뒤쪽. 등쪽. (=mặt trái)	back side
			2	엎드리다	(lying) prone
		sập	1	끌어내리다. 함몰시키다. 침몰시키다	to collapse. to fall down. to bang shut
			2	침대. 상과 걸상 겸용의 단	low. wooden and ornate bed/platform
		sáp		밀랍	wax
		sạp		갑판. 대나무 또는 나무로 만든 평상 (잠을 자거나 물품진열대로 사용)	deck. a plain made of bamboo or wood
0767	sat	sát	1	근접한. 가까운. (운수. 운명) 죽을 운세인. 살기가 들은	very close to
			2	죽이다	to kill
		sạt		무너지다	to lose all
		sắt	1	강철. 쇠	iron (chemical element)
			2	단단하다. 경직되다	hard. stiffen
		sất		(부정의 강조) 전혀	(emphasis on negation) never
		sặt		cá sặt 논에 있는 작은 물고기	a small fish in a paddy field
0768	sau	sâu	1	곤충. 벌레	insect. worm
			2	(우물. 벽. 상처가) 깊은. 심원한	a deep (well.wall. wound). profound
		sầu	1	비탄. 슬픔	sorrowful. sadness
			2	근심이 있는. 슬픈	grieved. sorrowful. sad. melancholy
		sau		나중에. 후에. 뒤쪽(순서나 시간)	next. later. rear. hind. back

		sáu		여섯. 육. 6	six. 6
		sậu		빠른. 급한	fast. urgent
		sấu		악어. (=cá sấu)	crocodile
		sâu		깊다	deep. deeply
0769	say	sẩy	1	미끄러져 놓치다. 부주의하게 실수하다	to lose
			2	돌연. 갑자기	suddenly
		sảy	1	땀띠	prickly heat. heat rash
			2	전후좌우로 움직이다. (곡물) 키질하다	move back and forth. fling at. winnow
		say		~에 취하다. (연애. 색정 등에) 빠지다	be drunk. be inebriated
		sãy		갑자기	suddenly
		sây		긁다. 문지르다	to scratch. to scrub
		sậy		갈대	reed
		sấy		(열로) 말리다. 건조시키다	to dry (by heat)
		sầy		(피부가) 벗겨지다. 긁히다	scratched
0770	se	se	1	건조한. 마른	dry
			2	마르다	get dry
		sẽ	1	부드럽게. 온화하게. 가볍게	gently. in a mild manner. lightly
			2	~할 것이다 (조동사 역할. 미래시제를 표현)	will. shall. would
		sẻ	1	참새	sparrow
			2	나누다. 분배하다	to divide. to share
		sè		위로 향하다. 뒤로 자빠지다. 뒤집어서 펴다	face up. fall backward. turn over and spread
		sế		기울다. 저물다. 가라앉다	tilt. come to an end. sink down

		sẹ			어류의 정액	fish semen
		sệ			살찐. 뚱뚱한	fat. overweight
		sẽ			조금 흘러내리다. 조금씩 처지다	trickle down. fall slightly
		sề			크고 평평한 바구니. 소쿠리	a large flat basket. basket
0771	sec	séc			수표	(Am.) check. (Brit.) a cheque
0772	sep	sếp			보스. 우두머리. 상사	chief. boss
		sẹp			낮은. 평평한	low. flat
0773	sen	sen			연(蓮)	lotus
		sến			후박나무	machilus thunbergii
		sẻn			인색한	stingy
		sên		1	민달팽이. 굼뜬 동물	slug
				2	체인. 쇠사슬	chain
0774	seo	seo		1	주름살	wrinkles
				2	(종이를) 만들다	to make (paper)
		sẹo			상처. 흉터	wound. scar. hurt
0775	set	sét		1	녹슬다	to be rusty
				2	가득찬	full of
				3	번갯불	(weather) lightning
		sệt			질감이 매우 두꺼운	very thick in texture
0776	seu	sếu		1	두루미. 학	crane (bird)
				2	(몸이) 덜덜 떨리는. răng~ 이가 덜덜 떨리는	shivering with cold
		sều			침을 흘리다. 코를 흘리다.	drool. have a runny nose
0777	si	sỉ		1	도매의	wholesale

			2	창피. 불명예	shame. a dishonor to
	si			벵갈보리수. 용수(榕樹)의 일종	ficus benghalensis. banyan tree
	sĩ			학자. 지식인. 학생	scholar. expert. advisor
	sì			과도한. 심한	undue
	sị			슬픈	sad
0778	sieng	siểng		상자. 반합	box. case
		siêng		근면한	diligent. industrious. hardworking (=chăm)
0779	sieu	siêu	1	한약을 다리는 주전자	a pot for boil of a herbal medicine
			2	대단한. 매우. 초(超)~	super-. hyper-. super. very good
0780	sim	sim		(식물) 천인화(天人花)	rhodmyrtus tomentosa
0781	sinh	sinh	生(생)	1	태어나다. 세상에 나오다	to give birth (to). to produce. yield
				2	생원. 학생	student
		sình		1	부어오르다. 붓다	swell up. swell
				2	진창의	mud
		sính			~을 좋아하는. ~에 미친	fond of. crazy about
		sĩnh			(점차로) 커지다	grow bigger and bigger
0782	so	sơ	疎(소) 初(초)	1	소홀히	inattentively
				2	보잘 것 없는	not worth a damn
		so		1	비교하다	to compare. to pair up
				2	(먼저) 태어난. 처음으로 태어난	(first) born
		sổ		1	기록. 등록	notebook. register book
				2	지우다	to erase. to delete

		sò			(먹는) 바지락	ark clam
		só			모퉁이. 틈새	corner. a crack
		sỗ			(일을) 소홀히 하는. 경솔한	inattentive. carelessly. imprudent
		sọ			두개골	skeleton skull
		sờ			만지다. (손으로) 더듬다	to feel. to touch
		sở	所(소) 楚(초) 礎(초)		사무소. 사무국	bureau. department. office
		sợ			두려워하다. 걱정하다	to fear. to be afraid
		số	數(수)		수. 숫자	number. size. amount. count
		sớ	疎(소)		(임금에게 올리는) 글. 상소	an address to the throne. appeal (to a higher court)
		sỏ			(가축의) 머리	head (of livestock)
		sô		1	버킷. 물통. 들통	bucket
				2	연주. 상영. 흥행. 공연	show. performance
				3	베옷. 상복	mourning (dress/clothes)
		sồ			큰. 부피가 큰	bulky
0783	soan	soán			(왕권. 권력 따위를) 빼앗다. 탈권하다. (=thoán)	(of royal authority, power, etc.) to deprive. divest
		soạn			준비하다. 작곡하다. 편찬하다. 편집하다	to prepare. to compose. to compile
0784	soat	soát			검사하다. 점검하다	to examine. inspection. test. check. check (out)
0785	soc	sọc		1	줄(무늬)이 있는	striped
				2	선. 줄(무늬)	stripe
		sóc			다람쥐	(zoology) squirrel
		sốc		1	충격. 쇼크	shocking. shocked.
				2	충격을 주다	to shock (usually in an unpleasing kind of way)

		sộc		당당하게. 대담하게	proudly. boldly
0786	soi	sói	1	늑대. (=chó sói)	a wolf (animal)
			2	(머리가) 벗겨진. (=hói)	bald-headed
		soi	1	빛을 비추다.	to illuminated
			2	자세히 조사하다	to scrutinize
		sõi		확실하게. 잘. 또렷또렷하게	certainly. distinctly
		sồi	1	(거친) 옷감. 직물	textile fabric
			2	오크(나무)	oak
		sỏi		작은 돌. 자갈	pebble. gravel
		sòi		능력있는. 재주있는	competent. talented
		sới		투기장(鬪技場)	speculation field
		sọi		대머리의	bald-headed
		sởi		(의학) 홍역. 홍진	(medicine) measles
		sợi		(식물 따위의) 섬유질	thread. fiber
		sôi		끓이다. 끓인. 데친	(of riquid) to boil. to be boiled
0787	som	sóm		이가 빠진	toothless
		sòm		시끄러운	loud
		sọm		노쇠한. (=sòm sọm)	decrepit. old and infirm
		sớm		일찍이. 일찍. 곧	early. soon
		sỗm		노쇠한. (=sọm)	decrepit. old and infirm
0788	son	son	1	흔들리지 않는. 단단한	unshakable. firm
			2	루즈. 립스틱	lipstick
		sơn 山(산)	1	산. (=núi)	mountain
			2	칠을 하다	to paint
		són		(무의식 중에) 대소변을 싸다	have a bowel movement unconsciously

		sờn		(옷 따위가) 해어진	worn out
		sờn		오싹해지다. 곤두서다	to creep. to stand on end
0789	song	sóng	1	물결	wave
			2	고르게 흔들리다	to shake out even
		sống	1	삶	living
			2	살다. 생활하다	to live
		song	窓(창) 雙(쌍)	1	등나무의 일종 (의자, 지팡이 등 만들 때 씀)	a kind of rattan
				2	그렇지만	however
		sõng		1	(대나무로 엮은) 작은 배	a small boat woven of bamboo
				2	건방진. 무례한	cheeky. rude
		sòng		1	명백히. 분명히	plainly. clearly
				2	도박장. (=sòng bạc)	gambling-den
		sồng		1	(검은 염색에 쓰이는) 나무	a tree used in black dye
				2	조심스러운. 얌전한	cautious. well-mannered
		sổng			달아나다. 탈출하다	to escape. to break loose
		sông			강	river (large stream which drains a landmass)
0790	sot	sốt		1	열이 있는	steaming hot
				2	열병	to have a fever. to have a temperature
		sót			남겨두다	be remained
		sột			(무엇인가를) 긁거나 깨무는 소리. (=sồn sột)	the sound of scratching or biting
		sớt			(음식 따위를 다른 용기에) 옮기다	transfer (to another container)
		sọt			(등에 지는) 바구니. 대나무통	basket. cylindrical crate

0791	su	sư	師(사)	1	법사. 승려	a buddhist monk
				2	존사. 교사의 존칭. 대가(大家)	the honorific title of a teacher
		sù		1	부어오르다	swell up
				2	커다란. 뚱뚱한	big. fat
		sử	史(사) 使(사)	1	역사	history
				2	임지로 파견하다. 명령하다	dispatch to one's post
		sụ		1	극히. 매우	very. extremely
				2	거대한	huge. great. giant
		su			고무나무. (=su su)	a rubber tree
		sú			개다. 반죽하다	work a dough. paste
		sự	事(사)		일. 문제	deed. act. occurrence
		sứ	使(사)		중국 도자기. (=đồ sứ)	chinaware. porcelain
0792	sua	sữa		1	젖. 우유	milk
				2	어린	young
		sứa		1	해파리의 일종	jellyfish
				2	젖을 토하다	throw up one's milk
		sua			뽐내다	show off
		sưa			만취한. 술취한	drunken
		sửa			수정하다. 고치다	to repair. to correct. to put right
		sủa			(개가) 짖다. (경멸적으로) 말하다	(of a dog) to bark. (derogatory) to say. to tell
0793	suat	suất	率(솔)	1	정량	a portion. a fixed amount
				2	비율. 등급을 매기다	rate
				3	통솔하다	lead the way

0794	suc	súc	畜(축) 蓄(축)	1	통나무	a log
				2	씻다. 세정하다	to rinse
		sức		1	힘. 능력	strength. power
				2	꾸미다. 장식하다	decorate. decorate with
		sực		1	돌연히. 문득	suddenly
				2	강하게 퍼지다	spread strongly
		sục			찾다. 마구 뒤지다	to search (premises). to scour. to plunge deep into
0795	sui	sui			친척의 관계(인연)가 있는 사람	a relative
		sùi			거품이 일다	bubble up
		sủi			거품이 일다. 끓다. 비등하다	bubble up. to boil
0796	sum	sụm			쓰러지다. 무너지다	fall down
0797	sung	sưng		1	부은. 부어오른	(of a body part) be swollen
				2	붓다. 부어 오르다	(of a body part) to swell. to become swollen
		sung	充(충)	1	(식물) 무화과. (미국산) 플라타너스	fig. sycamore
				2	충족하다	to satisfy
		sùng		1	감자를 먹는 벌레의 일종	a kind of worm that eats potatoes
				2	숭배하다. 우러러 존경하다	worship. respect greatly
		sủng	寵(총)	1	영광. 은총. 축복	glory. grace. blessing
				2	사랑하다	to love
		súng	銃(총)		화기. 총	gun
		sững			움직이지 않는. 부동의(상태인)	immovable. motionless
		sửng			놀라운. 어이없어하는. (=sửng người)	amazing. dumbfounded

		sưng		부동의(상태인)	immovable. motionless
		sừng		뿔	horn
0798	suoi	sưởi	1	(몸을) 따뜻하게 하다	warm oneself up
			2	홍역. (=sởi sảy)	measles
		suối		개울	stream
0799	suon	sườn		늑골	rib
		suôn		곧은. 똑바로	straight
0800	suot	sướt	1	스치다. (=sượt)	pass by
			2	(피부가) 벗겨진	skinned
		suốt	1	처음부터 끝까지. 쭉	throughout
			2	원뿔모양으로 방추에 감은 실	a conical thread
		sượt		스치다. (=sướt)	pass by
0801	sut	sút		(축구) 슛하다	(soccer) to shoot
		sứt		국가에 내는 돈 (봉건시대. 식민지)	chipped (the feudal era. colony ear)
		sụt		감소하다. 저하하다	to tumble. to collapse. to go down. to drop. to fall. to decrease
0802	suy	suy	推(추) 1	곰곰히 생각하다. 헤아리다	to ponder over. to think carefully
			2	거절하다. 썩다	to decline. to decay
			3	실패하다	(medicine, of an organ) to fail
0803	ta	tả	瀉(사) 左(좌) 寫(사) 1	설사	diarrhea
			2	좌(파)	the left (wing/party)
		tà	邪(사) 斜(사)	사악한	crooked. wicked. dishonest. unjust. heretical. evil
		tá	借(차) 佐(좌) 1	타스	dozen
			2	구실을 만들다	make up an excuse for

		tã		1	(아기의) 기저귀	diaper
				2	오래되다. (낡아) 떨어지다	ragged
		tạ	謝(사) 籍(자)	1	감사하다	to thank
		ta	嗟(차) 些(사)		나. 자신. 우리	I. me. we. us
08 04	tac	tác	作(작)	1	연령. 고령	age. an advanced age
				2	만들다	to make
		tắc		1	금귤나무. 금귤	kumquat
				2	멈추다. 막히다	to be blocked. to be obstructed
		tấc			길이, 넓이 등에 쓰이는 단위	a unit used for length area, width, etc.
		tạc			(금속 등에 도안, 문자 등을) 새기다. 조각하다	to carve. to sculpt (statue, etc.)
		tặc	賊(적)		Hải tặc (해적)	pirate. sea robber
08 05	tach	tách		1	컵	cup (with a handle)
				2	나누다. 쪼개다. 분리하다	to separate. to split
		tạch			펑. 탁. 쾅 등의 의성어	pow! (sound of firecracker). clattered
08 06	tai	tai	災(재) 裁(재)	1	귀	ear
				2	쓸데없는. 보람없는	useless. fruitless
		tài	材(재) 裁(재)	1	재능. 능력	talent. gift
				2	능숙한. 재능있는	skillful. talented
		tái		1	하얀. 창백한. 희미한	of colors or shades that denote unhealthiness, defilement, fright, etc. pale
				2	창백해지다	turn pale
		tải	載(재)	1	싣다. 수송하다	to trasport. to convey. to carry
				2	운송용의	for trasportation purposes

			tãi			흩어지다. 흩뿌리다	to scatter
			tại	在	1	~에. ~안에. ~위에	at. in. on
					2	왜냐하면	because of. due to. because
08 07	tam	tầm		1	범위. 한도. 한계	range. scope
					2	찾다. 구하다. (=tìm)	look for. find
		tạm	暫(잠)	1	일시적인. 잠깐동안의	temporary
				2	즉각. 급히	immediately
		tam	三(삼)		셋. 삼(3)	three (3)
		tăm			이쑤시개	toothpick
		tâm	心(심)		마음. (=quả tim)	heart
		tám			여덟. 팔(8)	eight (8)
		tàm	蠶(잠)		잠. 누에. (=tằm)	silkworm
		tấm			(종이 등의) ~장	used to count wide, flat objects
		tẩm	浸(침)		젖다. 젖어들다. 깊이 스며들다	to soak
		tắm			뒤집어 쓰다. 샤워하다	to wash a body. to bath. to shower
		tằm	蠶(잠)		누에	silkworm
08 08	tan	tàn	殘(잔)	1	시들다. 떨어지다	to fade. to wither. to decay. to crumble
				2	재	ashes. remains. residue
		tân	新(신) 津(진) 賓(빈)	1	처녀	virgin
				2	처녀의. 동정의	vergin. maiden
		tần	瀕(빈)	1	삶다. 찌다	to steam
				2	(식물) 부추의 일종	(plants) a kind of leek
		tản	散(산)	1	분산되다. 흩어지다. 흩뜨리다	to be dispersed. to disperse
				2	우산. 낙하산	umbrella. parachute

		tận	盡(진)	1	없어지다. 다하다	disappear. run out	
				2	극단으로. 끝까지	to the extreme. until the end	
		tấn	進(진) 迅(신) 訊(신)	1	톤 (1,000킬로그램)	ton (1,000kilogram)	
				2	고문하다	to torture	
		tan			녹다. 액체상태로 되다	to melt	
		tán	傘(산) 贊(찬) 散(산)	1	양산. 큰 우산. 차양	canopy. parasol. sunshade	
				2	~의 환심을 사다. 구혼하다. (=tận)	win favor with. proposal of marriage	
		tẩn			(=tấn)	(=tấn)	
		tặn			tiện tặn 절약하다. 유익하게 사용하다	save. make good use of	
08 09	tang	tăng	曾(증) 增(증) 僧(승)	1	승려	monk	
				2	늘리다. 증가시키다	to increase	
		tảng		1	초석	foundation stone	
				2	~을 가장하다	to pretend. feign	
		tang	喪(상)	1	초상. 장례	funeral	
				2	(삼각법의) 탄젠트	(trigonometry) tangent	
		tàng	藏(장) 喪(상)		저장하다. 감추다	save. cover (up). hide	
		tâng			들어올리다. 아첨하다	to raise (moral value). to flatter	
		táng	葬(장)		매장하다	to bury the dead	
		tầng			계층. (건물의) 층	storey. floor. stratum. level	
		tạng	臟(장)		내장. 체형	innards. viscera	
		tặng	贈(증)		주다. 선물하다. 증정하다	to give as a gift. to get (something additional) for free	
		tằng			증손	great-grandchild	

08 10	tanh	tanh	1	고약한 냄새 (생선의 비린내)	having the smell of fresh fish
			2	정말로. 매우	really. very
		tánh		성격. 성품. (=tính)	personality. a cast of mind. nature. character
		tạnh		(비가) 그치다	(of rain or wind) to stop. to cease
08 11	tao	tảo	掃(소) 무(조) 藻(조)	1	쓸어버리다	sweep away
				2	기한 전의. 조기의	early
		táo		1	사과	apple
				2	변비에 걸리다	be constipated
		tạo		1	조화의 신. tạo hóa의 약어	the god of harmony
				2	창조하다. 만들다	to create. to make. to form. to cause
		tao			나 (자신을 스스로 높인말). 짐 (임금이 지칭할때)	(informal, familyar or self-conceited) I. me
08 12	tap	táp			(덥석) 물다	to snap. to bite
		tắp		1	다가서다	come close
				2	즉시. 정면으로	right off. head-on
		tập	集(집) 習(습)	1	(종이) 더미	ream (of paper)
				2	배우다. 학습하다. 연습하다	to learn. to practice
		tấp			표류하다. 떠돌다	drift on. float about
		tạp	雜(잡)		복잡한	complex. complicated
08 13	tat	tất	必(필) 畢(필)	1	양말. (=bít tất)	socks
				2	물론	then surely. of course
				3	전부. 전체의	all. the whole of
		tắt		1	스위치를 끄다	to switch off. to turn off
				2	짧은. 더 짧은	short. shorter

		tát			철썩 때리다. (손바닥으로 상대의 볼을) 때리다	to slap
		tạt			누군가에게 물(또는 다른 액체를) 붓다	to splash into. to pour water (or other liquids) onto someone
		tật	疾(질)		질병. 불치의 병	disease. an incurable disease
08 14	tau	tàu		1	Tàu 중국	Chinese
				2	낡고 더러운	old and dirty
				3	배. 함. (=tàu thủy)	boat. ship. vessel. craft
				4	기차	train
		tẩu	走(주)	1	(아편을 피울때 쓰는) 담배 파이프	tobacco pipe
				2	도주하다. 황급히 감추다	to flee
		tâu			(왕에게) 보고하다. 아뢰다	report (to the king)
		táu			가구용 목재의 일종	a kind of wood for furniture
		tàu			배. 보트. (=tàu)	ship. boat
		tậu			(가옥, 논 따위를) 구입하다. 사들이다	to buy (a house, a rice paddy, etc.)
		tấu	奏(주)		(왕에게) 보고하다	report (to the king)
08 15	tay	tay		1	손. 팔. 사내	a hand. an arm. a guy. a dude
				2	작다. 적다	small. few. little
		tày		1	~과 같다	be the same as ~
				2	무딘. 평평한	blunt. dull
		tây	西(서)	1	서쪽	west
				2	구미의	Western
		tấy		1	붓다	swell up
				2	(장사가) 번창하는. 번성하는	flourishing. thriving
		tầy			~와 같다. (=tày)	be the same as ~ (=tày)

		tẩy			씻다	to bleach, to clean, to wipe or rub off
08 16	te	te		1	찢어진	torn
				2	빠르게	quickly
		tệ	弊(폐)	1	폐해	harmful effect
				2	잔인한. 박정한. 나쁜	cruel, bad (at doing something)
		tế	祭(제) 細(세) 濟(제) 際(제)	1	(말이) 질주하다	gallop
				2	작은. 미세한	small, fine
		tề	薺(제)	1	동일하게. 일제히	in the same way, all together
				2	자르다. 베다	to cut
		tẻ		1	보통쌀. 멥쌀	non-glutinous rice
				2	쓸쓸한	lonely, lonesome
		tễ	劑(제)	1	환약	pill
				2	약을 제조하다	make medicine
		té			물을 튀기다. 적시다	splash water, get wet
		tè			소변보다. 쉬하다. (=đi đái)	to pee, to urinate
		tẽ			벗기다. 까다	peel off
		tể			동물을 죽이다	slaughter
		tê			(손발이) 마비된	to be numb
08 17	tem	tem			우표	postage stamp
		tém			쓸어모으다	gather up
		têm			구장 퀴드(씹는 담배)를 만들다	to make a quid of betel

08 18	ten	ten	1	구리의 녹	copper rust
			2	갈기갈기 찢긴	torn to shreds
		tẽn		부끄럽다. 부끄러워 얼굴을 붉히다	to be ashamed. blush with shame
		tên	1	화살	arrow
			2	이름. 명칭	given name
			3	사람. 놈	person
08 19	tep	tép		작은 새우. 참새우 무리	a small shrimp
		tệp		묶음	bundle (of). bunch (of)
08 20	tet	tẹt	1	우묵하게 들어간	hollowed in. sunk
			2	쪼개지다. 찢어지다	split apart. be split. tear
		tết	1	Tết. 축제일. 명절. 음력설	Lunar New Year (the first three days of the first lunar month). (by extention) used in the name of some other holidays/festivals. (rare, by extention, usually in simplified translation) a festival
			2	명절에 선물하다	present at a holiday
		tét		시험하다. 테스트하다	to test
08 21	tha	tha	他(타) 磋(차)	입에 물고가다. 입에 물다	to carry. to drag (usually by mouth)
			2	용서하다	to forgive
			3	다른 사람의. 다른	other people's. different
		thà		차라리. 오히려 (~하는 편이 낫다)	rather. would rather
		thả		해방하다. 석방하다. 놓아주다	to release. to let go
08 22	thac	thác	託(탁) 拓(탁) 鐸(탁)	1	폭포	waterfall
				2	죽다	dead

0823	thach	thách		도전하다	to challenge. to dare (someone)
		thạch	石(석)	우뭇가사리. 부레풀. 젤리 (디저트)	agar. isinglass. jelly (dessert)
0824	thai	thai	胎(태)	태아	fetus
		thái	太(태) 采(채) 彩(채) 態(태)	1 얇게 썰다. 저미다	slice thinly
				2 Thái. 태국	Thailand
		thải	採(채) 采(채) 貸(대)	없애다. 제거하다	to discard. to eliminate. to discharge. to dismiss
0825	tham	tham	參(참) 貪(탐)	1 보좌관. 참모	chief clerk. councillor. adviser
				2 탐하다. 욕심내다	to covet. to be greedy. to lust after
		thăm		1 추첨. 제비 (뽑기)	draw lots. drawing lots
				2 견학하다. 방문하다	to visit. to call on
		thấm		1 흡수하다	to imbibe. to absorb (liquids)
				2 흡수성의	absorptive
		thẫm		1 물들다. 스며들다	to permeate
				2 진한. 어두운	dark. deep
		thảm	慘(참)	1 융단	a rug. carpet
				2 비참한	tragic
		thám	探(탐)	찾다. 탐색하다. (=dò xét)	to find. make a search
		thâm	深(심)	깊은. 심오한	deep. profound
		thẩm	審(심)	심판하다	to judge
		thậm	甚(심)	심히. 몹시	very (much)
		thầm		비밀스럽게. 몰래	in the dark. in secret
		thắm		진하다	dark. deep

		thằm			깊은	deep
08 26	than	than	嘆(탄) 炭(탄)	1	석탄. 숯(炭)	coal. charcoal
				2	한탄하다(嘆)	to lament
		thán	炭(탄) 嘆(탄)	1	숯(炭)	charcoal
				2	한탄하다. 슬퍼하다(嘆)	to lament
		thân	親(친) 身(신) 申(신) 紳(신)	1	12지의 신(申). 원숭이	the Year of the Monkey (Chinese Zodiac)
				2	친숙한. 친애하는	intimate. dear
		thần	神(신) 臣(신) 晨(신) 辰(진)	1	신(神)	deity
				2	정교한	exquisite. delicate
		thăn			등심	sirloin
		thận	腎(신)		(해부학) 신장. (=quả cật)	(anatomy) a kidney
		thản	坦(탄)		평탄한	smooth
		thản			thẳng thản. 명백한. 확실히	clear and clear. of a certainty
08 27	thang	thẳng		1	~를 계속하여	continuously. consecutive
				2	곧은. 직선의	straight
		thăng	升(승) 昇(승)	1	되 (용량의 단위. 升). 높은 음표	a unit of measurement of volume. the treble clef
				2	승진하다	to go up. to rise. to advance. to ascend
		thặng		1	여분의	extra. spare
				2	초과하여	in excess of
		thắng	勝(승)	1	제동. 정지. 장치	break (of a vehicle, etc.)
				2	승리	victory
				3	제동을 걸다. (=thắng xe)	to stop (a horse, vehicle, etc.)

		thang	湯(탕)	1	뜨거운 물. 온천	hot water. hot spring
				2	사다리	ladder
		tháng	月(월)		달(月)	month
		thằng			손아래 사람에게 붙이는 말 (친밀한 사이만)	indicates a boy, a brat (used only for friendly relations)
08 28	thanh	thành	城(성) 成(성) 誠(성)	1	성(城)	castle
				2	~을 이루다. ~이 되다. 성장하다. 성공하다	to achieve one's goal. to become. to turn into. successful
		thanh	淸(청) 靑(청) 聲(성)	1	길고 얇은 것에 붙이는 말	a word that attaches to a long thin thing (swards, sabres, etc.)
				2	맑은. 상쾌한. 명백한(淸)	clear. fresh and fresh. clear and clear
		thánh	聖(성)	1	성인(聖人)	saint
				2	거룩한. 신성한	holy. sacred
		thạnh	盛(성)	1	번성하다. (=thịnh)	to flourish
				2	번성하는	thriving
08 20	thao	thảo	草(초) 討(토)	1	초목(草木)	plants and trees
				2	관대한	to be generous
		thao	操(조)	1	조견(組絹). 비단	silk
				2	훈련하다	to train
		thào		1	지나쳐버리다	pass by
				2	얇은. 약한	thin. weak
		tháo	操(조) 署(서)	1	풀다. 뜯다. 해체하다	to dismantle
				2	절개. 지조	principle and belief
		thạo		1	전문가	expert
				2	정통한. 숙련된	proficient. skilled. experienced

0830	thap	tháp	塔(탑)	1	탑. 전망대	tower. stupa
				2	매다. 잇다	to tie. connect
		thập	十(십) 什(십)	1	열, 십, 10	ten. 10
				2	십자형의	cross-shaped
		thắp		1	(연필이나 볼펜의) 뚜껑. (=tháp)	cap. top
				2	점화하다. 밝히다	to light (candle, torch, lamp, incense stick, etc.)
		thấp	濕(습)	1	(의학) 낮은	(in height) short. low
				2	(의학) 류마티스	rheumatism
		thạp			병. 호리병	gourd bottle. gourd-shaped bottle
0831	that	thất	失(실) 七(칠)	1	칠. 일곱. 7	seven. 7
				2	잃다	to lose
		thắt			매다. 묶다	to tie. to fasten. to wear (belt, necktie)
		thật	實(실)		진실한. 올바른. (=thực)	real. true. correct. actually. for real
0832	thau	thau		1	놋쇠. 황동	brass
				2	용해하다	melt down
		thâu		1	처음부터 끝까지	from beginning to end
				2	모으다. (=thu)	to collect
		thấu	透(투)	1	완전한. 철저한	full and utter. complete. perfect. thorough
				2	꿰뚫다. 관통하다. 침투하다	pierce through. penetrate into
		tháu			휘갈겨 쓰다	scrawl. scribble (down)
		thàu			낙찰되다	win a sccessful bid
		thẩu			아편 (Á phiện. thuốc phiện)	opium

08 33	thay	thay	1	(형용사 또는 문장 끝에 붙이는 감탄사)	an adjective or exclamation attached to the end of a sentence.
			2	교대하다. 대체하다	to change. to replace
		thây	1	시체. 송장	corpse
			2	~의 자유에 맡기다. ~좋을대로 하게 하다	set free. freely
		thảy	1	던지다	to throw
			2	모두. 전부	all
		thày		선생. 교사. (=thầy)	male teacher. teacher
		thấy		보다	to see. to find. to feel
08 34	the	thế	替(체) 世(세) 勢(세)	1	기세. 세력	power. authority
				2	대신하다. 대체하다. (=thế chấp)	replace
		thể	體(체) 彩(채) 采(채)	1	시. 문장 형식	form. genre. linguistic form
				2	할 수 있다	can. may. to be able to
		the		1	얇은 비단. 시폰	thin silk. chiffon
				2	(맛) 떫은	bitter. astringent
		thè			혀를 내밀다	to stick tongue out
		thé			(사람소리) 째지는. 찢어지는	a ripping voice
		thệ			맹세하다. (=thề)	to swear. to vow. to pledge
		thẻ			표(회원, 클럽). 증명서	card
		thề			맹세하다. 서약하다	to swear. to vow. to pledge
08 35	them	thèm		1	탐내다. 좋아하다	to want
				2	약간 부족한	a bit lacking
		thềm			베란다	veranda
		thêm			더하다. 보태다. 합치다	additional. more. plus

08 36	then	then	1	빗장, 걸쇠	latch, clasp
			2	검은	black
		thẹn		부끄러워하다, 얼굴을 붉히다	to feel shy, to be bashful, to feel embarrassed
08 37	theo	thẻo	1	소량, 작은 덩어리	a small quantity, a small mass
			2	자르다	to cut
		theo		따르다, 뒤따르다 (đi theo, đưa theo)	to follow, come with, to obey
		thẹo		극히 적은 양	a very small amount
08 38	thep	thép	1	철, 강철	steel
			2	견고한	soild
		thếp	1	등잔	oil lamp
			2	금(은)박의	gilded, silver-thinned
08 39	theu	thêu	1	수를 놓다	to embroider
			2	삽 (카드의) 스페이드	spade
08 40	thi	thì	時(시)	1	때, (=thời)	time, period
				2	~에 대해서	about~
		thi	詩(시) 施(시) 試(시)	1	시(詩)	poetry
				2	시험하다, 겨루다	to take an examination
		thị	市(시) 是(시) 侍(시) 視(시) 示(시) 氏(씨)	1	보다	to see
				2	흔히 여성의 이름 사이에 붙이는 말	a common word for a woman's name
		thỉ	失(실) 始(시)	1	화살	arrow
				2	비로소	for the first time
		thí	施(시) 試(시)		희생하다	to sacrifice for

08 41	thia	thìa		숟가락	spoon (for eating or serving)
08 42	thich	thích	適(적)	1 불교	buddhism
				2 팔로 가볍게 밀다	push lightly with one's arm
				3 좋아하다	to like
		thịch		(의성어) (물건을 세게 내려놓을 때) 쾅. 쿵	(onomatopoeia) thump
08 43	thien	thiển	淺(천)	얕은. 피상적인. (=nông. cạn)	shallow. superficial
		thiền	禪(선) 蟬(선)	(불교) 선	(Buddhism) Zen
		thiện	善(선)	착한	kind. good-natured. good-hearted
		thiến		거세하다	to castrate
		thiên		1 장편의 문학 작품. 대작	a literary work of feature
				2 기울다. ~의 경향이 있다. (=thiên lệch)	tend to
				3 하늘	sky. heaven. nature. god
08 44	thiet	thiết	設(설) 切(절) 鐵(철)	1 철. 쇠. (=sắt)	iron (chemical element)
				2 마련하다. 만들다	make arrangements
		thiệt	實(실) 舌(설)	1 혀	tongue
				2 손해 보다. 잃다	suffer a loss. to lose
08 45	thieu	thiếu	少(소)	1 연소(年少)의. 어린. (=ít tuổi)	young
				2 부족하다	to be short. to lack
				3 빚지다	to owe
		thiều	韶(소)	(생선) 메기의 일종	a kind of catfish
		thiểu	小(소) 消(소)	적은	a little
		thiệu	紹(소)	giới thiệu 소개하다	to introduce
		thiêu		화장하다. 태우다. 소각하다	to burn

0846	thinh	thinh		1	침묵하다. (=lặng thinh, làm thinh)	to be silent
				2	소리	sound
		thính	聽(청)	1	햅쌀가루	newly harvested rice powder
				2	음성 감지능력이 있는	voice-sensitive
		thỉnh	請(청)		종을 치다. (=đánh chuông)	ring a bell
		thịnh	盛(성)		번영하다. 번성하다	to prosper, flourish, thrive, boom
		thình			불시의. 갑작스러운	sudden
0847	thit	thít			단단히 묶다	tie tight
		thịt			살	meat, flesh
0848	thiu	thiu		1	부패한. 오래된	rotten, get stale
				2	잠을 청하다	try to sleep
		thìu			탄광의 갱도를 받치고 있는 침목	a wooden column supporting a shaft
0849	tho	thó		1	점토. 찰흙	clay
				2	소매치기하다	pick a pickpocket
		thơ		1	시	poetry, poem, verse
				2	젊은	young, tender
		thồ		1	안장	saddle
				2	말 등에 지우다(맡기다)	load on a horseback
		thổ	土(토) 吐(토)	1	땅. 흙	earth
				2	토하다. 침을 뱉다	throw up, to spit
		tho			열등하다	be inferior to
		thò			돌출하다	to jut, to stick out

		thố		궤		tub
		thỏ		토끼. 산토끼		rabbit. hare
		thở		호흡하다		to breathe. to respire
		thờ		숭배하다		to worship
		thợ		수공예 등에 종사하는 사람의 총칭		workman
		thớ		고기, 나무, 돌 등의 세로줄		vertical lines of meat, wood, stone, etc.
		thọ	壽(수)	오래 살다. 장수하다. (=sống lâu)		to live long
		thô		조잡한. 굵은. 거친		coarse. husky
0850	thoa	thoa		1	비녀	hairpin
				2	칠하다 (=xoa). 문지르다	to rub (liquids)
		thòa		청동		bronze
		thỏa	妥(타)	온화한. 부드러운		gentle. pleasant. satisfied
0851	thoai	thoái	退(퇴)	후퇴하다. 물러나다		fall back. step down
		thoải		완만한. 약간 언덕진		(of terrain) gentle
		thoại	話(화)	말. 담화		speech. talk. language
0852	thoang	thoáng		1	짧은 시간	a short time
				2	휩쓸고 지나가다. 빨리 지나가다	to sweep past. to pass quickly
				3	통풍이 잘 되는. 바람을 쐬다. 환기의	airy. open to the wind. ventilated
		thoảng		(바람. 향기가) 떠다니다. 감돌다		(of wind, odour, etc.) to sweep past. to be fleeting
		thoắng		빠르게. 신속하게		quickly. at a rapidity
0853	thoat	thoát	脫(탈)	탈출하다. 나가다		to escape. to exit
		thoạt		~하자마자. 곧. 바로. (=vừa mới)		as soon as~. soon enough time. at once. right away

		thoắt			돌연. 갑자기	all of a sudden. suddenly. abruptly. all at once
0854	thoi	thoi			직조기	handloom
		thối	退(퇴)	1	악취를 발산하다	fetid. putrid. stinking. foul-smelling
				2	썩은. 상한	rotten
		thòi			노출하다. 튀어나오다	to expose. expose to. stick out
		thói			습관. 습성	habit usually bad. custom. practice. manner
		thơi			깊은	deep
		thỗi			식탁	(dining) table
		thỏi			조각	piece (of)
		thời	時(시)		시간	time. moment. season
		thổi			불다	to blow
		thôi			단지 ~이다. 다만 ~이다. 중단하다	it's just~. it's only~. to stop (forever). to cease
0855	thom	thơm		1	파인애플	pineapple
				2	향기로운	fragrant of a pleasant aroma
		thòm			(북의) 울리는 소리	a drumbeat
		thỏm			(제한적) 톡 떨어지다	fall lightly
0856	thon	thốn	寸(촌)		길이. 치수	length. size
		thon			야윈. 홀쭉한. 가는. 호리호리한	slender
		thộn			바보같은. 멍청한	stupid
		thôn	村(촌)		촌. 마을	hamlet

0857	thong	thõng		1	좁고 긴병	narrow long bottle
				2	늘어지다. 흔들거리다	droop. sag
		thống	統(통) 痛(통)	1	큰 토기그릇	large porcelain vase. large earthenware bowl
				2	포괄적인	comprehensive
		thòng			(줄을) 늘어뜨리다	hang (a rope) down
		thông		1	솔. 소나무	pine (tree of the genus Pinus)
				2	통과하다	pass through
0858	thot	thót		1	꽉 조르다	tighten one's grip on
				2	한순간에. 신속하게	in a moment. in a swiftness
		thốt		1	말하다	to utter. to speak. to tell
				2	갑자기	all of a sudden. suddenly. all at once
		thọt		1	절름발이인. 절름발이의	having a one leg longer than the other
				2	빠르게	quickly
		thớt			도마	a cutting board. a chopping board
0859	thu	thư	書(서) 舒(서)	1	편지	letter (a written message)
				2	한가로운. 자유로운	inactive. idle. unoccupied. free
		thú	趣(취) 首(수) 守(수)	1	동물. 짐승. 야수	animal. beast. wild animals
				2	기분좋은. 유쾌한	pleasant
		thứ	次(차) 庶(서)	1	종류. ~종류의 물건	kind. order. rank. sort. type. category
				2	관용하다. 용서하다	forgive. excuse. pardon
		thu	收(수) 秋(추)	1	얻다. 거두다. 모으다	get. gain. gather
				2	가을	autumn. fall

		thù	殊(수) 酬(수) 讐(수)	1	원한. 적시(敵視)	a feud
				2	원망하다. 적시하다	to detest
		thụ	樹(수) 受(수) 授(수)	1	나무. 수목. (=cây)	tree. plant
				2	받다. 참다. 견디다	to receive. to bear. to endure. to suffer
		thử	署(서)	1	검사	inspection. test. check
				2	(새로운 것을) 시험하다. 실험하다 시도하다. (술을) 맛보다. (사람을) 시험해보다	to test. to try
		thủ	首(수) 手(수) 守(수) 取(취)	1	머리	head
				2	훔치다	to steal
		thừ			기진맥진하여	be utterly exhausted. be worn out
08 60	thua	thưa		1	(손윗사람에게 말씀드릴 때 사용하는 말)	to tell somebody something in a respectful way
				2	공손히 말씀 올리다	speak politely
		thùa		1	동을 많이 섞은 금	gold mixed with a lot of copper
				2	단추구멍을 내다	to buttonhole. to work buttonholes
		thừa	乘(승) 承(승)	1	남은. 나머지의	leftover
				2	과잉의	superfluous
		thua			(전쟁에서) 지다. 패하다	to lose
		thửa			경작지. 농지	farming ground
		thủa			시간. 시대. (=thuở)	time(s). period. epoch. era. age
08 61	thuan	thuận	順(순)	1	찬성하다. 동의하다	give one's assent. agreement. agree. approval. consent
				2	~에 순종하는	submissive to

		thuần	純(순) 淳(순) 醇(순)		순종적인. 다루기 쉬운	submissive. easy to handle
		thuẫn	盾(순)		방패	shield
08 62	thuat	thuật	術(술) 述(술)	1	예술	art
				2	말하다. 이야기하다. 진술하다	to speak. to talk. make a statement
08 63	thuc	thực	食(식) 蝕(식) 植(식) 實(실)	1	(단독으로 사용되지 않음) 음식	(not used exclusively) food
				2	(단독으로 사용되지 않음) 먹다	(not used exclusively) to eat
				3	실제	true. real
		thúc	促(촉) 束(속) 叔(숙)	1	삼촌	uncle
				2	압력을 가하다. 억누르다	to push. to shove. to jab
		thức	識(식) 式(식) 軾(식)	1	옷차림 모양. (=vẻ)	the appearance of one's dress
				2	잠에서 깨다. 일어나다	to wake (up)
		thục	熟(숙) 贖(속) 淑(숙)	1	글방. 학원	a private school. academy
				2	익숙해지다	get used to
08 64	thue	thuế	稅(세) 說(세) 了(료)	1	세금. 의무	tax. duty
				2	납세하다	pay one's taxes
		thuê		1	세를 얻다. 임대하다. (=mướn)	get rent. to lease
				2	고용하다	to employ. to hire
08 65	thung	thung	椿(춘)		산골짜기	a mountain valley
		thưng		1	되 (용량의 단위. 升)	a unit of measurement of volume
				2	위로 들어 올리다	lift up
		thủng		1	(비밀 등이) 누설되다	to leak (a secret, etc.)
				2	뚫린. 구멍난	perforated
		thúng			바구니	basket

		thũng		(의학) 수종. 각기. (=bệnh phù)		edema
		thùng		통. 나무통		a barrel
		thững		서두르지 않는. 느긋한		in no hurry. laid back. relaxed. carefree. easygoing
		thừng		밧줄. 노끈		rope. string. twine
		thụng		넓은. 널찍한		broad. large. spacious. extensive. roomy
0866	thuoc	thuốc	1	약		medicine. drug
			2	독살하다		to poison
		thuộc	1	소속되어 있다		to belong to
			2	알다		to know (lesson, road, etc.)
			3	가죽을 무두질하다. 햇볕에 태우다		to make tanning (leather)
		thước	1	까치		magpie
			2	자 (길이 등을 재는 도구)		ruler (measuring device). meter (measuring stick)
0867	thuong	thương	槍(창) 傷(상) 商(상) 倉(창) 滄(창)	1	창(槍)	long-handled spear
				2	사랑하다. 좋아하다	to love
		thượng	上(상) 尙(상)	1	맨 위에. 최고의	uppermost
				2	오르다	go up
		thường	常(상) 裳(상) 賞(상) 償(상)	1	보상하다	make amends
				2	보통의. 통상의	frequent. usual. ordinary. common. average
		thuổng		삽. 가래		shovel. spade
		thưởng	賞(상)	보상하다. 보답하다. (=thưởng thức)		to award
		thướng		(=thưởng)		(=thưởng)

0868	thut	thụt	1	펌프	pump
			2	(몸을) 숨기다	hide oneself
0869	thuy	thụy 睡(수)	1	죽은 사람에게 붙이는 이름	a name given to a dead person
			2	좋은	good
		thúy 翠(취)	1	(보석) 비취	jade
			2	푸르다. (=xanh biếc)	deep blue
		thủy 水(수) 始(시)	1	수은. thủy ngân의 약자	mercury. quicksilver. hydrargyrum
			2	정절있는. 절개있는. thủy chung의 약자	chasty. dependable
		thùy 垂(수) 滿(만)		둥글게 튀어나온 부분. 귓불. 엽	ear lobe. lobe
0870	thuyet	thuyết 說(설)	1	말씀. 교리	doctrine
			2	설득하다. 납득시키다	to persuade. convince
0871	ti	tí	1	극히 소량	a little bit
			2	작은. 조그만	tiny. small
		tị 己(기)	1	소량. 조금	a small quantity. a little bit
			2	질투하다	get jealous
		tì (tỳ)	1	(팔, 다리를) 의지하다. 기대다 (몸을 의지할 때는 dựa를 쓴다)	lean on (one's arms and legs) (dựa : lean on one's body)
			2	흠. 티	flaw
		tĩ		직장 (항문과 연결되는 소장의 끝부분)	(bodily organs) rectum
		tỉ		(숫자) 10억	(numeral) billion. milliard
		ti (ty) 絲(사) 司(사)		실	thread

0872	tia	tia		1	광선. (=tia sáng)	ray, beam
				2	분사하다	to spray
		tía		1	자주빛	purple
				2	자색의	purple
		tỉa		1	다듬다. 가지치기를 하다	to trim, to prune
				2	하나씩. 한사람씩	one by one
0873	tich	tịch	席(석) 籍(적) 夕(석)	1	몰수하다	to confiscate
				2	적막한	quite, lonely
		tích	昔(석) 惜(석) 跡(적) 績(적) 積(적)	1	고사(故事)	historical event, ancient event
				2	축적하다	accumulate
0874	tiec	tiếc		1	후회하다. 유감으로 생각하다. 아쉬워하다. 탄식하다	to regret, to be regretful, to lament
				2	안타까운. 유감스러운	sad, regrettable, unfortunate
		tiệc			잔치. 향연. 연석. 연회	banquet, party, dinner
0875	tiem	tiệm	店(점)	1	상점. 가게	shop, store
				2	조금씩. 차례로. (=dần dần)	little by little, gradually
		tiềm		1	삶다	to boil
				2	도자기로 만든 식기	ceramic tableware
		tiếm	損(손)		탈취하다. 찬탈하다	to usurp power, extort
		tiêm			주사를 놓다	to inject (medicine), to give a shot
0876	tien	tiền	錢(전) 前(전)	1	돈. 현금	money
				2	전의. 앞의	preceding
		tiễn	餞(전) 箭(전)	1	배웅하다. 전송하다	to see off
				2	화살	arrow

		tiện	便(편)	1	적절한	proper
				2	편리한	convenient. handy
		tiến	進(진)		나아가다. 전진하다. (tiến bộ)	advance. march forward
		tiên		1	첫(번)째의. 선(先)의	first. prior. before
				2	요정. 선녀	fairy
0877	tieng	tiếng		1	말. 언어. 소리	voice. language. sound
				2	시간	hour(s)
0878	tiep	tiệp	摺(접)		(색깔) 잘 조화되어 어울리는. 민첩한	well-matched in color. nimble
		tiếp	接(접)		접속하다. 결합하다. 연결하다. 받다. 계속하다	to join. to graft. to receive. to continue
0879	tiet	tiết	節(절) 泌(필)	1	동물의 피	animal blood
				2	분비하다. 배설하다	to secrete. to emit
				3	시기. 시간. 철	period. time. season
		tiệt			끝나다. 다하다	end. run out
0880	tieu	tiểu	小(소)	1	소변보다. 방뇨하다	to urinate. to pee
				2	작은 관. 널	a small coffin
		tiếu	笑(소)		웃다. (=cười)	to laugh. smile
		tiều			나무꾼	lumberjack. woodcutter
		tiễu			섬멸하다. 진압하다. (=trù đi. diệt đi)	annihilate. exterminate. wipe out. put under control
		tiêu		1	후추(가루)	pepper
				2	플룻. 피리	flute
				3	(돈을) 쓰다. 소비하다. (=chi tiêu)	spend (money). to spend
0881	tin	tin		1	믿다. 신뢰하다	believe
				2	뉴스. 소식. 통지	news
		tín	信		신용. 신뢰	credit. trust

0882	tinh	tình	情(정)	1	애정. 사랑. 느낌. 감정	affection. love. feeling. sentiment
				2	애정의. 사랑의	affectionate. love
		tịnh	靜(정) 淨(정)	1	깨끗한. 조용한	clean. quiet
				2	물품의 총수량을 계산하다	calulate the total amount of goods
		tỉnh	省(성) 醒(성)	1	성(행정기관으로 한국의 도 (道)에 해당됨)	province. perfecture
				2	눈 뜨다. 깨다. 의식을 되찾다. 깨닫다	be awakened (to). be awake (to). become aware (of)
		tinh	精(정) 星(성) 旌(정)	1	성(星), 별	star
				2	정액. 정자	semen. sperm
				3	총명한. 영리한	intelligent. clever. shrewd
				4	정제된. 순수한	refined. pure
		tính	性(성) 姓(성)	1	성격, 버릇, 성질, 품성	personality. habit. temper. character. nature
				2	계산하다. 셈하다	to calculate
		tĩnh	淨(정) 靜(정)	1	제단	altar
				2	고요한. 조용한	still. silent. calm. quiet. peaceful
0883	to	tố	訴(소) 遡(소) 素(소)	1	폭풍	storm
				2	원소	(cheminal) element
				3	소송하다. 고소하다	to sue
		tợ		1	닮다	to be like
				2	유사한	similar
		to		1	큰. 거대한. 커다란	big. large. great
				2	높다	high

		tơ		1	비단. 명주실	silk (the raw material, not the finished fabric). thread
				2	(치킨, 여자 등) 어린. 부드러운	(of a chicken, girl, etc.) young. tender
		tó		1	지팡이	walking stick
				2	절뚝거리는. 취한듯이 흔들거리는	limping. wobbly as a drunken man
		tỏ		1	(~에) 밝다	to know clearly
				2	빛나는. 영리한	clear. bright. shining
		tớ		1	나	I. me
				2	나의. 나 자신의	my. my own
		tổ	祖(조) 組(조)	1	선조. 조상	forefathers. ancestor
				2	조직	group. organization
		tờ			종이	sheet. paper
		tở			흩어지다	to scatter. disperse
		tộ			큰 사발. (=bát to)	large bowl
		tồ			부족하고 서툰. 어색한	clumsy. awkward
		tô		1	사발. 주발	bowl
				2	칠하다. 바르다	to apply color to
0884	toa	toa		1	철도 차량	a railroad car
				2	처방전	a prescription
		tóa			흐르다. (=túa)	to flow
		tòa		1	큰 건조물. 건물	building
				2	법정	court of law
		tỏa			퍼지다. 전개하다. 펴다	to spread
0885	toan	toan	酸(산)	1	~할 예정이다. 즉시 ~을 시도하다. 꾀하다	to intend (to). to attempt (to). to contemplate
				2	초. 식초	acid. vinegar

		toàn	全(전)	1	완전히. 전부. (=hoàn toàn)	compete. perfect
				2	모두의. 전부의. 모든	entire. whole. total
		toán	算(산)		계산	mathematics. math(s)
08 86	toc	tốc	速(속)	1	걷어올리다	roll up
				2	급히. 빨리	in a hurry. quick
		tóc			머리카락	headhair
		tộc	族(족)		일족. 가족. 종족	family. clan. tribe
08 87	toi	tơi		1	비옷. (=áo tơi)	raincoat
				2	흩어 날리다. 흩뿌리다	to scatter
		tối		1	밤. 저녁 (오후 6시경부터 오후 8시경까지)	the duration from the late evening to the early night
				2	어두운. 깜깜한. 침울한	dark
		toi		1	(동물이) 페스트에 걸려 죽다	(of domestic animals) to die in epidemic. to die
				2	쓸모없는. 무익한	to be lost. to go. to waste
		tới		1	도착하다. 오다. 닿다	to arrive (at)
				2	다음의	next
		tội	罪(죄)	1	죄. 과오. 과실. 죄과	crime. offense. felony. fault. guilt. sin. delinquency
				2	가련한. 가슴 아픈. (=đáng thương)	pitiful. pitiable. heartbreaking
		tói			밧줄	rope
		tòi			밖으로 뻗쳐 나오다	stick out
		tỏi			(식물) 마늘	garlic
		tời			도르래	a pulley
		tồi			보잘것 없는. 하찮은. 안 좋은. 뒤지는	poor. bad. mediocre
		tôi		1	나. 나는. 내가	I
				2	나에게. 나를	me

0888	tom	tom		1	노래가락에 어우러진 대북소리	the drumming of a song
				2	모으다	gather up
		tõm			물건이 수면으로 떨어지는 소리. (=tòm)	the sound of objects falling to the surface of the water
		tòm			(=tõm)	(=tõm)
		tóm			잡다. 붙들다.	to grab (by hands). to catch. to apprehend
		tởm			구역질나는. 역겨운	gross. disgusting
		tôm			새우	shrimp. prawn
0889	ton	tốn	遜(손) 巽(손)	1	소비하다	to pay for. to spend. to cost. to consume
				2	값비싼. 소비하는	expensive. consuming
		tợn		1	대담한. 굉장한. 사나운	bold. mighty
				2	강하게. 심하게	strongly. badly
		tồn	存(존)		존재하다. (=còn lại)	to exist
		tởn			놀라다. (=khiếp sợ)	frightened
		tổn	損(손)		소비하다	to pay for. to spend. to cost. to consume
		tôn		1	철판	iron plate
				2	존경하다. 높이 받들다	respect (for). respect (to)
0890	tong	tổng	總(총)	1	총괄하다	take charge of
				2	모든. 총	all. total. a sum
		tong			완전히 잃다	be completely lost
		tòng	從(종)		(남편을) 따르다. (=tòng phu)	follow one's husband
		tỏng			분명한. 명확한	distinct. plain. clear
		tọng			채우다. 채워넣다	fill up. fill in
		tống	送(송)		배웅하다	see off

		tông	1	가계. 혈통	family line. pedigree. lineage.
			2	(색깔) 톤. (소리) 톤	(color) tone. (sound) tone
			3	세게 부딪히다	to crash into
08 91	top	tóp	1	오그라들다. 줄어들다	shrink. shrivel
			2	지방을 뺀. (=tóp mỡ)	reduce fat
		tợp	1	(한 입의) 양	(a bite's) amount
			2	(한 번에) 마셔버리다. (=tợp một hơi)	drink at a gulp
		tốp	1	무리. 집단	group. crowd. party. bunch
			2	(엔진) 정지시키다	stop an engine
			3	어떤 것의 상위 번호를 나타내다	indicates a top number of something
		tớp	1	덤벼들어 물다. (=táp)	pounce and bite
			2	당장에. (=ngay lập)	at once
		tọp		쇠약하다. 병약해지다. 야위어지다. (=gầy tọp)	become weak. become infirm. grow thin
08 92	tot	tốt	1	(장기의) 졸(卒)	(xiangqi) soldier
			2	좋은. 훌륭한. 고급의	good
		tót		깡충 높게	to jump
		tột		정점	peak. the top
		tọt		빨리. 재빨리	quick. quickly. rapidly. fast
08 93	tra	trả	1	물총새 (chim sả)	a water gunbird
			2	돌려주다. 돈을 내다	to return. to give back. to pay
		tra	查(사)	검사하다	to investigate. to examine. to inspect
		trã		큰 냄비	a large pot
		trá	詐(사)	(금, 은 등을) 씻다	to wash (gold, silver, etc.)

		trà	茶(차)	차. (=nước trà, chè)	tea
0894	trach	trách	責(책)	1 작은 냄비	a small pot
				2 비난하다. 책망하다	give a reproach
		trạch	宅(택) 澤(택) 擇(택)	저택	mansion. residence
0895	trai	trái	債(채)	1 과일	fruit
				2 어기다. 이치에 맞지않는. 편협한	(rare) morally wrong. unreasonable. illogical
				3 왼쪽	left (side. direction)
		trại	寨(채)	병사(兵舍) 야영지. 막사	a barrack
		trải		1 카누(배)	canoe
				2 경험하다	to have experienced. to have gone through
		trai		소년. 남자	boy. male
		trài		지붕을 이다. (=lợp nhà)	roof. tile. thatch. shingle
0896	tram	trăm		1 100. 백	hundred. 100
				2 (빨리) 말하다	speak (quickly)
		trầm	沈(심)	1 침향	an aloeswood
				2 가라앉다. 침하하다. 저하하다	to sink (into). to plunge (into)
		trám		1 감람나무	canarium album (tree)
				2 막다. 메우다. (통로, 구멍 따위를) 폐쇄하다	to fill. shut (down)
		tràm		(식물) 벌레가 먹다	worms eat
		trắm		1 숨기다	to hide
				2 싹이 돋지 않는	not sprouting
		trâm		비녀	hairpin
		trẫm	朕(짐)	짐 (황제의 자칭)	I. me (the emperor's call himself)

		trăm			(증류기의) 작은 구멍. (=ống trăm)		a small hole in the distiller
		trảm	斬(참)		참수하다. (=chém đầu)		to behead
		trạm	站(참)		중계소. 정류장		stop. station
		trăm			(방언) 귀걸이		(dialect) earrings
08 97	tran	tràn		1	체. 조리		sieve. strainer
				2	넘치다		to overflow. to run over the edge
		trần		1	천장		ceiling
				2	드러내다		to exhibit. to display
		trân	珍(진)	1	(멍석을 짜기 위한) 새끼줄. (=trân chiếu)		a straw rope for making a straw mat
				2	얼굴이 두꺼운. 뻔뻔스러운.		thick-skinned. shameless
		trấn	鎭(진)	1	진 (현재의 행정기관에 상당한다)		old administrative agency
				2	막다. 차단하다		keep out. block off
		tran			대(垈). 단(壇). (=trạn)		an altar
		trán			이마		forehead
		trăn			큰 뱀. 보아뱀(열대 기후에 사는 독이 없는 큰 뱀)		a python. a non-venomous constricting snake
		trắn			(월경이) 없는		temporarily menstrual-free
		trận	陳(진)		전형. 싸움. 전쟁. 전투		a battle formation. a battle. a match
		trắn			살짝 피하다(빠져나가다)		get away from
		trạn			대(垈). 단(壇). (=tran)		an altar
08 98	tranh	tranh	爭(쟁)	1	그림. 족자		painting. picture
				2	경쟁하다. 싸우다		to compete. to fight for
		tránh			옆으로 비키다		to stay out of the way
		trành			한쪽으로 기울다		lean to one side

		trạnh			바다 거북이	sea turtle
0899	trang	trang	裝(장)	1	페이지	page
				2	재능, 덕이 있는 사람 앞에 붙이는 말	a word that comes before a person's name who has talent and virtue
		trắng		1	비게 하다	empty
				2	흰. 새하얀. 하얗게 된	white
		tràng	長(장)	1	연속음. (=trường)	continuous sound
				2	옆으로 빗나가다	miss to the side
		tráng		1	장정	strong young man
				2	헹구다	to rinse. to dip in water
		trạng	狀(상)	1	원상. (=trạng nguyên)	original state
				2	숙련된. 뛰어난	master. expert
		trăng			달	the Moon
		trảng			불모지. 황무지	wasteland. wild land. wilderness. barren land
0900	trao	trao			주다	to pass (to). to hand over (to)
		trào	朝(조) 潮(조)		넘치다. (=triều)	to overflow. to brim over
		tráo			(진짜를 가짜로) 바꿔치기 하다	convert the real thing into a fake (to deceive)
0901	trap	tráp			(보석. 귀중품을 넣는) 작은 상자	casket
		trập			늘어져 내리다	droop down
0902	trat	trát		1	근거. 이유(보증이 되는 것)	basis. grounds
				2	~을 바르다	to plaster. to coat. to smear
		trật		1	계급. 등급. (=thứ bậc)	class. stratum. rank. rating
				2	빗나가다. 실패하다	be missed (a target). be incorrect. be dislocated

		trắt		깨물어 부수다. (=cắn trắt)	break by biting
		trạt		무성한	thick. overgrown
09 03	trau	trau		(매끄럽게) 갈다	grind (smooth)
		trấu	1	곁겨. 왕겨	chaff. rice husks
			2	매우 많은	very many
		trâu		물소	water buffalo
		trầu		(식물) 구장(후추나무과)	betel
09 04	tre	trẽ	1	교살. 교수형	death by hanging
			2	늦게	late
		tre		(식물) 대. 대나무. 죽순	bamboo. a bamboo shoot
		trẻ		젊은. 어린. 연소한	young. a child. children in general
		trề		뾰로통하다	get sulky
09 05	tren	trẽn		뻔뻔한. 건방진	shameless. saucy
		trên	1	~의 위에. ~에	on
			2	(범위) ~이상. ~을 넘어서	upper. higher. superior
09 06	treo	treo	1	(법률) 집행유예. 일시적 경감	suspended sentence
			2	걸다	to hang
		trèo		기어오르다. (=leo)	to climb
		tréo		꼬다. 교차하다	cross
		trẹo		탈구하다	dislocate
09 07	treu	trệu	1	제거하다. 생략하다	to remove. to omit. drop. skip. leave (sth) out
			2	~을 탈구한	dislocated from~
		trếu		우스꽝스러운. 익살맞은	ridiculous. ludicrous. funny
		trêu		놀리다. 괴롭히다. 귀찮게 하다	to tease. to poke fun

09 08	tri	trì	池(지) 持(지)	1	연못. (=ao)	pond
				2	유지하다. (=giữ)	keep up
		tri	知(지)		알다. (=biết)	to know
		trĩ			꿩. (=chim trĩ, bệnh trĩ)	pheasant
		trí	智(지)		지능. 지성. 총명	mind. clever
		trị	治(치)		고치다. 치료하다	to treat medically. to cure
09 09	trich	trích	摘(적) 謫(적)	1	정어리의 일종	a kind of sardine
				2	적출하다. 발췌하다. 뽑아내다. 인용하다	to remove. extract. pluck out. to quote
		trịch			무겁다	heavy
09 10	trien	triền		1	유역. (=triền núi)	basin (of river). slope (of mountain)
				2	경사지다. 비탈지다	slant. slope. incline
		triện			도장	seal. stamp
		triển	展(전)		넓어지다. 늘이다	widen. extend
09 11	trieu	triệu	兆(조) 召(소)	1	백만. 1,000,000	million
				2	부르다. 소환하다	call in. summon up
				3	징조	an omen
		triều	朝(조) 潮(조)		조정(朝廷). 궁중. 밀물	royal court. tide
09 12	trinh	trinh	貞(정)		순결한. 성적으로 순결한	virgin. chaste
		trình	呈(정)		(표 등을) 보이다. 제시하다	to submit. to show. to present. to report
		trình			잘 달라붙는. 끈적끈적한. (고무, 아교 등) 접착성의	glued to. sticky. adhesive
09 13	triu	triu			(테니스에서) 공을 강타하다. 때리다. 치다	(tennis) drive. smashing
		trĩu			무거워서 구부러짐	bending. curling down (due to having too much weight on it)

		tríu		'붙다'의 강조어	stick tight
09 14	tro	tro	1	재	ash (solid remains of a fire)
			2	회색의	grayish
		trò		생도(生徒). học trò의 약어. 희극. 오락 게임. 익살 맞음	pupil. comedy. amusement. play. game. facetiousness
		trơ		움직이지 않는. 변경할 수 없는. 수치를 모르는	motionless. unchangeable. shameless. brazen
		trở		돌아오다(가다)	to turn. to change
		trở		갑자기. 돌연. (=bất thình lình)	all of a sudden. suddenly. abruptly. all at once
		trộ		겁주다	to scare off
		trợ	助(조)	돕다. (=giúp)	to help
		trọ		임시 머물러 살다. 체재하다. 숙소를 정하다	to stay overnight (at another place). to lodge
		trố		감시하다	to monitor
		trớ		길을 잃다. (=đi lạc đường)	get lost
		trổ		(=trỗ)	to flower. to bloom. widen
		trỗ		꽃이 피다. 넓히다. 확대하다	to flower. to bloom. widen
		trỏ		가리키다. (=tỏ ra)	to point
		trõ		칭찬하다. (=trầm trồ)	to compliment. to praise. credit. (formal) commend
09 15	troc	trốc	1	정상. 윗쪽. 상부	top. summit. the upper side. the upper part. a head
			2	벗기다	strip off. take off
		tróc		탈락하다. (칠 등이) 벗겨지다	to scale off. to flake off
		trọc		머리카락이 없는. 대머리인	bald

09 16	trom	trộm		1	좀도둑	thief
				2	훔치다	to steal. to burgle
		trõm			움푹 들어간	recessed
		trờm			덮혀지다	covered
09 17	trong	trộng		1	다소 큰	rather large
				2	씹지 않고	without chewing
		trọng	重(중)	1	소중히 여기다. 중요시하다	to cherish. attach importance to
				2	무거운	heavy
		trống		1	태고(太鼓). 북	(music) drum
				2	비어있는	empty. (of a bird) male
		trong			~안에	in. inside. within
		tróng			족쇄. (=cái cùm chân)	a shackle
		tròng			눈동자. 안구	iris. pupil (of the eye)
		trỏng			(방언. 구어) 그안	in there. inside that place
		trồng			심다. 재배하다	to plant
		trổng			(자치기 놀이) 짧은 막대기. 자	a short stick
		trông		1	보다. 바라보다	to look at
				2	보살피다. 돌보다	to watch. to look after
09 18	tru	trừ	除(제)	1	(수) 빼다. 없애다. 제외하다	to eliminate. to exclude. to substract
				2	~이외의	~other than
		trứ	著(저)	1	저술하다	write a book
				2	유명한. 저명한	famous. distinguished
		tru	誅(주)		(개, 늑대 따위가) 울다. 없애다	(of an animal) to howl. to eliminate
		trú	駐(주) 住(주)		주류하다. 잠시 체재하다	to stay. to reside

		trù	呪(주) 籌(주)		주문을 외다	chant a spell
		trủ	紬(주)		견(실크)	silk
		trụ	柱(주) 胄(주)		기둥. (=cột)	pillar
		trữ			돈. 금액	money. amount (of money)
		trữ	貯(저)		저금하다. 저장하다. (=chứa)	store (up)
09 19	trua	trưa		1	정오. 낮. 한낮의	noon. midday
				2	늦게	late
		trụa			상처	wound
09 20	truc	trúc	竹(죽)	1	대나무. (=cây tre)	bamboo
				2	쓰러지다. (=ngả xuống)	fall down. trumble down
		trực	直(직)	1	정직한	honest
				2	숙직. trực nhật의 약자	a night duty. Short for trực nhật
		trục	軸(축) 逐(축)	1	(차바퀴의) 굴대. 축	axle. axis
				2	들어올리다	to lift (up)
09 21	trung	trùng	蟲(충) 重(중)	1	일치하는. ~와 동시에 일어나는	to coincide (with something in time)
				2	겹치다. 거듭되다	overlap. be repeated
				3	벌레	insect. bug
		trung	忠(충) 中(중)	1	충성	loyalty
				2	충성스러운	loyal
				3	가운데	middle
		trúng	中(중)	1	명중하다. 맞다. 이득을 보다	to hit (a target). to win. to gain
				2	옳은	right. proper
		trũng			오목한	be lower than the surrounding earth's surface

		trưng		징수하다. 징발하다		to collect. requisition
		trụng		삶다		to dip in boiling water. to scald
		trứng		달걀. (=trứng gà)		egg
		trừng		노려보다. (=trừng mắt)		glare (at). stare (at)
09 22	truoc	trước		이전에		before (earlier than in time)
09 23	truong	trương	章(장)	1	책장. (=trang)	page of a book
				2	(다시) 빌려주다	lend back
		trướng	帳(장)	1	막. 커튼	curtain
				2	부풀다	inflate. to swell
		trường	場(장) 長(장) 腸(장)	1	학교. trường học의 약자. 넓고 트인 장소	school. a domain. an area. a field
				2	긴	long
		trưởng		1	(장) 긴	long
				2	두목. 장	head. leader
		truồng			알몸의. 나체의	without anything covering the genitals. pantslessly
		trượng	丈(장)		길이	a unit of length. (dated) stick. cane. staff. rod
09 24	truu	trừu			면양(綿羊). (=cừu)	sheep
09 25	truyen	truyện	傳(전)		이야기. 소설	story
		truyền	傳(전)		전하다	to communicate. to transmit. to pass down
09 26	tu	tư	私(사) 思(사) 司(사) 資(자) 滋(자)	1	이. 이것	this
				2	재능	talent
				3	4의. 네번째의	four. fourth

		tự	自(자) 字(자) 似(사) 寺(사) 序(서) 嗣(사)	1	절(寺)	buddhist temple
				2	스스로	oneself
		từ	慈(자) 辭(사) 詞(사) 磁(자) 祠(사) 徐(서)	1	품사. 단어	word
				2	사양하다. 거절하다	to refuse. decline. reject.
				3	~부터	from. since
		tử	死(사) 子(자) 紫(자) 仔(자)	1	아들	child. son
				2	죽다	to die
		tụ	聚(취)	1	모으다. 집합시키다	gather. bring together
				2	(전기를) 응축시키다	condense electricity
		tu	修(수) 羞(수) 須(수)		(종교계에) 투신하다. 수도하다	enter the religious world. practice asceticism
		tù	囚(수)		죄수	prisoner. convict. jailbird
		tủ			찬장. 캐비넷. 옷장	cabinet. cupboard
		tứ	四(사) 思(사)		사륜마차	a four-wheel carriage
09 27	tua	tưa		1	아구창(病). (=tưa lưỡi)	thrush. aphtha
				2	잡아찢다	tear apart
		tựa		1	머리말. 서문	preface. foreword
				2	의지하다. 기대다	to lean (on). to rely (on). to recline (on)
		tua			테두리. 장식	border. decoration
		túa			흐르다	flow through
		tủa			(불꽃. 섬광이) 날다. 한꺼번에 밀려들다	sparkle, flash. rush in at once
		tứa			쏟아져 나오다. 우유를 토하다	to pour out. to throw up the milk

09 28	tuan	tuần	旬(순) 訓(훈) 巡(순)	1	(10일 또는 일주일) 기간	week
				2	순찰하다	to patrol
		tuân	遵(준)		(법. 규칙을) 따르다. 복종하다. 명령에 따르다	follow (the law, rules, etc.). obey. obey an order
		tuẫn	殉(순) 徇(순)		희생하다. 순교하다	make a sacrifice. have a martyrdom
		tuấn	俊(준) 駿(준)		재주가 뛰어난	talented
09 29	tuc	tức	即(즉) 息(식)	1	이식(利息). 이자	interest
				2	압박을 느끼다.	feel pressure
		túc	足(족) 宿(숙)	1	발. (=chân)	foot
				2	가난한 사람을 구제하다	relieve the poor
		tục	俗(속) 續(속)		세속의. 현세의	common. mundane. worldly
09 30	tue	tuế	歲(세)		해 년(年). (=tuổi năm)	year of age
		tuệ	慧(혜) 彗(혜)		영리한. 현명한	smart. wise
09 31	tui	tui			단련하다. (철) 연마하다.	train. sharpen iron
		tụi		1	무리	group (of people). party
				2	패거리	gang
		túi			주머니	bag
		tủi			개탄하다. 한탄하다	to deplore. to lament. to grieve. to self-pity
09 32	tum	tum			차바퀴의 축을 받치는 부분	the part that supports the axle of a car
		túm		1	손 안에 잡아쥐다. 붙잡다	grab (by hands). to catch
				2	한줌. 한손의 분량	a handful
		tũm			[의성어] 물건이 물에 빠질 때 나는 소리	[onomatopoeia] the sound of a thing falling into the water
		tùm			(=tũm)	(=tũm)

		tụm		한자리에 모이다	gather in one place
		tủm		입 벌리지 않고 킥킥거리며 웃다. (=tủm tỉm)	giggle without opening one's mouth
09 33	tung	tung	縱(종)	1	던지다	toss. throw
				2	종적. 흔적	whereabouts. trace
		tùng	松(송) 從(종)	1	소나무. 전나무. (=cây thông)	pine. fir tree
				2	북소리	the pounding sound of a drum
		từng	層(층)	1	낱개	every. each
				2	(일정한) 양	(a certain) quantity. amount
		tụng	誦(송) 訟(송) 頌(송)	1	암송하다. 염불을 외다. 성가를 부르다	recite. sing a hymn
				2	곧바르지 않고 축 늘어진	droopy
		tưng			(공) 튀게 하다	to rebound
		túng			부족한. 모자란	insufficient. lack
09 34	tuoi	tươi		1	신선한	fresh
				2	날것이	raw
		tuổi			나이. 연령. 세	age. (of age) year
		tuồi			처지다. (=tụt xuống)	to droop
		tưới			흠뻑 적시다. 끼얹다	to water (plants)
09 35	tuong	tường	墻(장) 詳(상)	1	벽. 담. 성벽(墻)	a wall
				2	자세한. 상세한(詳)	detailed
		tương	相(상) 醬(장)	1	된장. 장	a generic term meaning "sauce"
				2	(함부로) 사용하다	use recklessly
		tướng	相(상) 將(장)	1	장군(將)	general
				2	보통 이상인	aboce average
		tuồng			베트남의 전통 고전극	traditional Vietnamese classical play

		tượng	像(상) 象(상)	1	형상. 조상(彫像). 조각상	statue
				2	코끼리. (=con voi)	(xiangqi) elephant
		tưởng	想(상) 獎(장)		생각하다. 간주하다. 추측하다. 믿다	to think that. to deem
0936	tuot	tuốt		1	제거하다. 벗기다. 떼어 내다	to detach
				2	전부. (=tất cả)	all
		tuột		1	미끌어져 떨어지다	to slip. to slip out of alignment. to come off. to slide
				2	단숨에	at a gulp
0937	tuy	tuy			~에도 불구하고. 비록 ~일지라도. (tuy~nhưng의 구문형식)	although. though
		tùy	隨(수)		tuỳ의 대체	alternative spelling of tuỳ
				1	의지하다. 믿다	lean (on/against). depend (up) on. rely on
				2	~에 따라서. (=phụ thuộc vào. theo. căn cứ)	according to~. to follow
		túy	醉(취)		순수한	pure. purity
		tủy	髓(수)		tuỷ의 대체 뼈(骨). 골수	alternative spelling of tuỷ bone. bone marrow
		tụy			tuy.의 대체 췌장. (=tụy tạng)	alternative spelling of tuy. pancreas
		tuy.	膵(췌)		췌장. (=tụy tạng)	pancreas
		tuỳ			~을 따르다	to follow. to be up to
		tuỷ			골수	marrow (of bone)
0938	tuyen	tuyền	泉(천)	1	샘	(water) spring
				2	단지. 오로지	just. only. simply. merely
		tuyển	選(선)		선택하다. 고르다. (=kén chọn)	choose. select
		tuyến	腺(선) 線(선)		선. 샘	line. gland

		tuyên	宣(선)		선언하다	to declare, to proclaim
09 39	tuyet	tuyệt	絶(절)	1	자르다	to cut off, to exhaust, to use up
				2	절묘한	nice, great, wonderful, terrific, excellent, perfect
				3	엄청나게, 뛰어나게	immersely, extremely (good), exceptionally
		tuyết	雪(설)		눈	snow
09 40	ty	tỷ (tỉ)			(숫자) 10억	(numeral) billion, milliard
		ty			12지중 여섯번째, 뱀	snake (of 12 Chinese zodiacs)
		tý (tí)			12지중 첫번째, 쥐	mouse (of 12 Chinese zodiacs)
09 41	u	ù		1	이명이 있는	having tinnitus
				2	빨리, 단숨에	quick, at a gulp
		u	幽(유)	1	어머니	mother, mom
				2	어둡다 (=tối)	dark
		ú		1	살찐, 뚱뚱한	fat
				2	아주 많이	(very) much
		ủ		1	따뜻하게 하다	warm up
				2	시무룩한	sullen, gloomy
		ư			문장 끝에 붙여서 의문을 나타내는 말	a question mark at the end of a sentence
		ứ			물이 고이다	to be stagnant (water)
		ừ			(대답) 응! 아니! (동등 위치나 손아랫사람에게)	yeah, nope
		ụ			(공사판 따위에서) 흙을 쌓아 올림. (=mô đất cao)	mound

09 42	ua	ùa		1	쇄도하다. 밀려오다. 많은 사람들이 밀려 들어오다	pour in. rush. flood in
				2	황급히	on the double. hurriedly
		ứa		1	흘러 넘치다. 솟아나오다	to ooze
				2	대단히 많은. 풍부한	plentiful. rich (in). ample. (formal) abundant
		úa			시들다	to wither
		ưa			좋아하다. 애호하다	to like. to be fond of
		ủa			놀람을 나타내는 소리. (=uở)	a sound of surprise
		ụa			토하다. 토해내다. (=nôn mửa)	to vomit. bring up. throw up. puke up. spew up
		ựa			토하다. 게우다	to vomit. bring up
09 43	uan	uẩn	蚊(문)	1	축적하다	to accumulate
				2	깊이 숨겨진	deep hidden
09 44	uat	uất		1	화내다	get angry
				2	게으름 피우지 않고	without laziness
09 45	ue	uế	穢(예)		더러운. 불결한. 부정한. (=nhơ bẩn)	dirty. filthy. mucky. dishonesty. uncleanly
09 46	ui	úi		1	(물고기가) 뜨다	(fish) float
				2	오! 아이쿠! 어머나! (=ối)	an expression of surprise. Oh!
		ũi			(돼지가) 코를 들이대고 파다	(a pig) digs with its nose
		ủi			다림질하다	to iron. to press (clothing)
09 47	um	um			(초목 등이) 무성한. 번성. 울창한	lush. thick. overgrown. heavily wooded
		ùm		1	(물건이) 물위로 떨어지는 소리	the sound of things falling on the water
				2	(어린아이) 밥을 먹다	(a child) eats a meal
		úm			속이다. 우롱하다	to deceive. make a fool of

09 48	ung	ủng		1	(옛 무관들의) 승마구두	boot
				2	난숙(爛熟)한. 너무 익어서 냄새가 나는	be overripen
		ung	癰(옹)	1	악성종기. 부스럼	malignant tumor. boil.
				2	썩은	rotten. addled
		ưng	應(응) 鷹(응)	1	매	(zoology) hawk
				2	동의하다. 응하다	to like and accept
		ứng	應(응)	1	대응하다	respond to
				2	상응의. 어울리는. tương ứng 의 약자	corresponding
		úng			(과일 등이) 상한	spoiled (fruit, etc)
		ửng			(얼굴에) 홍조를 띠다	(of cheeks) to blush (to become red)
09 49	uoc	ước	約(약)	1	바라다. 희망하다. 열망하다	to wish
				2	대략. 추정치. 근사치인	estimate. approximate
09 50	uon	ươn		1	(생선 등이) 상하다	(fish, etc.) go bad
				2	병색이 나는. 기분이 언짢은. 몸상태가 좋지않은. (=ươn mình)	to feel sick. in bad shape
		uốn			구부러지다. 구부리다	to bend. to curl. to curve
		ưỡn			(몸을) 벌리다. 내밀다	spread oneself out. lean out
		ườn			펼치다. 쭉 뻗다	spread out. stretch out
09 51	uong	ương	央(앙) 殃(앙) 鴦(앙)	1	어린 묘목	young seedling
				2	모종을 심다	plant seedlings
		uống			마시다	to drink
		uổng	枉(왕)		헛된. 무익한	vain. useless
		ưởng			메아리가 들리는	echoing

09 52	uot	ướt		1	젖은	wet
				2	젖다	get wet
09 53	up	úp		1	가리다. 덮다	cover up. cover (sth with sth)
				2	상승하다. 뒤집다	to upturn. to turn over
		ụp			(순서, 방향 등을) 뒤집어 놓다. 뒤집히다. 전복시키다. (=đổ ụp)	turn upside down. turn inside out. flip over. subvert
09 54	uu	ưu	優(우) 憂(우)	1	장점. ưu điểm의 약어	advantage. strength. merit. strong point. virtue
				2	우수한	excellent. superb. outstanding
09 55	uy	uy	威(위)		권위. 위신. 권한. 위력. (=oai)	authority. prestige. dignity. power. force. might
		úy	尉(위)		위관	officer. company grade officer
		ủy	委(위)		위탁하다. 맡기다	leave. entrust.
09 56	uyen	uyển	婉(완) 宛(완)	1	정원	garden
				2	유연한	flexible
09 57	va	và		1	(찰싹) 때리다	to slap
				2	게다가. 더욱이. (=và chăng)	besides. again
		vá		1	(옷, 천을) 깁다. 수선하다	to sew. to mend (to repair a tear in clothing)
				2	반점이 있는. 얼룩덜룩한	speckled
		va		1	그. 그녀	he. she
				2	맞부딪치다. (=va phải)	to bump into (something)
		vã		1	(땀에) 흠뻑 젖다. 적시다	be dripping (with sweat). get wet
				2	두서없이	discursively. incoherently
		và		1	(젓가락으로) 긁어먹다	to use a pair of chopsticks to shovel rice from a rice bowl to one's mouth
				2	~와. ~과. ~및	and

		vạ	1	재앙. 재난	disaster. misfortune. calamity
			2	더 쌓아올리다. 더 북돋우다	pile up. encourage more
0958	vac	vạc	1	큰 솥. (세발달린) 무쇠솥	a large caldron. three-legged iron caldron
			2	새기다. 조각하다. 가늘게 깎아내다	to carve
		vặc	1	욕을 하다. 싸우다	to curse. to fight
			2	밝은. (=sáng vặc)	bright
		vác		어깨에 지다	to carry (on shoulder)
0959	vach	vạch	1	분리하다. 열다	to separate. to open up
			2	선을 긋다	to make a line. to draw. to outline
		vách		벽. (=vách ngăn)	wall
0960	vai	vai	1	어깨	shoulder
			2	계급. 지위	rank. status
			3	부문. 역할. 임무	part. role
		vãi	1	여자 수도승	a female monk
			2	어지럽게 쏟아붓다. 흩뿌리다	to spill (something) all over. to strew. to broadcast (of rice, seeds, etc.) to be spilled all over. to be scattered
			3	(불법적으로) 배설하다. 내뱉다. (우연히) 소변이나 오줌을 누다	to excrete (involuntarily). to let out. to urinate or pee (by accident)
		vái		기도하다. 손을 모아 탄원하다	to pray. to beg to gods, spirits, deities or ancestors
		vài		몇몇의. 두셋의	some. approximately two or three
		vại		큰 항아리. 큰 컵	a large jar. a big cup
		vải		옷감. 천	cloth. fabric

0961	van	van		1	빌다. 간청하다	to beg
				2	(댄스) 왈츠	waltz
		vẩn		1	탁한. 흐린	turbid. cloudy
				2	파문을 일으키다	cause a stir
		vàn		1	만(萬). vạn의 변한음(音)	ten thousand. myriad
				2	(논) 약간 높은 지대에 있는	(a rice paddy) on a slightly high ground
		văn	晚(만) 挽(만) 娩(만)	1	(거의) 마치다. 종료하다	(almost) finish. to terminate
				2	저녁때. 해질녘	at that time of the evening. at dusk
		văn	文(문) 紋(문) 汶(문) 問(문)	1	문학. Văn học의 약어	literature. letters. culture. civilization
				2	감다. 말다	wind up. roll up
		vần	韻(운)	1	음절	syllable
				2	운을 달다. 시를 짓다	rhyme
		vận	運(운)	1	운. 운명	luck. fortune
				2	입다	to wear (clothes)
		vằn		1	줄(무늬)이 있는	striped
				2	(화가 나서) 얼굴이 붉어지다	to blush (with anger)
		vẫn	殞(운) 吻(문) 隕(운)	1	여전히. 아직	still. yet
				2	목을 베다	behead
		ván			판자. 널판지	a plank (long, broad and thick piece of timber)
		vân	云(운) 雲(운) 步(보)		구름. (=mây)	cloud
		vạn			만(萬). (=mười nghìn)	ten thousand. myriad
		vấn	問(문) 紋(문)		묻다. 물어보다. (=hỏi)	to ask
		vắn			짧은. (=ngắn)	short

		vặn			비틀다	to twist
09 62	vang	vang		1	포도주	short for rượu vang. wine
				2	울려퍼지다	to echo. to resound
		văng		1	갑자기 빠르게 내던지다	to throw out suddenly and swiftly
				2	대나무 받침대	bamboo pedestal
		váng		1	(기름, 우유 위에 생기는) 얇은 피막	a thin film (of oil, forming on milk)
				2	현기증이 나는	giddy
		vàng		1	금. 황금	gold
				2	황색의	yellow
		vâng		1	따르다. 복종하다	follow. to obey
				2	동의. 승락의 대답. 예 (대답하는 말)	yes
		vẳng		1	(뿔 따위로) 찌르다	stab sb (with a horn or something)
				2	낫의 일종으로 벼를 벨때 쓴다	a kind of sickle used to cut rice
		vãng	往(왕)		가다. 지나가다. (=đi. qua)	go. pass (by). go by
		vẳng			울려퍼지다	to resonate
		vạng			황혼	twilight. dusk
		vắng			인적이 드문. 황량한. 적막한. 아무도 없는	deserted. desolate. absent
		vầng			후광	halo
09 63	vanh	vanh			(가위로) 자르다	to cut (with scissors)
		vành		1	꽃부리. 화관	corolla
				2	(손으로) 원을 그리다	draw a circle (with one's hands)
		vánh			빠르게	quickly
		vảnh			올리다. 세우다. (=vểnh)	raise. lift. put up. stand. pull up. erect. make sth stand

		vạnh		둥근	round
0964	vao	vào		들어가다(오다). 가입하다	to enter. to become a member of. to join
0965	vat	vát	1	(배가) 순풍을 타고 가다	(a ship) goes with a fair wind
			2	(전기) 와트	watt
		vắt	1	거머리. 산(山)거머리	leech
			2	(빨래를) 짜다	to wring (clothes)
			3	(확장) 쥐어짜다 (과일 한 조각으로 즙을 짜는 것)	(by extension) to squeeze (a piece of fruit to get juice out of it)
		vặt	1	적은. 하찮은. 사소한. 잡다한	trifling. petty. odd. miscellaneous
			2	쥐어 뜯다. 뽑다. 벗기다	to pluck (feathers). to strip
		vạt		(비스듬하게) 자르다. 날카롭게 하다	cut obliquely. sharpen
		vật	物(물) 勿(물)	1	물건	thing. object
				2	맞붙어 넘겨뜨리다. 씨름하다	to wrestle
		vất		1	던지다. (=vứt)	to throw
				2	매우 힘든. 곤란한. 괴로운. vất và의 약어. 수고하다	very hard. in distress. take the trouble (to do)
0966	vay	vay	1	빌리다. 차용하다	to borrow
			2	문장끝에 붙여서 의문이나 아쉬움의 뜻을 나타내는 말	a word attached to the end of a text to indicate a question or regret
		váy	1	스커트. 치마	skirt (women's garment)
			2	귀를 후비다. (=váy tai)	pick one's ears
		vày	1	(옷감짜는) 기계. 방직기	(clothing) machine. a textile machine
			2	헝클어지다. 구기다	make a mess of. crumple
		vây	1	지느러미	(anatomy) fin
			2	포위하다. 에워싸다	to encircle

		vầy	1	모이다		to gather
			2	(=vậy)		(=vậy)
		vảy	1	(물고기와 파충류의) 비늘		scale (of fish and reptiles)
			2	뿌리다. 살포하다		sprinkle (sth on/over sth). distribute. spray
		vấy	1	얼룩진. 더러워진		smeared. stained. spotted. dirty. get dirty
			2	잘못을 남에게 전가하다		pass the blame on to a person
		vạy		멍에. 굴레		yoke. bridle
		vãy		움직이다. 흔들리다		to move. to be shaken
		vẫy		흔들리다. 손짓하다		(of hand, tail and flag) to wave
		vẩy		물고기 비늘		fish scales
		vậy		그와 같이. 이와 같이. ~처럼		so. thus. like that
0967	ve	ve	1	매미		cicada
			2	장난치다. 희롱하다		play jokes. make fun of
		vè	1	풍자시. 풍자민요		a satirical poetry. satirical folk song
			2	접안하다		come alongside the pier
		về	1	돌아오다. 돌아가다		to return. to come back
			2	~에 관하여		about. on
		vé		표		ticket
		vế		넓적다리. 허벅지		thigh
		vẻ		모양 (모습, 태도, 기색 등의)		look. appearance
		vẽ		그리다		to draw. to paint
		vệ	衛(위)	지키다		to guard
		vê		말다		to roll

09 68	ven	ven		가장자리	shore. bank. side
		vẹn	1	완전한	to be complete. to be intact. to be whole
			2	실천하다. 완수하다	put into practice. carry through. fulfill
		vén		끌어올리다. 걷어올리다	to roll up. to lift up. to tuck up
		vện		얼룩이 있는. 주름진	brindled
09 69	venh	vểnh		위로 올리다 (=vảnh). 활기를 띠다	be perking up
		vênh		휜. 비뚤어진. 뒤틀린	warped
09 70	vet	vét	1	긁어내다. 준설하다	to dredge. to cleanse the bottom
			2	정장	(clothing) suit
		vẹt		앵무새	parrot
		vệt		줄.선	line
		vết		얼룩. 흠. 오점	spot. stain. blemish
09 71	vi	vi	爲(위) 韋(위) 違(위) 圍(위)	1	둘레	circumference
				2	둘러싸다. (=vây)	to encircle
		vì			~때문에. ~의 이유로	because. for. for the sake of
		ví		1	지갑	wallet. purse
				2	비교하다	to compare. to link to. to liken
		vị	味(미) 未(미) 爲(위) 位(위)	1	위치	position. location. site
				2	불공평한. 편파적인. (=bênh ~)	unfair. unjust
				3	맛	taste
		vĩ	偉(위) 緯(위) 渭(위) 尾(미)		끝(꼬리)	(the tail) end
		vỉ			대나무 발. 대나무 체	bamboo net. bamboo sieve

09 72	via	via			[구어] 아버지. 어머니	[spoken language] father. mother
		vía			혼	soul. spirit
		vỉa		1	광층	seam (underground layer of a mineral)
				2	가장자리. 국경. 도로 경계석	edge. side. border. kerb
09 73	viec	việc			일. 사항	job. work. business. thing. matter. affair
09 74	vien	viện	援(원) 院(원)	1	기관. 협회	institution
				2	돕다	to help
		viễn	遠(원)		먼 (=xa)	far (from). distant
		viền			가장자리	hem. edge
		viên	(員)원 (圓)원	1	어떤 분야에 종사하는 사람에게 붙이는 것	agent, actor, worker, etc.
				2	작고 둥글고 단단한 것	small round solid things
09 75	vieng	viếng			방문하다	to visit (a person or a place)
09 76	viet	viết		1	쓰다	to write
				2	펜	pen
		việt Việt	越(월)	1	넘다	cross over. jump over
				2	베트남	Vietnam
09 77	vin	vin			꺽다. 잡아내리다	bereak down. catch down
		vịn			손을 기대다	to lean one's hand on
09 78	vinh	vinh	榮(영)		영광. 광영	glory. honor
		vịnh	泳(영) 半(반)	1	[지리] 만(灣)	gulf. bay
				2	읊다. 암송하다	to recite
09 79	vit	vít		1	끌어내리다. 비틀다	to pull down, to wrest down
				2	나사	screw
		vịt			오리. 집오리	duck. domestic duck

0980	vo	vò		1	술병. 항아리	jar (pot used to contain liquid)
				2	구기다	crumple
		võ	武(무)	1	무(武). (=vũ)	martial art
				2	수척해진. (=gầy ốm)	lose a lot of weight. become emaciated
		vơ		1	쓸다. 일소하다	sweep
				2	모호한. 불확실한	obscure. imprecise. uncertain
		vố		1	속임수. 장난	cheating
				2	세게 치다. 내리치다	hit hard. smash
		vồ		1	불쑥 튀어나온	protrude from
				2	한움큼	handful
		vọ		1	올빼미	owl
				2	(타인에) 붙어서 살다	live off. sponge off
		vớ		1	잡다. 얻다	get. gain
				2	양말. 스타킹	socks. stockings
		vờ		1	(곤충) 하루살이	mayfly
				2	속이다. 가장하다	to pretend
		vồ		1	나무 망치	mallet
				2	낚아채다. 쥐다. 잡다	(of animals) to pounce
		vo			둥글게 하다	round up
		vó			발굽	hoof (of a horse)
		vỏ			외피. 껍질	cover. bark. shell. sheath. husk. skin. peel. pot. crust
		vợ			부인. 아내	wife
		vở			연습장. 노트	paper book. exercise book
		vỗ			파도치다	go overboard
		vỡ			(그릇 등이) 깨진	broken

		vô	1	없는	without. ~less. un~
			2	들어오다. (=vào)	to enter. to go into
0981	vom	vòm	1	아치. 홍예	arch
			2	(바다의 바위에 붙어사는) 굴의 일종	a kind of oysters (living on rocks at sea)
0982	von	von	1	(전기) 볼트	volt
			2	아주 날카로운. 아주 뾰족한	sharp as a razor
		vờn		(~앞에서) 맴돌다. 놀다	to play (with)
		vốn	1	자산. 자본	capital. bond. fund
			2	원래. 본래. 이전에. 예전에	originally. formerly
		vón		한덩어리로 만들다	lump together
0983	vong	vong	忘(망) 亡(망)	잃다. 죽다	lose. die
		vòng	1	원. 둥근모양	circle. ring
			2	돌아서 출발점으로 되돌아오는 모양	returning to the starting point
		võng		(볼이) 튀다	(a ball) bounces
		vọng	望(망) 妄(망)	1	울리다	to echo. to resound
				2	망루. 감시탑	watchtower. lookout tower
		võng	妄(망) 罔(망) 網(망)	그물침대	net bed. hammock
		vổng		위로 튀어오르다	spring up. bounce
0984	vot	vót	1	날카롭게 하다	sharpen
			2	가파른. 깍아지른 듯한	steep. sheer. precipitous
		vọt	1	매. 채찍	rod. whip
			2	(물따위가) 솟아나오다. 뿜어나오다	(water) gushing up. spout out
		vợt		라켓. 방망이	racquet. bat

		vớt		(물속에서) 건지다. 꺼내올리다	to pull something out of water
0985	vu	vụ	務(무) 霧(무)	1	(한부서의) 사령부	specialized department within a ministry
				2	도모하다. 기도하다	make an attempt. to try
		vu	誣(무) 于(우) 盂(우)		비방하다	to slander. to libel
		vú			(포유류의) 유방	breast
		vũ	舞(무) 武(무) 宇(우) 雨(우)	1	깃털	feather
				2	춤추다	to dance
0986	vua	vua			왕	king
		vùa		1	쓸어버리다	sweep away
				2	나무로 만든 그릇	wooden bowl
		vữa		1	모르타르	mortar
				2	상한. 부패한	go bad. spoil. go stale. decayed. rotten. decomposed
		vừa		1	맞다. 어울리다	to fit. to suit
				2	만족시키다	to satisfy. to please
		vựa			저장소. 보관소	storage. storage house
0987	vui	vui			즐거운	merry. joyful. gay
		vùi		1	(땅에) 묻다	to bry (to the ground)
				2	인사불성의. 완전히 취한	insensible. unconscious. intoxicated
0988	vung	vung		1	(단지, 항아리들의) 뚜껑	lid. cover
				2	(돈, 일생을) 허비하다. (칼, 채찍 등을) 휘두르다. 흔들다	to waste (money, life). to wield (a knife, whip, etc.)

		vùng	1	지역	region. area
			2	(몸을) 세게 용트림하다. (묶인것을) 풀어 버리려고 애쓰다	to try to untie (a knot)
		vụng	1	어색한. 미숙한. 서투른	awkward. clumsy
			2	비밀리. 몰래	secretly. stealthily
		vưng		따르다. 응하다. (=vâng)	follow. accept. respond to
		vũng		웅덩이	puddle (a small pool of water)
		vững		안정된. 견고한	firm
		vừng		(참)깨	sesame
		vựng		현기증나는	dizzy
0989		vườn	1	밭	(dry) field. farm. grove. garden
			2	서툴은. 미숙한	clumsy. be unskilled
		vươn		기지개를 펴다	to stretch
		vượn		유인원. 오랑우탄	an ape. a orangutan
0990	vuong	vương	王(왕)	1	왕. 임금	a king
				2	옴짝못하게 걸려들다	be caught in a trap
		vượng	旺(왕)	1	왕성한. 번영한. (=hưng thịnh)	prosperous
				2	번영하다. 성공하다	to prosper. to succeed
		vướng			걸리게 하다. ~에 휘감기게 하다.	to be entangled in. to be involved in
		vưởng			vất vưởng=불확실한. 불안정한	vất vưởng=uncertain. unsettled
		buông			정방형의. 정사각의	(geometry) square
0991	vuot	vuốt		1	(호랑이 등의) 발톱	claw
				2	쓰다듬다. 어루만지다	to caress. to stroke (as in "to stroke a dog's head")

		buột		문질러서 비비다. 비벼서 벗기다	rub off
		bượt		넘다. 초과하다	to pass over
0992	vut	vút	1	재빠르게 움직이다	to move swifly (like an arrow)
			2	채찍질하다. 매질하다	to lash
		vụt	1	갑자기. 급히	all of a sudden. in a hurry
			2	(누군가를) 때리다. 채찍으로 때리다	to flog (someone). to lash with a whip
			3	(스포츠) (공을) 때리다	(sports) to smash (ball)
			4	갑자기 아주 빠르게 움직이거나, 뛰거나, 도망치다	to move, run or flee suddenly and very quickly
		vứt		던지다. (=vất)	to throw away
0993	vy	vỹ	尾(미)	꼬리. 꽁지. (=vĩ)	(the tail) end
0994	xa	xa	車(차)	1 (거리가) 먼. 멀리 떨어진	far
				2 (장기의) 차	(xiangqi) xe
		xà	蟟(택)	대들보. 도리	girder (in a house)
		xá	舍(사) 赦(사)	숭배하다	to worship
		xã	社(사)	마을	village
		xả	捨(사) 舍(사)	물로 씻다. 헹구다	wash with water. rinse with water
		xạ	射(사) 麝(사)	쏘다	to shoot
0995	xac	xác	確(확)	1 사체. 시체	corpse
				2 확실한	definite. certain. sure. confident. positive
		xạc		꾸짖다. (=mắng nhiếc)	to scold. rebuke. tell (sb) off
		xấc		무례한. 건방진. 오만한	rude. impudent. haughty
		xắc		핸드백. 손지갑	handbag. hand wallet

0996	xach	xách	1	손잡이를 잡고 운반하다. 들다	to carry (suitcase, etc.) by the handle
			2	끌어올리다. 끌어당기다	to pull up. to hitch up
		xạch		덜컹거리는	rattling
0997	xang	xang	1	(양손을 벌려) 들다	lift one's hands apart
			2	오음 계 중의 하나. 오음. hò. xừ xang. xế. cống (도레파솔라)	one of the five tone scale (Do, Re, Fa, Sol, La)
		xẳng	1	신랄하게. 거칠게	acrimoniously. roughly
			2	짜다	salty
		xáng		준설기. 준설선. (굴 따위의) 채취선	dredging machine. dredging boat
		xăng		가솔린 (=dầu xăng)	gasoline
		xẳng		(맛) 매운. 신랄한. 퉁명스러운. 거친. (=xẳng)	(taste) spicy. acrid. gruff. rough
		xẳng		엉망으로. 품위없이	in a mess. without dignity
0998	xam	xam	1	잡다한. 가지가지의	miscellaneous. sundry
			2	뒤섞이다. (대화에) 참여하다	be mixed up. engage (in a conversation)
		xẩm	1	어두워지다	get dark
			2	땅거미지는	duskous
		xám	1	회색의	ash-coloured. grey
			2	회색	gray
		xăm	1	찌르다. 문신하다	to tattoo
			2	신탁 (신의 말씀)	prophecy. oracle. fortune stick (in temples)
		xảm	1	메우다	fill up. fill (in). plug (up)
			2	무미건조한	dull and dry
		xàm		엉망진창으로. 횡설수설. (=xàm bậy)	of the bollocks, bullshit. untrue

		xâm	侵(침) 寢(침)		침입하다. 침략하다.	to invade
		xạm			값싼	cheap
0999	xanh	xanh		1	푸른 (초록색 또는 파란색)	grue (green or blue in languages that do not distinguish the two colors)
				2	청록색 (과일). 익지 않은	(of fruit) "green". unripe
1000	xao	xao		1	소란한	noisy
				2	소요하다. 동요하다	be agitated. be shaken (up). waver
		xạo		1	위조하다	to forge. fake
				2	거짓말하다	to lie
		xào			튀기다. 볶다	to fry. stir-fry
		xáo			뒤집다. 섞다. 휘젓다	to mix up (mix or blend thoroughly and completely)
		xảo	巧(교)		교묘한. 교활한. (=khéo)	artful
1001	xau	xàu		1	시들다	to wither
				2	우울한. 풀이죽은. 수심에 찬	gloomy. downcast. pensive
		xâu		1	꾸러미. 다발(열쇠따위)	a bunch. bundle
				2	꼬챙이로 찌르다	pork with a skewer
		xạu			우울한. 수심에 찬. 슬픈	gloomy. pensive. sad
		xấu			못생긴. 추한. 보기 흉한. 나쁜	ugly. unsightly. bad. evil
1002	xay	xay			정미하다. ~의 껍질을 벗기다. 깍지를 까다. 가루로 만들다	be refined. peel a pod. to grind
		xây		1	건축하다. 건설하다	to build
				2	턱받이(식사동안 아이들의 턱밑에 놓는다)	a bib
		xáy			파다. 퍼내다	to dig (with a pointed tool). to hollow. to excavate. to scoop out

		xảy			발생하다. 생기다. 일어나다. (=xảy ra)	usually of something bad and used with "ra" to occur. to happen (by itself)
10 03	xe	xẻ		1	찢겨지다. 파손되다	be torn apart. be damaged
				2	찰과상을 입은. 벗겨진	bruised. abrasion. scratch
		xe		1	차. 운반하는 것. 탈것	wheeled vehicle (except for airplanes and trains)
				2	차로 운반하다	carry by vehicle
		xễ (xệ)		1	(의학) 탈장하다. 탈수하다	have a hernia. get dehydrated
				2	(의학) 축 늘어진. 활기없는	droopy
		xé			찢다. 찢어 버리다. 종이를 찢다	to tear
		xế			(해, 달) 기울다	to decline. to be on the wane. to be sinking (of the sun, moon)
		xê			접근하다. 가까이 오다	to approach. to access
		xẻ			톱질하다. 썰다	to cut up. to shred. to divide up. to cut into strips
		xê			물러서다. 길을 비켜주다	to et out of one's way
10 04	xem	xem			구경하다. 보다	to see. to watch
		xém			거의. 가까운. 막 되려는 참	nearly. just about to be
10 05	xen	xen			끼어들다. 참견하다. 간섭하다	to interfere (in). meddle (in). to intervene
		xén			자르다. 잘라내다	to shear. to trim. to clip. to prune
		xến			양도하다	hand over (to). transfer (to)
10 06	xeo	xeo			말로 남의 마음을 찌르다	speak into a person's heart
		xéo		1	짓밟다. 경멸하다	to trample on. to despise. scorn. look down on
				2	비스듬한. 경사진	oblique. slanting

		xèo		기름을 데울 때 나는 소리. (=xèo xèo)	the sound of heating oil
		xèo		잘게 썰다	chop up
		xẽo		조그만 도랑. 개천. (=lạch)	a small ditch, small stream
		xẹo		경사진	inclined, slant, sloping
10 07	xep	xép	1	(작은) 해협. 수로	small strait, waterway
			2	작은	small
		xẹp	1	떨어져서 파인. 오목해진	concave
			2	수축하다. 바람빠지다	to shrink, be deflated
		xếp	1	정리하다	to arrange, to put in order
			2	장. 장관(프랑스 식민시대 정부기관의 장)	the head, minister, the head of a gavernment agency
		xệp		축 늘어지다. 침착하게 앉아있다	be droopy, sit still
10 08	xet	xét		고찰하다	to examine, to consider, to check
		xẹt		스치다. (=vụt qua)	pass by, brush past
10 09	xi	xi	1	봉인	seal
			2	어린이에게 소변 봐주는 때의 소리. (=xi xi)	the sound you make when you ask a child to urinate
		xí	企(기) 熾(치)	1	화장실. (=nhà xí, cầu xí, chuồng xí)	toilet
				2	먼저 차지하다	take first
		xỉ	齒(치) 侈(치) 紳(신)	1	이빨	teeth
				2	손가락질하다. 욕하다	point a finger at, curse at
		xì		1	불발된	undone
				2	새다	leak out, escape
		xị			늘어져 내린	stretched, drooped

10 10	xich	xích	赤(적) 尺(척) 斥(척)	1	쇠사슬	chain
				2	쇠사슬로 묶다	to bind in chains, to chain up
		xịch			(자동차가 급브레이크를 걸어서 멈추는) 소리	the sound (of a car stopping by a sudden brake)
10 11	xiec	xiếc			서커스. (=xiệc)	circus
10 12	xiem	xiêm			자수 스커트	embroidered skirt
10 13	xieng	xiềng		1	족쇄. 쇠사슬	shackle, chain
				2	족쇄를 채우다	to shackle
10 14	xin	xin			청하다. 요구하다	to ask (for), to beg
		xìn		1	광택이 없어지다	lose luster
				2	인색한. 몹시 아끼는	stingy, dearly cherished
10 15	xinh	xinh			귀여운. 예쁜. (=đẹp mắt, dễ coi)	nice, pretty
		xình			충분한. 넓은	sufficient, broad
10 16	xit	xít			다가오다	come near, approach
		xịt			~을 뿌리다. (물보라를) 날리다	to sprinkle, blow (a spray of water)
10 17	xiu	xìu			잿빛이 되다	change color, darken
		xíu			아주 작은. 극소의. (=nhỏ xíu)	tiny
		xỉu			실신하다. 기절하다	pass out, black out, to feel faint, lose consciousness
		xịu			시무룩해 보이다	look sullen
10 18	xo	xơ		1	섬유질. 가는 실	fibre, filament
				2	수녀	a sister (a nun)
		xổ		1	뛰어 나오다. 달려들다	pounce upon
				2	털이 복실복실하게 난. (=xù)	shaggy
		xo			위축되다. 움츠리다	be daunted, be intimidated

		xó		모둥이. 귀퉁이		corner. nook
		xõ		마른. 야윈		thin
		xỏ		실을 꿰다		to reeve. to thread
		xọ		(이야기를) 전환하다. 돌리다		change the topic
		xộ		잘못된. 실수의. 틀린		wrong. mistaken.
		xổ		(머리카락이) 풀어지다		one's hair comes loose
		xở		넓히다. 크게하다		widen
		xô	1	버킷. 물통		a bucket (container)
			2	밀다		to push. to shove
10 19	xoa	xoa	1	문지르다. 비비다. 바르다		to use hand to rub
			2	비녀의 일종. (=thoa)		a kind of hairpin
		xõa		(머리카락) 흘러내리다. 늘어뜨리다		have one's hair flowing down. to droop. to sag
		xóa		말소하다. 삭제하다. 지우다		to erase. to delete
		xòa		늘어지다. 늘어뜨리다		to droop. to sag
10 20	xoai	xoai		지쳐있다		exhausted
		xoài	1	망고		mango
			2	큰 대자로		in a (long) sprawl
		xoải		(날개를) 펴다. (팔, 발) 벌리다		spread (wings). open (one's arms and feet)
10 21	xoay	xoay		회전하다. 돌다		to turn. to swivel
		xoáy		소용돌이 치다. 회오리치다		to awirl. to whirl
10 22	xoe	xoe	1	꼬다. 둥글게 말다		twist up. roll up round
			2	더할나위 없이		pefectly
		xòe		넓히다		to spread. to stretch. to open (wings, tail, fingers)

1023	xom	xom	1	작살	harpoon
			2	(작살로) 찌르다	to stab (with a harpoon)
		xờm	1	늘어지다	to droop
			2	흐트러진 (머리카락이)	disheveled (hair)
		xòm		매우	very
		xõm		매우	very
		xơm		충돌하다	come into conflict
		xóm		부락. 작은 마을	a small village. a hamlet
		xổm		쭈그리다. 웅크리다	to crouch. to curl up
		xồm		털많은	hairy
1024	xong	xong	1	끝난. 완성된	finished. complete. done
			2	끝나다	to end. to complete
		xỗng		무례하게. 불손하게	rudely. arrogantly
		xống		스커트. 치마. (=váy)	skirt
		xổng		웅크리다	to curl up. to crouch
		xông	1	돌진하다. 돌격하다	to rush
			2	풍기다. 발산하다	give off
			3	들이마시다. 숨을 내쉬다	to exhale
1025	xop	xộp	1	스폰지	sponge
			2	체포하다. 붙잡다	to arrest. catch
		xọp	1	야윈	thin
			2	움츠러들다. 수축하다. 작아지다	shrink in. shrink down. get smaller. become smaller
		xốp	1	부드러운. 말랑말랑한	soft. tender
			2	물을 잘 흡수하다	absorb water well
		xóp		오목한	concave
		xợp		혼란해지다. 헝클어지다	get confused. disheveled

		xớp		거칠거칠한	rough
10 26	xot	xót	1	아픔을 느끼다	usually of a body part be hurt. be in pain
			2	욱신거리는	throbbing. aching
		xợt	1	돌진하다	to rush
			2	갑자기	suddenly. abruptly. unexpectedly. all of a sudden. all at once
		xốt	1	소스	sauce
			2	재촉하다. 독촉하다	to hasten. hurry. rush. press. urge on. push
		xớt		살짝 스치다	brush past slightly
		xọt		(절구 등으로) 찧다. 빻다	to pound. crush (with a mortar, etc.)
10 27	xu	xù	1	털이 덥수룩한	shaggy. bushy
			2	매우. 아주	very
		xu 驅(구)	1	쑤 (동의 1/100)	xu (1/100 of Vietnam dong)
			2	빨리 걷다	to walk fast
		xủ	1	처지는. 늘어지는	drooping. sagging
			2	늘어져 내리다	to droop. to sag
		xụ	1	늘어져 내리다. (=xủ)	to droop. to sag
			2	슬퍼 보이는. 슬픈	sad-looking. sad
		xũ		관. 상여. (=quan tài)	(funeral) bier
		xử 處(처)		대처하다	to cope with
		xừ		놈. 녀석 (남성을 조롱하면서 부르는 말)	guy (a derision of a man)
		xứ 處(처)		지구. 지방	country. region
10 28	xua	xua		(손으로) 내쫓다	to dispel. to make something go away

		xưa		1	옛날	a long time ago, old times
				2	옛날의	old, ancient
10 29	xuan	xuân	春(춘) 椿(춘)		봄	spring
		xuẩn			어리석은. 바보같은	foolish
10 30	xuat	xuất	出(출)		나가다. (돈) 선불하다	get out, go out, to leave, to advance (money)
10 31	xuc	xúc	觸(촉) 促(촉) 蹴(축)		푸다. 퍼내다	to scoop
		xức			(기름을) 바르다	to grease oil
		xực			먹다. (=ăn)	to eat
10 32	xui	xui		1	불행한	unlucky
				2	자극하다. 유도하다. 선동하다. (=xúi)	to stimulate, to incite, to induce
		xụi		1	불구가 된	crippled
				2	축 늘어뜨리다	droop down
		xúi			부추키다. 자극하다. (=xui)	to stimulate, to incite, to induce
10 33	xum	xúm			모으다. 그룹을 만들다	to gather, to form a group
		xụm			넘치다	to overflow
10 34	xung	xung	衝(형)		성난. 격노한. (=tức giận)	angry, furious
		xửng		1	찜통	steamer
				2	싸우려고 털을 일으키다	raise hair for a fight
		xứng	稱(칭)	1	알맞다. (=xứng đáng, tương xứng)	harmonize (with), match, suit
				2	~와 상응한	commensurate with
		xưng	稱(칭)		칭하다. 이름 부르다. 지칭하다	call oneself
		xửng			(닭) 싸우기 위해 깃털과 목털을 일으키다	(chicken) raise feathers and neck hair to fight

10 35	xuoc	xước		1	벗겨지다	come off. pee off
			2	(피부가) 까진. 벗겨진	be skinned
		xược		거만한. 뻐기는. 건방진. 오만한. (=xấc xược)	haughty. arrogant. impudent
10 36	xuoi	xười	1	너덜너덜하게 되다	be worn to tatters
			2	단정치 못한	untidy
		xuôi		내려가다	go down
10 37	xuong	xương	昌(창) 菖(창)	1	뼈	bone
				2	뼈만 앙상한. (문제) 풀기가 매우 어려운	bony. (problem) very difficult to solve
		xuống		1	내려가(오)다	to go downwards. to descend
				2	(차에서) 내리다	to get off (a vehicle)
		xuổng			삽. (=thuổng)	shovel. spade
		xuồng			모터 보트. 카누	motor boat. canoe
		xướng	唱(창) 倡(창)		제창하다. 시작하다	originate
		xưởng	廠(창)		공장	workshop. factory
10 38	xuyen	xuyến			팔찌	bracelet
		xuyên			관통하다	to pierce. to go through
10 39	xuyt	xuýt		1	거의	nearly
				2	(나쁜일) 부추기다	encourage (bad things)
		xuyt		1	쉿(조용히 하라는 신호)	a signal for to be quiet
				2	조용하게 하다	keep quiet
10 40	y	y	醫(의) 衣(의) 依(의) 伊(이)	1	의학. (=y học)	medical science
				2	같은	like. same
		ỷ	倚(의) 椅(의)	1	신위(神位). 제단	memorial tablet. the altar
				2	의지하다	rely on. lean (on/against)

		ý	意(의)	생각. 뜻	idea. meaning
10 41	yem	yếm		브래지어	bra. brassiere
		yểm		부적을 묻다. 액땜을 하다	bury an amulet. exorcise evil spirit
10 42	yen	yến	燕(연)	제비. (=chim én)	swallow
		yên		1 안장	saddle
				2 평화로운. 조용한. 고요한	calm. peaceful
10 43	yeu	yếu		약한. 연약한. 허약한	weak. feeble
		yêu		사랑하다	to love romantically
		yểu		단명한. 요절한	short-lived. die young. die at an early age. premature

초판 1쇄 발행 2024년 6월 28일

지은이 이상범
펴낸이 김영근
편집 김영근, 최승희
마케팅 김영근, 최승희
디자인 강초원
펴낸곳 마음 연결
주소 경기도 수원시 팔달구 인계로 120 스마트타워 1318
이메일 nousandmind@gmail.com
출판사 등록번호 251002021000003
ISBN 979-11-93471-08-1
값 18000원

이 책은 저작권법에 의해 국내에서 보호받는 저작물입니다.
저작권자의 승인 없이 본문의 내용을 무단으로 복제하거나
다른 매체에 기록할 수 없습니다.